Practical Counselling
and Helping Skills

2000

Practical Counselling and Helping Skills

Helping clients to help themselves

Second edition

Richard Nelson-Jones

Cassell

Cassell Educational Limited
Artillery House
Artillery Row
London SW1P 1RT

First edition published in 1983 by Holt, Rinehart and Winston Ltd.
This edition first published 1988

British Library Cataloguing in Publication Data

Nelson-Jones, Richard
  Practical counselling and helping skills :
  helping clients to help themselves. —
  2nd ed.
  1. Counselling
  I. Title
  361.3′23   BF637.C6
ISBN: 0-304-31469-2

Phototypesetting by Inforum Limited, Portsmouth
Printed and bound in Great Britain by Biddles Ltd.

Last digit is print no: 9 8 7 6 5 4 3 2 1

Contents

List of Exercises

Chapter 5   A Model for Managing Problems

Chapter 6   Focusing on Feeling

Chapter 7   Focusing on Thinking

Chapter 8   Focusing on Action

Preface

This is unashamedly a how-to-do-it book. I aim to provide a down-to-earth presentation of practical counselling and helping skills. An important assumption throughout is that practical counselling and helping skills are not used just by professional counsellors and psychologists. Rather, they are used by voluntary counsellors and by numerous helpers as part of their jobs: for example, teachers, supervisors, managers, doctors, nurses, social workers, probation officers, community workers and priests. Additionally, counselling and helping skills are used by informal helpers, in roles such as those of partner, spouse, parent or friend.

There is no getting away from the fact that practical skills are at the heart of counsellor and helper training. Though people can learn about these skills by reading, writing and talking about them, if they are to become competent practitioners, sooner or later they have to learn by *doing*. This book is written to support trainers charged with the responsibility of imparting practical skills. However, it also aims to help those who do not have either the time or resources for, or ready access to, formal training. Additionally, I hope practitioners, even if familiar with much of its material, may find it a useful book for their continuing education.

What are the main changes between this book and its predecessor, *Practical Counselling Skills*? It is a substantial revision and enlargement. All the chapters have been reworked and updated. I have added four new chapters: those on further facilitation skills, a model for managing problems, focusing on feeling, and life skills training. There is a clearer emphasis on counselling and helping skills as series of choices that may be either well or poorly made, and so helpers are given the existential message that they are responsible for *making* their helping lives through the adequacy of their choices. The book is more thoroughly referenced. However, so as not to disrupt its flow, the references for each chapter are combined in a separate section at the end. Last, I have attempted to impart skills not just through earnestness, but through humour. Yes folks, this book contains many more helping jokes than the first edition.

My aim has been to write in the language of the educated layperson. I have endeavoured to use clear and simple English. I apologize in advance for any unwitting slips into psychobabble. On this score I hope I will not suffer the same judgement as Belshazzar: 'Thou art weighed in the balance and found wanting.'

The book starts with a thorough introduction to facilitation skills such as listening and communicating understanding, and thus making it easier for your clients to disclose, explore and experience themselves. Then a five-stage model for managing problems is presented, followed by chapters on interventions focused on feeling, thinking and action. There are then two chapters on group work: facilitating groups and life skills training. The book ends with a chapter on maintaining and developing your skills, followed by a glossary (retained from the first edition by popular demand), before the references and the name and subject indexes.

The approach to each skill or component part of a skill is to start by describing it clearly and then to provide an exercise involving its use. There are sixty-nine exercises in the book. Most of the exercises may be done in a number of ways: on your own, in pairs or in a training group. Where appropriate, suggested responses for exercises are provided at the end of chapters. I encourage you to take a flexible approach to the exercises. For instance, if you are a trainer you may wish to modify some exercises so that they better suit your setting. If you are a student or on your own, stay with any one exercise only so long as you find it useful.

What about my credentials for writing this book? Well, to start with I was a pretty screwed-up young man. I have now been in counselling and helping some twenty-five years, though not all as a client! Though British born, in the early to mid 1960s I trained at Stanford University in the United States. I acquired my basic counselling skills not least from being the recipient of numerous individual sessions from the then director of the Stanford Counseling and Testing Center, Dr John Black. I also attended a number of groups at the Stanford Medical Center, where one of my group therapists was Irvin Yalom. Throughout the 1970s I was a counsellor trainer at the University of Aston in Birmingham, England. There I also worked on a sessional basis as a counselling psychologist at the University Health Service. Now, in the 1980s, I coordinate what is probably Australia's largest tertiary counsellor training programme, at the Royal Melbourne Institute of Technology. There I teach practical skills for individual counselling, group counselling and life skills training. Additionally, I teach a human relationship skills course for undergraduates. Also, as something of a hobby, I run a small private practice. Over the years I have developed an integrative theoretical and practical approach which is outlined in my book, *Personal Responsibility Counselling and Therapy*. In a nutshell, I am very committed to helping people acquire, develop and use the skills of self-help.

I thank the following people who have contributed to the writing, preparing and publishing of this book: at Cassell in Britain, Juliet Wight-Boycott, my editor, and her colleagues who worked on this publication; at Harcourt Brace Jovanovich in Australia, Jeremy Fisher, who supervises its Australasian distribution; at the Royal Melbourne Institute of Technology, Jenny Tserkezidis and her colleagues in the Wordprocessor Section of the Communication Services Unit, for typing the manuscript so diligently; and from everywhere, all those friends and colleagues who have benefited my thinking and practice, been good mates and even provided some jokes for this book.

I hope that you find *Practical Counselling and Helping Skills* stimulating and useful, and also that it helps you to make better choices in your counselling and helping work. Though I'm responsible for writing this book, you are responsible for what you get out of it. I wish you all the best in your endeavours.

Melbourne   *Richard Nelson-Jones*
Australia   June 1987

1 Counselling, Helping and Self-Help

Below are concerns that people might wish to share with another.

'I'm feeling depressed, lonely and very tense.'
'Now I've had a heart attack I must learn to live more sensibly.'
'I carry my parents around in my head all the time, even when they are miles away.'
'I wish that I could relate better and have more social life.'
'There is continuous conflict in our marriage.'
'I get very tense over exams and never seem to do myself justice.'
'I'm undecided about my career.'
'I'm so worried about my job. Being made redundant would be disastrous.'

There are four main categories of other people who might offer help with such concerns.

- *Helping professionals.*   Persons specializing in helping others with their problems. Such people include counsellors, psychologists, psychiatrists and social workers.
- *Voluntary counsellors and helpers.*   People trained in counselling and helping skills who work on a voluntary basis in settings such as marriage guidance councils, young people's counselling services and numerous other voluntary agencies.
- *Those using counselling and helping skills as part of their jobs.*   Here the main focus of the job may be: teaching; managing; supervising; providing religious, medical, financial or legal services; trade union work, etc. These jobs require people to use counselling and helping skills some of the time if they are to be maximally effective in them.
- *Informal helpers.*   All of us have the opportunity to assist others, be

it in the role of marital partner, parent, relative, friend or workmate.

Just because people are available to help does not necessarily mean that they are helpful rather than retarding or harmful. The question then becomes 'What is effective help?' or, to put it even more specifically, 'What are the skills of effective helping?'

DEFINING COUNSELLING AND HELPING

A word about my use of terms in this book. Possibly, in relation to the above fourfold classification of people who offer help, the word 'counsellor' refers more to helping professionals and voluntary counsellors, whereas the word 'helper' refers more to those using counselling and helping skills as part of their jobs, and to informal helpers. Some would even query this distinction and view counselling and helping as synonymous.[1] For the sake of brevity, mostly I use the word *helping* instead of 'counselling and helping'. Except where I refer specifically to counsellors, mostly I use the word *helper* to cover both counsellors and helpers. I use the word *client* to refer to the person receiving help. Throughout the book the notion of help is that of validating clients by fostering self-help rather than invalidating them by creating dependency.

Helping takes place within different kinds of contracts. Kanfer and Goldstein state three of the main differences between professional and informal help.[2] First, professional help is *unilateral*, in that the focus of the relationship is on solving the problems of the client. Second, it is *formal*, in that the relationship between helper and client is usually confined to specific times and places. Third, it is *time-limited*, with the relationship terminating when stated goals and objectives are reached. An additional difference is that professional help is often of a *free-for-service nature*. Furthermore, there is the assumption that professional helpers are *suitably trained and qualified*. I mention the above because, although I use the word 'helping' on its own, I do not wish to obscure the fact that there are many important differences in the provision of helping services.

What is Counselling and Helping?

There are a number of ways to approach a definition of counselling and helping. Some of these are explored below prior to arriving at a composite definition.

- It is a *relationship*. The emphasis here is on the quality of the relationship offered to the client. Characteristics of a good helping relationship are sometimes stated as non-possessive warmth, genuineness and a sensitive understanding of the client's thoughts and feelings.[3]
- It involves a *repertoire of skills*. This repertoire of skills both incorporates and also goes beyond those of the basic relationship. Another way of looking at these skills is that they are interventions which are selectively deployed depending upon the needs and states of readiness of clients. These interventions may focus on feeling, thinking and acting. Furthermore, they may include group work and life skills training. Another intervention is that of consultancy. This may deal with some of the problems 'upstream', with the systems causing them, rather than 'downstream', with individual clients.[4]
- It emphasizes *self-help*. Helping is a process with the overriding aim of helping clients to help themselves. Another way of stating this is that all clients, to a greater or less degree, have problems in taking effective responsibility for their lives. The notion of personal responsibility is at the heart of the processes of effective helping and self-help.[5]
- It emphasizes *choice*. Elsewhere I have defined personal responsibility as 'the process of making the choices that maximize the individual's happiness and fulfilment'.[6] Throughout their lives people are choosers. They can make good choices or poor choices. However, they can never escape the 'mandate to choose among possibilities'.[7] Helping aims to help clients become better choosers.
- It focuses on *problems of living*. Helping is primarily focused on the choices required for the developmental tasks, transitions and individual tasks of ordinary people rather than on the needs of the moderately to severely disturbed minority. *Developmental tasks* are tasks which people face at differing stages of their life span: for instance, finding a partner, developing and maintaining an intimate relationship, raising children, and adjusting to declining physical strength. The notion of *transitions* both applies to progression through the life stages, and acknowledges that changes can be unpredictable and not necessarily in accordance with normative developmental tasks: for instance, getting fired, as contrasted with maintaining a steady job. The notion of *individual tasks* represents the existential idea of people having to create their lives through their daily choices. This is despite constraints in themselves, from others and from their environments. Though helping skills may be used with

vulnerable groups like psychiatric patients, helpers are mainly found in non-medical settings.

● It is a *process*.   The word 'process' denotes movement, flow and the interaction of at least two people in which each is being influenced by the behaviour of the other. Both helpers and clients can be in the process of influencing each other.[8] Furthermore, though some of this process transpires within sessions, much of it is likely to take place between sessions and even after the contact has ended. What begins as a process involving two people ideally ends as a self-help process.

Below I draw together the six characteristics mentioned above into a composite definition of counselling and helping.

Counselling and helping is a process whose aim is to help clients, who are mainly seen outside medical settings, to help themselves by making better choices and by becoming better choosers. The helper's repertoire of skills includes those of forming an understanding relationship, as well as interventions focused on helping clients change specific aspects of their feeling, thinking and acting.

AREAS FOR COUNSELLING AND HELPING SKILLS

Below I identify six different areas for using helping skills. Though in practice these six areas overlap, each may require different skills.

Nurturing and Healing

Karen, an only child aged eighteen, grew up in a home where her parents were in constant conflict. Both tried to get her to take their side and neither spent time trying to understand her point of view. Instead she was being constantly put down. Her father started drinking heavily. Her home atmosphere was characterized by anger, tension and unhappiness with rare glimpses of fun. Karen is now shy, tense, depressed and fearful of intimacy.

Young people require emotional nourishment when growing up. They need to feel secure. This is not just physical but emotional security. British psychiatrist John Bowlby talks of the concept of a secure base. He calls this provider of a secure base an attachment figure.[9] Another way of approaching the concept of a secure base is to emphasize the growing person's need for empathic understanding. Through being sensitively listened to by an attachment figure, children not only learn to experience and acknowledge their own feelings, but also feel confident to engage in exploratory behaviour.

In the above vignette it is probable that Karen's confidence in herself has been insufficiently encouraged. Furthermore, she may have learned from her parents some poor relationship skills. Karen requires a healing relationship from a helper in which she can receive some of the nurturing and affirmation that her life to date has lacked. This relationship might be viewed as more *person-* than *problem*-oriented. Though assisting her to solve problems is important, the major aim is to foster Karen's overall development as a person. Karen and people with similar adverse experiences may require long-term contact of possibly twenty sessions or more.

There are many people in any society who have had emotionally tough upbringings. Partly for financial reasons, there appears to be a growing trend for trained helpers to do short-term problem-management work. This may be insufficient to meet the needs of people like Karen.

Problem Management

Geoff is a married man in his mid-forties with two boys, aged fifteen and thirteen. He is getting increasingly concerned at his deteriorating relationships with his sons. He resents the fact that they spend so much time away and complains that they treat a good home just like a hotel. His wife tells him that she wishes that he would control his anger with the boys.

Problem management helping assists clients to make better choices in one or more problem areas in their lives. Clients tend to approach helpers with specific problems. For instance, Geoff may be seeking help in improving his relationship with his sons. Presenting problems can be many and varied. Examples are: the communication problems of marital partners; the learning difficulties of pupils and students; adjusting to a bereavement; the stress problems of an executive; and coming to terms with a physical disability. Not surprisingly, problem management helping usually starts with assessment. This is in order to understand and define the problem(s) and to set goals.

Problem management helping is sometimes viewed as inelegant.[10] This is because it tends to have a specific focus and last for only a few sessions. Nevertheless, it may be all that the client wants and the helper has time for. Furthermore, it may be approached in such a way that clients learn some useful self-help skills.

Decision Making

Ken, aged twenty, is at the end of his first year on a university engineering course. He has just received his results for the year and has failed three out of his nine subjects. He acknowledges that not only does he have considerable difficulty with two of the subjects, but also that he is not particularly interested in the whole course. He now wonders whether he should change his course.

In this book the aim of all helping is to aid people in making better choices and in becoming better choosers. However, decision making can be viewed as a distinct area. In decision-making helping, the focus is on helping clients make one or more specific decisions. Much occupational work is concerned with clients' decisions in such areas as: choosing a job or career; the educational route to obtaining qualifications; whether or not to accept redundancy, or early retirement; whether or not to change jobs in mid-career; use of leisure time; and what to do when retired. There are many other important decisions that clients may wish to think through with the help of skilled and unbiased helpers; for example, getting married or getting divorced. Decision-making helping can both help clients with particular decisions and also impart self-help skills.

Crisis Management

Judy's husband left her a year ago to live with another woman. Since then she has been taking refuge from her loneliness by involving herself for long hours, including much overtime, in her stressful job as nurse in a busy operating theatre. Today she had an ugly row with one of the doctors. She is now tense, agitated, depressed, pessimistic and hurting all over. She feels she can't go in to work any more and is clearly at the end of her tether.

In crisis management helping, clients feel that their coping resources are under great strain, if not overwhelmed. They are often stuck in unproductive and repetitive patterns of thinking, living in states of heightened emotions, and unable to view dispassionately the range of their choices. Crisis management, sometimes conducted by telephone, requires helpers to make speedy assessment of situations, including: suicide risk, clients' coping resources, availability of support and whether medication and/or hospitalization is desirable. Additionally, helpers are likely to work with clients on managing their problems, at least to the extent of getting them through the worst of the crisis.

Support

Kim and Winnie Lee are an Asian couple in their mid-thirties who migrated with their three children to a western country five months ago. The whole family has found it a major change involving differences in culture, language, climate, physical environment, employment and friends, and also absence from relatives. While the family are coping well, Kim and Winnie feel in need of support during their transition.

Supportive helping assists clients who, while not going through a major crisis, may nevertheless consider extra support necessary to help them through an awkward phase. For instance, Kim and Winnie might arrange to see a migrant counsellor on an occasional basis. In fact, just knowing that a counsellor was available might help them. Such counselling may give them the opportunity to express and then start sorting out their thoughts and feelings in a safe environment. Ideally supportive helping quickly puts clients back in touch with their own strengths and resources so that they feel better able to cope with life on their own.

Life Skills Training

> Michelle and Rudy are in a close relationship and thinking of getting married. Both sets of parents were divorced and they do not want history to repeat itself. Accordingly they have enrolled in a relationship skills training course for couples. This is to be held one evening each week for twelve weeks.

Increasingly it is recognized that helpers need not restrict their activities to those who already have problems. Helping skills can be used to conduct life skills training programmes with a preventive and developmental, as contrasted with a remedial, focus. Such training programmes can be in any area in which people require skills: work, leisure, study, relationships and sexuality, to mention but some.

Helping skills can also be used to impart life skills without going so far as offering structured programmes in specific skills. For instance, teachers can manage learning environments in such a way that pupils develop skills of self-directed learning and group participation. Supervisors can supervise workers in such a way that they develop both initiative and teamwork skills. Youth club leaders can run activities programmes that have the side effect of helping young people develop autonomy and relationship skills.

I have tried in the above section to provide illustrations of six areas in which counselling and helping skills can be used. These six areas, albeit overlapping, are: (1) nurturing and healing; (2) problem management; (3) decision making; (4) crisis management; (5) support and (6) life skills training. I stress the need for effective helping skills to be offered by a wide variety of people. Paraphrasing the French statesman Talleyrand's aphorism that 'War is much too serious a thing to be left to military men', I assert that 'Helping skills are much too serious and valuable a thing to be left to professional helpers.'

COUNSELLING, HELPING AND CHOOSING

There are many ways in which participants in the helping process are choosers. Some of these are examined below.

Goals for Counselling, Helping and Living

An assumption of this book is that all people are ultimately personally responsible for their survival and unique fulfilment. Thus, it is assumed that both helpers and helped share a common responsibility *for* creating and making their lives. Do not be put off by the notion of personal responsibility. It is not a 'heavy' concept conducive to engendering guilt and depression. Rather, if rightly understood, it is a liberating concept that assists people in becoming and staying effective choosers.

Effective living involves people in making appropriate choices in the areas of feeling, thinking and acting. Without going into detail at this stage, appropriate *feeling* choices enable people to be open to their experience, acknowledge their feelings, and be aware of their wants and wishes. Appropriate *thinking* choices help people to regulate self-defeating feelings, avoid defensiveness, problem-solve and plan. Appropriate *acting* choices enable people actively to meet their needs through mutually satisfying and enhancing relationships and through gaining meaning in work and leisure.

Problems as Deficits in Choosing

Many problems that clients have are either caused by or compounded by deficits in choosing. This is not to deny that many clients have also to cope with problems that may be largely outside their influence: for example, ill health, accidents, poverty, poor housing. Effective living involves effective choosing. The people in the previous vignettes – Karen, Geoff, Ken and Judy – were needing outside assistance so that they could choose more effectively. Karen lacked both the confidence and skills to make the choices that could help her to meet her needs. Geoff was too blocked to be able to make effective choices in managing his anger and rebuilding his relationship with his sons. Ken seemed to have made one inappropriate educational and career choice and was at risk of making another. Judy had made some poor choices in coping with the departure of her husband and was now in a crisis where her capacity to choose appropriately was greatly diminished. Even Kim and Winnie might be viewed as needing outside assistance to give them the support and strength to continue making effective choices. Michelle and Rudy wanted to learn to become better choosers before they were married, as a way of preventing marital problems.

Counsellors and Helpers as Choosers

Counsellors and helpers are choosers both in their personal and working lives. In their working lives they may be viewed as making role, treatment and responding choices.[11] *Role* choices relate to how they distribute their time between various activities such as either helping individuals, or facilitating groups, or life skills training. Role choices for helpers like managers and supervisors may focus on how to incorporate helping skills into their overall role. *Treatment* choices refer to what methods helpers adopt with which clients and when. Even informal helping may require strategies and tactics. *Responding* choices refer to how helpers respond to individual statements or series of statements from those with whom they work. To provide an imprecise analogy from daily life: role choices relate to how much time you spend on vacation; treatment choices to how, where and when you go; and responding choices are all those choices that you actually make on your vacation.

Counselling and Helping as a Choosing Process

The choices counsellors and helpers make both influence and are influenced by those with whom they work. Figure 1.1 provides a representation of the process of choosing that transpires during any helping relationship. All the time both of you cannot avoid making choices. Even deciding not to make a choice is a choice.

Skilled helpers make appropriate choices. The purpose of a book like this is to improve readers' choices so that you can help others better. By emphasizing helpers as choosers I hope to put you in the driver's seat and to encourage you to take responsibility for the quality and appropriateness of your choices.

Clients are also continuously making choices. Some of these choices

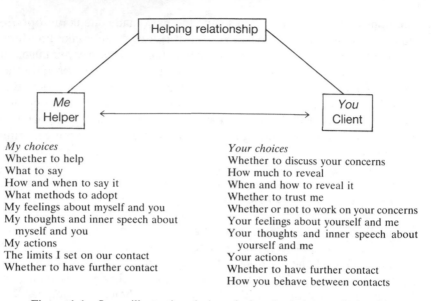

Figure 1.1   Some illustrative choices during the helping relationship

are at the very basic levels of whether to give you the opportunity to help and how much of themselves to reveal to you. Other choices may concern either resisting or working for change and whether to alter their behaviour between sessions.

Client self-help is the ultimate goal of helping. This involves clients not only in requiring the skills of making appropriate choices but also in maintaining their ability to choose appropriately. By emphasizing clients as choosers I encourage you to put them in the driver's seat so that they can increasingly assume responsibility for their choices. Effective living involves making the daily smaller choices correctly, not just the big choices. As Maslow observed: 'To make the growth choice instead of the fear choice a dozen times a day is to move a dozen times a day towards self-actualization.'[12]

WHAT ARE COUNSELLING AND HELPING SKILLS?

What are Skills?

The meanings of the word *skill* include proficiency, competence, and expertness in some activity. However, the essential element of a skill is the ability to make and implement an effective sequence of choices so as to achieve a desired objective.[13] For instance, if you are to be a good listener, you have to make and implement the choices entailed in being a good listener. The fact that all skills involve choices does not mean that the activities have to be carried out in a mechanistic way. Rather the skills approach to helping may free you to be more spontaneous.

The concept of skill is best viewed not as an either/or matter in which you either possess or do not possess a skill. Instead it is preferable to think of yourself as possessing skills *resources* and *deficits* or a mixture of the two. If you make good choices in a skills areas, for instance, either in listening or in helping clarify a problem, this is a skills resource. If you make poor choices in a skills areas, this is a skills deficit. In all helping skills areas you may possess resources and deficits in varying degrees. For example, in the skills areas of listening, you may be good at understanding clients but poor at demonstrating your understanding to them. The object of this book is to help you shift the balance of your resources and deficits more in the direction of resources.

Relationship Approach versus Skills Approach

A distinction can be made in helping between a *person* orientation and a *task* orientation.[14] With a person orientation the major emphasis is on the quality of the human relationship offered by counsellors and helpers. In an emotional climate of safety, freedom and being understood at a deep level, technical skills become secondary. The client's own capacity for self-direction is released. Providing good relationships with clients is considered both 'necessary and sufficient' for change to occur.[15] This is an underlying assumption of the client-centred or person-centred approach to helping.

In this book, offering a good relationship is seen as consisting of a number of skills; for example, the ability sensitively to understand others and to communicate to them that they are understood. These skills of good relating involve both self-awareness and technique. However, offering a good relationship alone, even if defined in skills terms, may be insufficient to help clients move beyond *describing* their problems, to *understanding* their contribution to sustaining them, and then to *working* actively for change. Thus most often, as well as the *person* orientation of a good relationship, clients need their helpers to be *task* oriented. This entails possessing a further repertoire of skills beyond the basic relationship.

As helpers you should view not only your own functioning in skills terms but also, where appropriate, encourage your clients to view their functioning the same way. The notion of skills can help clients to help themselves. They are in a much better position to monitor and work on their skills deficits if they are clear what the required skills are than if they do not have this knowledge.

The quality of your counselling and helping relates to the quality of your choices. Skills are sequences of choices. It is now time to move on to identifying some specific skills areas and to try and help you become a better chooser within them.

2 Becoming a Good Listener

Two counsellors meet up in the bar at the end of a working day. One looks fresh, the other tired.
Tired-looking counsellor: 'I don't know how you can look so fresh after all that listening.'
Fresh-looking counsellor: 'Who listens?'

Despite my cynical introduction, the capacity to be a good and understanding listener is the most fundamental helping skill of all. Clients come to helpers in pain, with problems, with decisions, in crisis and in need of support. From the start you are faced with the need to make good listening choices. At many times in your contact with clients, the following observation holds true: 'It is the province of knowledge to speak and it is the privilege of wisdom to listen.'[1]

DEFINING LISTENING

In this chapter I make a distinction between hearing and listening. *Hearing* involves the capacity to be aware of and to receive sound. *Listening* involves not only receiving sounds but, as much as possible, accurately understanding their meaning. As such it entails hearing words, being sensitive to vocal cues, observing movements and taking into account the context of communications.

You may wonder why accurate listening is so important when there are so many opportunities for people to be listened to in their everyday lives. Here, at the risk of overstating the case, it is possible to make a distinction between a social and a helping conversation. A *social* conversation is geared towards meeting the needs of both participants. In fact, social conversations have facetiously been described as 'two people, both of whom are taking turns to exercise their ego'. Though hearing may take place, listening may not. A *helping* conversation emphasizes meeting the psychological needs of clients. As such it places a high premium on listening to them.

Listening, however, does not just take place between people, it also takes place *within* each. Indeed your *inner* listening, or being appropriately sensitive to your own thoughts and feelings, may be vital to your *outer* listening involving understanding another. Furthermore, if you listen well to another, this may be very helpful to the quality of their inner listening. There is a beautiful saying of Lâo-Tse which indicates the effect that outer may have on inner listening:

> It is as though he listened
> and such listening as his enfolds us in a silence
> in which at last we begin to hear
> what we are meant to be.

Listening involves choices regarding both receiving and sending messages. Sometimes terms like 'active listening'[2] and 'empathy'[3] are used to describe this process. Barrett-Lennard observes that there are three main phases in what he terms 'facilitative relational empathy'.[4] Phase 1 is *empathic resonation* by Person A in response to B's message. This is an inner receiving process on the part of the listener. Phase 2 is A's attempt to *communicate responsive understanding* to B. Here the listener becomes the sender of a responsive understanding message. Phase 3 is B's *reception and awareness* of A's responsive understanding message. Briefly these three phases can be labelled empathic resonation, expressed empathy and received empathy.

The focus of this chapter is on receiving messages accurately, phase 1 of Barrett-Lennard's 'empathy cycle'. However, listening also entails communicating to clients so that they feel understood. Furthermore it involves creating a safe emotional climate. The next chapter focuses on the sender skills of becoming a good listener.

Importance of Listening

Accurate listening and communicating understanding is important in helping for a number of reasons.

● *Creating rapport.* You are more likely to develop an effective working relationship with your clients if they feel you have understood them than if this is not the case. For example, a study of helpful and non-helpful events in brief counselling interviews identified eight kinds of events perceived as helpful by clients. These helpful events were grouped into two 'superclusters' corresponding to task and interpersonal aspects of counselling. Understanding was the predominant cluster in the interpersonal grouping.[5]

- *Creating an influence base.*   The object of helping is to help people to help themselves. To do this effectively, helpers may choose not always to be passive, but to influence their clients actively in developing self-help skills. Listening accurately to your clients is one way you can build your position as an influencer. It contributes to their perceiving you as competent, trustworthy and attractive.[6,7] Furthermore, understanding clients from different cultural groups both as individuals and also in terms of their culture contributes to your ascribed status and credibility.[8] This may require special knowledge and cross-cultural sensitivity on your part.

- *Creating a knowledge base.*   A psychologist colleague of mine once quipped about another psychologist that he had to ask everyone whether they were female or male. He was incapable of gathering information without asking questions. If you listen well, most clients collaborate in providing relevant information about themselves. This helps you both in your initial assessment and also in any later interventions you make.

- *Helping clients to talk.*   All of us have some fears about revealing ourselves to others. Clients are often shy and anxious. They may be divulging highly sensitive information. They may have received much rejection in their pasts. Good listening helps them to feel affirmed, safe, accepted and understood. This in turn helps them to make the choices that allow them to share their world with you.

- *Helping clients to experience and to express their feelings.*   Earlier I made a distinction between hearing and listening. Many clients have been inadequately listened to in the past. Also, they have been exposed to people who modelled or demonstrated poor inner listening skills. Consequently, they may have relinquished, temporarily at least, some of their capacity for emotional responsiveness to themselves and to others.[9,10] Accurate listening can help clients to acknowledge more of their inner flow of experiencing. The message some clients may need to receive is that it is OK to acknowledge, experience and express their feelings.

- *Helping clients to own responsibility and to problem-solve.*   Clients who are listened to sharply and accurately are more likely to assume responsibility for working on their problems than those who are not. One reason is that good listening may reduce defensiveness. This may increase their willingness to focus on their own behaviour rather than on what others do to them. Another reason is that good listening provides a base for the offering of well-timed confrontations and of different perceptions that encourage clients to assume rather than to avoid responsibility. Furthermore, good listening provides clients with psychological space and support for their self-exploration and problem-solving.

INTERNAL AND EXTERNAL FRAMES OF REFERENCE

If your clients are to feel that you receive them loud and clear, you need to develop the ability to 'get inside their skins', 'walk in their moccasins' and 'see the world through their eyes'. The skill of listening to and understanding your clients is based on your choosing to get into their internal rather than to remain in your external frame of reference.[11] At the heart of listening to another is a basic distinction between 'you' and 'me', between 'my view of me' and 'your view of me', and between 'my view of you' and 'your view of you'. Now, 'my view of me' and 'your view of you' are both inside or internal viewpoints. However, 'your view of me' and 'my view of you' are both outside or external viewpoints.

To the extent that I understand 'your view of you' I choose to be inside your *internal frame of reference*. If I then chose to respond in a way that demonstrates an accurate understanding of your viewpoint, I am responding *as if inside* your internal frame of reference. If, however, I choose not to understand 'your view of you' or lack the skills to do so, I remain in the *external frame of reference* with regard to your world. Furthermore, even if I have understood you accurately, I may still choose to respond from my frame of reference, which is external to you, rather than as if inside your frame of reference. In short, if I respond to you as if inside your frame of reference, I respond to you from where you are. If I step outside your frame of reference, I respond in an external way.

Below are some counsellor and helper comments that are from an *external frame of reference* to that of the client.

'I'm here to help you.'
'People say you whinge a lot.'
'You should always be kind to others.'
'I'm glad that you are making progress.'
'You're behaving like a manic-depressive.'
'Why don't you stop taking tranquillizers?'

The internal frame of reference involves you in understanding clients on their own terms. This involves choosing to listen carefully and to allow clients the psychological space to tell their own stories. It involves paying attention to vocal and bodily as well as to verbal messages. In the following examples, helpers have chosen to respond as if inside the client's *internal frame of reference*.

> 'You're feeling extremely low and wonder whether you have the strength to continue.'
> 'You think you drink when the going gets rough.'
> 'You feel unappreciated by your children.'
> 'You think you will let your parents down if you fail your exams.'
> 'You're elated at having found a girlfriend.'
> 'I'm hearing the intensity of your hatred for your boss.'

Developing Skills in a Training Group

Exercise 2.1 focuses on the distinction between internal and external frames of reference. It can be done either individually, in pairs or in a training group. In learning basic helping skills I strongly suggest that, if possible, this be done in a training group of about six members plus an experienced and competent trainer. A six-member group can be sub-divided into either three pairs or two triads. If the group is small enough your trainer will be able to present skills verbally, demonstrate them, and still have time for coaching and providing feedback for individual members. The members of a training group can give you practice and feedback, help you develop observation skills, provide models of good and poor helping skills, let you receive as well as give help, and offer you care, support and challenge. The training group provides a stepping stone to working with real clients. For those of you who are already in helping roles, it can give you the opportunity, away from your daily pressures, to review and improve existing skills and to acquire new ones. Incidentally, it may save training group time if many of the exercises in this book are first done as homework.

Exercise 2.1 Getting inside another's frame of reference

This exercise may be done either on your own, in pairs or in a training group. The answers are provided at the end of the chapter.

A *On your own*
    This exercise consists of a number of statement–response excerpts from

different helping relationships. Three responses have been provided to each statement. On a piece of paper write 'IN' or 'EX' for each response, according to whether you consider it is predominantly *as if inside* the speaker's internal frame of reference or from a frame of reference *external* to the speaker.

B   *In pairs*
Either independently make your ratings for the responses to all statements, then discuss;
or independently rate the responses to one statement at a time, then share and discuss your answers.

C   *In a training group*
The trainer introduces the concept of internal versus external frame of reference. The trainer gets different pairs of group members to read out the statement–response units as realistically as possible. After each statement–response unit, the trainer gets members to share their answers and reasons for them before moving on.

Example
Client to social worker
Client: I'm worried sick. I'm not sleeping good and afraid for the kids. We're desperately short of money and my husband's on the booze again.
Social worker:
(a)   A lot of people are hard up these days.
(b)   You're ill with worrying about money, about your husband's drinking and about what's going to happen to the kids.
(c)   You poor thing. You have got a load on your mind.
Suggested answers and comments:
(a)   External. A patronizing generalization.
(b)   Internal. A sincere attempt at paraphrasing.
(c)   External. This is what the social worker thinks and feels however sympathetic he/she may be.

Exercise
1.   Pupil to teacher
Pupil: I hate it when the other boys tease me. Don't they realize I've got feelings too?
Teacher:
(a)   You loathe being teased and having your feelings hurt.
(b)   Self-pity won't get you anywhere. Why don't you stand up to them more?
(c)   You're hurt and extremely upset at the way you're being treated.
2.   Husband to family counsellor
Husband: I work my butt off all day and I dislike coming home to a sulking wife and demanding kids.
Family counsellor:
(a)   How long has this been going on?

(b)   I wonder whether you could be handling the situation differently.

(c)   After a hard day's work the last things you want is further pressure from your wife and kids.

3. Widow to bereavement counsellor

Widow: When Jim and I were together we did a lot for others. Now I'm on my own I'm much more selfish.

Bereavement counsellor:

(a)   You need to give yourself more time and not be so harsh on yourself.

(b)   You're noticing you do a lot less for others now Jim's dead.

(c)   You're still in pain. Losing Jim was a big blow.

4. Worker to supervisor

Worker: Bloody hell. The job's difficult enough without having to work with that lazy bastard.

Supervisor:

(a)   You've got enough on your plate without having to carry him.

(b)   It would make my life easier too if he worked harder.

(c)   Does he know how you feel?

ATTENDING AND SHOWING RECEPTIVENESS

How can you make good listening choices? Carl Rogers particularly emphasized the importance of listening in helping. However, Rogers had this to say about his mother: 'I would never have thought of telling anything significant to my mother, because I know that she would have a judgement about it and it probably would be negative'.[12] There are many aspects of being a safe and rewarding person with whom to talk. *Receiving information* skills include attending and showing receptiveness, disciplined hearing, and accurately observing body messages. *Sending information* skills include communicating your understanding and checking its accuracy.

Psychological Receptiveness

Being open to another person's experience of life is more difficult than it appears on the surface. Carl Rogers knew that his mother was not going to be psychologically available to him as a listener. However, often the blocks and distortions are subtle rather than as obvious as in his mother's case. Furthermore, many carry round the illusion that they listen well, despite the pervasiveness of anxiety and of set ways of perceiving in most people's everyday communication.

As a helper you need to be present to your clients. This entails an absence of defensiveness and a willingness to allow the expressions and experiencing of your clients to affect you. Ideally you should be 'all there' – with your body, your thoughts, your senses and your emotions. You offer a person-to-person contact to another. Bugental observes that the process of presence has two chief aspects: accessibility and expressiveness.[13] *Accessibility* entails 'a reduction of the usual social defences against being influenced or affected by others. It implies a measure of trust and vulnerability.' *Expressiveness* entails 'making available some of the contents of one's subjective awareness without distortion or disguise. It implies a measure of commitment and a willingness to put forward some effort.'

Sensitivity and vulnerability are qualities in counsellors and helpers that can be for good or ill. At best, they allow for a deep accessibility to and understanding of clients.[14] Also, they are necessary for your own personal development. At worst, they block understanding and contribute to the manipulation and depersonalization of others.

Physical Attending

To be a rewarding person with whom to talk you need physically to convey your receptiveness and interest. Sometimes this is referred to as attending behaviour. Some of the main non-verbal ways you can demonstrate your interest and attention as a listener are as follows:

- *Availability.* It may seem obvious, but helpers may sometimes be rightly or wrongly perceived as unavailable to help. It may be that they are genuinely overworked and simply do not have time for everyone. Some may be poor at letting their availability be known. Others may be giving out messages, possibly without realizing it, that create distance. For instance, a teacher may physically withdraw if a pupil seems to want to discuss a personal concern. You need to be clear about any formal and informal messages you convey about availability and access.
- *Relaxed body posture.* A relaxed body posture, without slumping or slouching, contributes to conveying the message that you are receptive. If you sit in a tense and uptight fashion, your clients may either consciously think or intuitively feel that you are so bound up in your personal agendas and unfinished business that you are not fully aware of them. Depending on how they are done, crossed arms, crossed legs, a stiff body posture, finger drumming, leg bouncing and fidgeting may each indicate tension.

- *Physical openness.* Physical openness means facing the speaker not only with your face but with your body. Trainers such as Egan[15] and Carkhuff[16] recommend sitting square to the other person – your left shoulder to their right shoulder and vice versa. However, another option is to sit at a slight angle to your client, but still in a position where you can both receive all of each other's significant facial and bodily messages. The advantage of this is that it provides each of you with more opportunity to vary the directness of your contact than if you are sitting opposite to each other. This may be especially appreciated by highly vulnerable clients.
- *Slight forward lean.* Leaning forward is a sign of your involvement. However, if you lean too far forward you look odd and your clients may consider that you invade their personal space. If you lean back, they may find this distancing. Especially at the start of relationships, a slight forward trunk lean can, without being threatening, encourage the talker.
- *Good eye contact.* Good eye contact means looking in your client's direction so that you allow the possibility of your eyes meeting reasonably often. Staring threatens clients. They may feel dominated or seen through. Some clients even feel threatened at seeing their own reflections in shop windows. Looking down or away too often may indicate tension and boredom. Good eye contact also means that you see all the facial messages your clients send.
- *Appropriate facial expression.* A friendly, relaxed facial expression, including a smile, usually demonstrates interest. However, if your client comes in agitated or weeping, a smile would be inappropriate. Your facial expression needs to show that you are tuned into their verbal, vocal and bodily messages.
- *Use of head nods.* Each head nod can be viewed as a reward to the client giving the message that you are paying attention. Head nods need not signify that you agree with everything clients say, but rather that you are interested. As with all physical signals of attending, head nods can be used to control what clients say rather than to free them to communicate from their frame of reference. You need to become aware of whether, when and why you physically respond differently to your clients according to what they say: for example, encouraging either their negative or positive comments about themselves.

As your relationships develop, your clients get to know whether and when you are receptive to them. For instance, clients may know from past experience that when you lean back you still attend. However, based on the experience of innumerable hours of training people to listen, I can say that all too often people's bodily communication is much poorer than they think. Consequently, you may need to become more aware of your current behaviour as a step in remedying any skills deficits you possess. Exercise 2.2 gives you the opportunity to explore how you use your body when you listen. If possible, video-record your sessions. Not just being told, but actually seeing, how your body messages come across may sharpen your awareness and increase your motivation for any changes required.

Exercise 2.2   Demonstrating attention and receptiveness with body messages

This exercise may be done on your own, in pairs or as part of a training group.

A   *On your own*
Write down as many ways you can think of for choosing to demonstrate, by means of body messages, attention and receptiveness when you listen.
B   *In pairs*
Partner A talks for three minutes while Partner B demonstrates attention and receptiveness by means of body messages, but does not talk. Both partners are seated. Partner A should focus on: relaxed body posture, physical openness, slight forward lean, good eye contact, appropriate facial expressions, and use of head nods. At the end of three minutes Partner A gives Partner B feedback on his/her demonstration of attention and receptiveness as a listener. Partners then reverse roles. If possible, video-record each three-minute session and play it back to illustrate the feedback. This exercise may be repeated with progressively longer sessions.
C   *In a training group*
The trainer goes through ways of choosing to use body messages as a listener to show attention and receptiveness. The trainer then demonstrates showing attention and receptiveness through body messages with one of the trainees who talks for three minutes. The trainer then subdivides the group into threes – listener, talker and observer – and trainees are given the opportunity to be each. Where feasible, the trainer enables trainees to get video feedback on how they use their bodies when they listen. At the end of the subgroups, the trainer holds a plenary sharing and discussion session. Trainees are encouraged to practise in their everyday lives the use of good body messages to demonstrate attention and receptiveness when listening.

Giving Permission to Talk

Permissions to talk are comments that indicate that you are ready and willing to listen. They tend to be made at the start of each helping session. Also, they can be made on many occasions in informal contexts. These statements are 'door openers'. The message in all of them is: 'I'm interested and prepared to listen. I'm giving you the opportunity of sharing with me what you think and feel.' Permissions to talk are often best if they are *open-ended* questions that leave clients free to respond how they wish. This is especially so in an initial session. An example of an open-ended permission to talk is: 'What would you care to talk about today?'. An example of a close-ended permission to talk is: 'I hear you have difficulty speaking in public. Tell me about it.'

Examples of permissions to talk that might be used in *helping sessions* include:

> 'Hello, I'm —————. Would you care to:
> tell me why you've come to see me
> tell me what is concerning you
> tell me how you see your situation
> put me in the picture.'
> 'You've been referred by —————. Now how do you see your situation?'
> 'Where would you like to start today?'

In less formal helping contexts, a good time to choose to use a permission to talk is when you sense someone has a personal agenda that bothers them, but requires that extra bit of encouragement to share it. Permissions to talk that might be used in *informal helping* include:

> 'You seem upset. Is there something on your mind?'
> 'Would you like to share it with me?'
> 'I'm available if you want to talk.'
> 'I'm happy to listen to what you have to say.'
> 'I'd like to hear your viewpoint.'

DISCIPLINING YOUR HEARING

At its most basic level, good listening involves the capacity to hear and remember accurately what has been said. This may be easier said than done. For example, your clients may tell you more than you can easily remember, or they may not express themselves clearly, or may have distracting mannerisms. On your side, your own needs may get in the way of your hearing. You may be tired, angry or have unfinished business in your mind from a previous client. Additionally, you may have made up your mind what the client's problem is and consequently selectively hear mainly what fits into your formulation.

Choosing to listen well entails choosing to discipline your hearing. Put another way, you need to be able to hear the client accurately prior to choosing whether to respond from either their frame of reference or your own. I have noticed many times, when reviewing audiotapes and videotapes of counsellor trainees' sessions, that they sometimes respond as though they have not heard what the client has said. Certain of their responses ignore what has been said in the immediately preceding statement. On other occasions, the trainee may ask a question later which is unnecessary since the client has already supplied this information.

Exercise 2.3 is a disciplined hearing exercise. Though the exercise may seem artificial, some of you may be surprised to find how errors can creep into your listening even at this level. This is especially likely to be the case when client statements become longer.

Exercise 2.3   Repeating content in brief interviews

This exercise can be done in pairs or in a training group.

A   *In pairs*
Partner A, demonstrating attention and receptiveness, gives partner B permission to talk. Partner B spends five minutes discussing either a personal/work issue or evaluating his/her current experience and skills as a helper. Partner B should begin by speaking in short sentences, pause, allow partner A to give a precise repetition response (changing the first to the second person singular), before going on. Partner B feeds partner A progressively longer sentences. At the end of five minutes, partners discuss their experience of the exercise before reversing roles. It can also be helpful to audio-record and play back the interviews. The exercise may be repeated for progressively longer periods – ten minutes, fifteen minutes each way.

B   *In a training group*
The trainer demonstrates the above exercise with a group member for five minutes. Group members then do the exercise either in pairs or triads (talker, repeater and observer) with each person having the chance to be the repeater. Afterwards, group members come back for a plenary sharing and discussion session. Again, the exercise can be repeated for progressively longer periods. Repeaters should use their attending and showing receptiveness skills, as well as emphasizing precision in their responses.

Hearing Vocal Messages

Effective helpers are skilled not only at picking up what clients say, but also how they say it. Frequently *how* clients communicate is much more revealing than what they actually say, as their words may be more concealing than revealing. The client's communications consist of both verbal messages and vocal and body 'framing' messages which may or may not match the verbal messages. Table 2.1 presents some dimensions of vocal messages.

Table 2.1 *Some dimensions of vocal messages*

Dimension	*Illustrative characteristics*
Volume	Loudness, quietness, audibility
Pace	Fast, slow, ease of following
Stress	Monotonous, melodramatic
Pitch	High pitched, low-pitched, shrill, deep
Enunciation	Clear, mumbled, slurred
Intensity	Very intense, light-hearted
Accent	National, regional, social class variations
Speech disturbances	Stammering, repetition

At one level, helpers need to hear the vocal messages accurately. At another level, they need to understand their meaning. Much emotional content is conveyed by voice messages. Sometimes these come over loud and clear, as when a client says with intensity she hates her partner. On other occasions, the vocal expression may not match what the client says: for instance, using a flat voice to express happiness and joy about a relationship. Exercise 2.4 is a simple consciousness-raising exercise in relation to vocal messages, your own and other people's.

Exercise 2.4   Hearing vocal messages

The exercise can be performed in a number of different ways.

A   *On your own*
Write out an assessment of your vocal messages on each of the dimensions listed in Table 2.1
B   *In pairs*
Speak in a manner as close to your usual one as possible, and hold a conversation with your partner for two to five minutes. It may help to

audio-record the conversation. At the end of this period, on each of the dimensions listed in Table 2.1, give feedback to your partner on his or her vocal messages and then allow your partner to give similar feedback to you. Both of you may wish to illustrate your feedback with examples from the recording. This exercise may also be done in triads, with each person taking a turn as observer.

C   *In a training group*
One option is to break the group down into either pairs or triads and perform the exercise as in B above, but come back together at the end for a plenary sharing and discussion session. Another option, especially if group members have had some prior contact, is to ask one member to assess his or her vocal communication on the Table 2.1 dimensions, then to get the other members to provide feedback on how they see that person's vocal messages. Each group member should have the opportunity to be the focus of attention.

OBSERVING BODY MESSAGES

Good listening involves choosing to see as well as to hear. Both you and your clients are always sending body messages, some dimensions of which are listed in Table 2.2.

Table 2.2   *Some dimensions of body messages*

Dimension	Illustrative characteristics
Eye contact	Staring, looking down or away, signalling interest
Facial expression	Expressive of thoughts and feelings, vacant, smiling, hostile
Hair	Length, styling
Gesture	Amount, variety, e.g. arm movements
Grooming	Neat, unkempt, tidy, untidy, clean, dirty
Smell	Body odour present, deodorized, fragrant, pungent
Touch	Part of social ritual: illustrating companionship, sensuality, aggression
Physique	Thinness, fatness, muscularity
Physical distance	Near, far, ability to touch
Trunk lean	Forwards, backwards
Trunk orientation	Facing, turned away
Posture	Upright, slouched
Degree of tension	Tight, relaxed
Fidgeting	Fiddling with hair, fingers, etc.
Perspiration	Sweating, absence of sweating
Breathing	Regular, shallow and rapid
Blushing	Presence or absence, location of blushes

There are many reasons why paying attention to clients' body messages is important. If you are to receive and resonate their communications, you cannot miss out on a major means by which they send messages. For instance, body messages may convey clients' general state of psychological wellbeing, energy level, vitality and health. They also help you to understand the genuineness or congruence of specific communications. Where people communicate openly, verbal, vocal and body messages match each other. When they put on a facade, wear a social mask or 'present a self' to you, their vocal and body 'framing' messages tend not to match what they say. Additionally, accurate observation of body messages helps you to assess the impact your own responses have on clients. For instance, do they show attention and receptiveness to what you say? In the final analysis, do they turn up or not?

Exercise 2.5 is a consciousness-raising exercise to encourage you to observe and accurately label other people's body messages. During the exercise you may get some interesting feedback about the way you communicate with your body.

Exercise 2.5   Mirroring and reading body messages

This exercise can be done either in pairs or in a training group.

A   *In pairs*
Partner A talks to partner B for two minutes. During this period, partner B copies or mirrors all of partner A's body messages, but does not speak. At the end of the two minutes, partner B shares how he or she interpreted or read partner A's body messages. Partner A comments on this. Afterwards, reverse roles. This exercise may also be done in triads with each person taking a turn as external observer.

B   *In a training group*
The trainer demonstrates the above exercise by acting as partner B with a group member as partner A. The group is then divided into threes (partner A, partner B, and external observer) with trainees rotating until they have played all three roles. The external observer always gives feedback before roles are changed. Afterwards, the trainer holds a plenary sharing and discussion session. Alternatively, the group can perform the exercise in pairs prior to a plenary sharing and discussion session.

SOURCES OF INTERFERENCE

In an ideal world clients would be readily and easily understood by their helpers. In the real world, life is not that easy. An analogy may be made between two amateur radio operators who are trying to communicate. When all goes well, the receiver receives the sender 'loud and clear'. However, on a number of occasions there is likely to be poor communication due to static or interference. The reasons for this interference may be located in the sender's radio, the receiver's radio or both. Making good listening choices can be difficult. There are numerous barriers and filters to accurate reception of information.

Table 2.3 lists some possible sources of interference, located in your clients, to your receiving their messages loud and clear.

Table 2.3   *Possible sources of interference to listening located in the client*

Client characteristic

Lack of trust in the helper
Shyness
Inner rules that inhibit disclosure
Anxiety and tension
Diminished self-awareness
Difficulty acknowledging and/or expressing feelings
Exhibiting threatening emotions, e.g. anger, appreciation, sexuality
Engaging in competitive power contest
Not seeming to listen to the helper
Lacking clarity regarding the intentions of a message
Leaving material out by mistake
Leaving material out because of incorrect assumption that it is known
Encoding message rather than communicating it directly
Not matching vocal and body with verbal messages
Sending distracting body messages
Having poor vocal communication, e.g. speaks quietly, stammers
Having heavy accent
Having poor command of language
Talking too much, delivering monologue
Coming from a different culture
Coming from a different socio-economic group
Being of a different gender, age group, religion, etc.

Clients are often clients precisely because they have difficulty communicating. With you they may be shy, find it hard to trust you and have all sorts of inner rules about what it is appropriate to disclose: for instance, some clients may be reluctant to talk about their parents, homosexual tendencies, etc. Clients may exude a level of anxiety and tension that you find distracting. Because some of them are out of touch with their own thoughts and feelings, they have difficulty articulating and expressing these clearly to you. You may find some of your clients' emotions threatening. For example, anger, appreciation and sexuality can each be expressed either about third parties or towards you. Some clients may threaten you by competing with you and frustrate you by not listening.

It may be hard for you to be clear about messages when your clients are unclear themselves. They may leave material out either unintentionally or because they assume that you know it already. Many messages are not sent loud and clear, but encoded. This requires the receiver to decode the verbal, vocal and bodily components of the message to understand the real communication. For instance, a client may say 'I'm not upset' with a choked voice. The more clients communicate in code rather than direct, the more chance there is for misunderstanding on the part of listeners through errors in decoding. Additionally, if clients have distracting mannerisms and awkward voice characteristics, this may contribute to poor reception. Clients who talk too much, or 'ear-bash', risk closing their helpers' ears. Also, there are numerous considerations centred on clients' differences from you – such as culture, age and gender – which may present barriers to your listening to them well.

Part of the skill of becoming a good listener is the ability to overcome many of the sources of interference located in others. However, an even more important part of the skill, though related to coping with external sources of interference, is the ability to assume responsibility for becoming aware and dealing with your own barriers and filters to listening with understanding. As Burley-Allen observes: 'Not many adults realize that they have listening problems'.[17] You need to acknowledge that, as you have grown up, you have had a training in perception that has taught you both what to see and also what to ignore. Furthermore, your own anxieties and level of acceptance will mediate the level of acceptance, and hence quality of listening, that you offer to clients. The level of self-acceptance of some helpers is so low, because they have been inadequately listened to when growing up, that, like some clients, they require a nourishing and healing helping relationship to remedy their earlier misfortune. All helpers need to acknowledge that effective listening is a learned skill that requires constant vigilance to be maintained. None of us can afford the luxury of considering listening difficulties to be solely the preserve of clients.

Table 2.4 identifies possible sources of interference located in helpers.

Table 2.4 *Possible sources of interference to listening located in the helper*

Helper characteristic
Attention sources of interference Hearing difficulties Sight difficulties Distractability, e.g. by noise

Table 2.4 (*contd.*)

Fatigue, illness
Low attention span
Unfinished business, personal agendas, thinking of something else
Time pressure
Time lag, daydreaming

Receiving messages sources of interference
Memory difficulties
Leaving out, adding, substituting material
Limited intelligence
Being out of touch with feelings, and hence unable fully to receive another's feelings
Poor skills of identifying and labelling feelings
Poor skills at reading and understanding vocal and body messages
Selective listening in areas of personal need and prejudice
Anxiety and threat
Insufficient cross-cultural awareness
Theoretical blinkers
Premature conceptualization of client's difficulties
Anxiety about how to respond
Feeling under pressure to get results
Sympathy rather than empathy
Lacking decoding skills
Lacking assertion skills
Inability to identify crux of matter

Sending discouraging messages to clients
Demonstrating poor attention and receptiveness
Sending discouraging body messages
Lacking capacity for empathic responding
Lacking capacity for helpful questioning
Being perceived as less than competent
Being perceived as less than trustworthy
Being perceived as less than attractive
Language deficits, e.g. for communicating with ethnic minorities

---

The client sends a message, even if imperfect, that may then be either received accurately or distorted so that the message ultimately received differs from the message originally sent. In some instances, incoming messages are totally denied.

Some of those barriers and filters affect the level of *attention* you offer your clients. Obvious ones include: poor hearing, poor vision, distracting noise, fatigue, illness, low energy level, low attention span and time pressure. Unfinished business either from a previous client, from other aspects of your work, or from your personal life may seriously interfere with attention. Indeed, you may catch yourself not having heard a section of what your client has said because other things have been on your mind. Time lag refers to the possibility that your rate of processing information may be considerably faster than your rate of speech. This may contribute to loss of attention through, for instance, daydreaming. Alternatively, time lag could be used constructively both to understand the material better and to think about how best to respond.

As well as poor attention, there are numerous barriers and filters that affect helpers' abilities to *receive* their clients' messages accurately. Memory difficulties may have at least two causes. First, receivers may not have sufficient discipline to be able to memorize precisely. Second, some people's capacity for retention is worse than others. Partly because of difficulty memorizing and partly for other reasons (for example, selective listening), you may leave out, substitute or even add material to what your client has said. Limited intelligence blocks some helpers from clearly understanding their clients. Listeners who are distant from their own feelings have some of their sensitivity blocked for receiving and resonating to others' feelings. Furthermore, they may have poor skills at observing, understanding and labelling clients' feelings. Helpers who have rigid inner rules regarding their own and others' behaviour may be blocked from adequately processing information that runs counter to their thoughts. Moreover, their listening may be affected by their personal needs; for example, some may encourage and others discourage clients from openly discussing their sexuality, depending upon their own anxieties and interests.

Anxiety and threat are present to a greater or lesser degree in all relationships. Virtually everybody, in varying degrees, likes approval and fears rejection. To the degree that helpers either feel anxious in themselves or are helped to feel anxious by their clients, there is a greater chance that this anxiety harms rather than helps their listening and subsequent communication. Feelings of shyness, emotional instability and threat may each contribute to poor and defensive listening. Some helpers may be vulnerable to specific *situations*. These include: initial sessions, handling silences, handling clients in crisis, and working with a group. Some helpers may feel vulnerable in relation to client *feelings*, especially if expressed strongly and directed towards them. Such feelings may include anger, dissatisfaction, frustration, appreciation and sexual attraction. Helpers may also find discussion of certain *topic areas* to be threatening. Sometimes this is because they have had or are undergoing similar painful experiences: for example, difficulty with a partner or child. Also, through not having developed sufficient awareness of their patterns of meaning and behaviour, some helpers may find it harder than is desirable to understand clients from different cultures.

Trained helpers are at risk of some barriers and filters that lay helpers are not. They may acquire theoretical blinkers that narrow their capacity to respond to all the information presented by clients. Based on their theoretical understanding, they may then rush into premature and incorrect conceptualizations of their clients' difficulties. This may lead them to listen in a self-fulfilling prophecy mode, in which they mainly hear what they want to. People undergoing training in helping, and even experienced practitioners, may get so anxious and involved in how to respond that this interferes with their listening. A contributory factor may be that of feeling under pressure to get results. Sometimes sympathy gets in the way of empathy. For example, helpers may wish to reassure or to rescue their clients rather than to listen to them accurately.

Helpers may be poor at receiving the crux of a client's message – they may fail to distinguish the wood from the trees. They may lack decoding skills, or they may not check the accuracy of their understanding. Sometimes helpers lack assertion skills. The effect of this may be that they allow clients to go on talking without checking out that they still understand their frame of reference.

Helpers can also *send discouraging messages to clients* that inhibit them from providing material to which they can listen. Mention has already been made of the need to show attention and receptiveness. Helpers require skills in creating a safe emotional climate in which clients can reveal themselves. They need to avoid unhelpful and threatening behaviour and to develop the skills of empathic responding and helpful questioning. Furthermore, clients are more likely to reveal themselves to people who communicate competence, trustworthiness and attractiveness. Additionally, not speaking the first language of certain clients may make it hard for them to understand you.

Exercises 2.6 and 2.7 are designed to help you become more aware of how you may interfere with receiving your clients' messages loud and clear. How do you introduce static into the relationship? What sources of interference prevent you from fully tuning into and staying tuned into another's wavelength? If you think you are totally immune to such considerations, there is a good chance that you may not yet possess sufficient insight into how you function to be an effective counsellor or helper! If you can identify some of your sources of interference, you have taken a first step in making the necessary choices to remedy them.

Exercise 2.6   Exploring your sources of interference to listening

This exercise may be done on your own, in pairs or as part of a training group.

A   *On your own*
Look at Table 2.4 on possible sources of interference in the helper. Write down your answers to the following questions.
1.   Identify and assess the likely impact of any sources of interference that either prevent or might prevent you from *attending* as fully as possible when you counsel or help.
2.   Identify and assess the likely impact of any sources of interference that either prevent or might prevent you from *receiving messages* from your clients as accurately as possible when you counsel or help.
3.   Identify and assess the likely impact of any *discouraging messages you may be sending to clients* that either prevent or might prevent their revealing themselves to you as fully as might be beneficial when you counsel or help.

B   *In pairs*
Either independently answer all the above questions, then discuss;
or work through the above exercise together from the start.

C   *In a training group*
The trainer introduces the idea of people having internal barriers and filters that interfere with accurate listening. The trainer may then take the whole group through the exercise question by question. Alternatively, the trainer may subdivide the group into pairs, threes or fours, get them to answer the above questions, and then end with a plenary sharing and discussion session.

Exercise 2.7   Listening to your reactions

The following exercise can be done on your own, in pairs, or in a training group.

A   *On your own*
Below are brief statements about a range of clients. Rate the degree of difficulty you might experience as a helper in listening accurately in an initial session to each of the clients below. Use the following scale:
   0   *No problem* in listening accurately
   1   *Slight problem* in listening accurately
   2   *Moderate problem* in listening accurately
   3   *Great problem* in listening accurately

Your rating   *Client characteristic*

_____ 1.   Sue, aged twenty-nine, starts questioning the adequacy of your listening and says you do not really understand her.
_____ 2.   Ted, aged thirty-five, name drops and tries hard to impress you with the importance of his social connections.
_____ 3.   Khalid, aged forty-eight, is a promiscuous homosexual Pakistani with an eye for younger white males.

———————— 4. Kate, aged twenty-two, has just left her husband and two young children.

———————— 5. Ellie, aged nine, is an orphan who is extremely unhappy with her foster parents.

———————— 6. Ariane, aged fifty-two, is a recent migrant from Indonesia with a poor command of the English language.

———————— 7. Ronnie, aged sixty, is a Salvation Army man who expresses strong religious convictions.

———————— 8. Ross, aged thirty-eight, is an aggressive and highly entrepreneurial businessman with marriage difficulties.

———————— 9. Tim, aged twenty-seven, is a timid and uptight bachelor who lives with his mother.

———————— 10. Jo, aged forty-two, is an ardent and militant feminist.

———————— 11. Di, aged eighteen, boasts about her good looks and frequent sexual conquests with older men.

———————— 12. Jack, mid thirties, has used physical violence with his wife.

———————— 13. Janet, aged eighty-eight, is a frail widow who feels lonely and depressed and weeps a lot.

———————— 14. Rita, aged twenty-seven, is a black woman who constantly complains about living in a racist society.

———————— 15. Hilda, aged fifty-seven, is a married woman who has just been told that she has terminal cancer.

———————— 16. Ellen, aged twenty-one, is on probation after a series of shoplifting offences.

———————— 17. Hank, aged fourteen, is very tense and withdrawn and says he has contemplated suicide.

———————— 18. Pierre, aged twenty-three, is a single man who says his preferred life-style is to live on the dole.

Write down your reasons for each rating in which you consider you might have a problem in listening accurately to the client. Are there any other categories of client whose characteristics might interfere with your effectiveness as a listener?

B *In pairs*
Answer the questionnaire independently, then discuss.

C *In a training group*
The trainer can break the group down into twos, threes or other subgroups, get them to answer the questionnaire, then discuss. This can be followed by a plenary sharing and discussion session. The trainer can get group members exploring current and prospective situations where the quality of their listening is at risk.

CONCLUDING COMMENT

The reason that babies get born with two ears and only one mouth is that the divine creator intended us to listen and knew how hard it would be.

RESPONSES FOR EXERCISE

Exercise 2.1
1. (a) Internal; (b) external; (c) internal
2. (a) External; (b) external; (c) internal
3. (a) External; (b) internal; (c) external
4. (a) Internal; (b) external; (c) external

3 Communicating and Facilitating Understanding

There is a story about Dr Ida Libido, a psychoanalyst who, like Freud, used to sit out of view behind the head of the couch on which her patients reclined. However, unlike Freud, who was addicted to nicotine, she was addicted to caffeine. Rather naughtily, she would nip out for cups of coffee, leaving her cassette recorder on to listen to her patients' free associations and dreams. One day Fanny Guilt, a patient who was meant to be on the couch, came into the coffee shop. With surprise the analyst said: 'What are you doing here? You're meant to be in analysis.' To which her patient replied: 'Don't worry, doc. I've left my cassette recorder on in your office speaking into your cassette recorder.'

In the next two chapters I focus on ways that, unlike our hypothetical psychoanalyst, you can send responsive or facilitative messages to your clients. The word *facilitative* is derived from the Latin word for 'easy'. As you respond to your clients facilitatively, you make it easier for them to disclose, explore and experience themselves. Staying largely within your clients' frames of reference is the distinguishing feature of these facilitation skills. They are the fundamental building blocks of your helping skills repertoire.

CONTINUATION MESSAGES

In Chapter 2, I mentioned the skills of attending, showing receptiveness and giving your clients permission to talk. Continuation messages are one of the main ways in which you can reward them for talking. Rightly used, continuation messages are brief helper responses that provide the message 'I am with you. Please go on.' Wrongly used, these messages cease to encourage clients to elaborate their internal frame of reference. Instead they have the effect of getting clients to respond to their helpers rather than to themselves. As such they are a travesty of a basic facilitation skill.

Many continuation messages are bodily rather verbal. Bodily continuation messages include responsive facial expressions, head nods, good eye contact, and appropriate body posture and orientation.

Possibly the main verbal continuation message is 'Uh-hmm'. Other verbal continuation messages include:

'Please continue.'
'I see.'
'Then,'
'OK.'
'Indeed.'
'That's interesting.'
'Tell me more.'
'So,'
'Go on.'
'Really.'
'Ah.'
'Yes.'

Clients require a human response from their helpers. If they are scarcely responded to at all, this is likely to extinguish their talking behaviour. On the other hand, if they are responded to too much this may both be artificial and block their process of inner listening. The pacing of the interaction, instead of being relaxed, may become pressurized.

The purpose of basic facilitation skills is not only to provide information for you, but also to help clients become more responsive to themselves. Helping is arguably less about what you do for your clients and more about what you enable them to do inside themselves. As Gendlin observes, if 'you only listen, and indicate only whether you follow or not, you will discover a surprising fact. People can tell you much more and also find more inside themselves, than can ever happen in ordinary interchanges.'[1]

Exercise 3.1 is designed to combine the use of continuation messages with an emphasis on facilitating clients' responsiveness to themselves. I focus at the start of this chapter on facilitating clients' inner listening in the hope that it provides a corrective to superficial forms of listening. These may collude in keeping clients out of touch with themselves.

Exercise 3.1   Using continuation messages to facilitate clients' outer expression and inner listening

This exercise can be done in pairs or in a training group.

A   *In pairs*
Each partner spends five minutes in silence on their own, listening to themselves in relation either to a personal or to a helping concern on which they wish to work. During this inner focusing period, pay attention to any feelings that emerge as well as to your thoughts. You may wish to focus on your breathing as a way into focusing on your body sensations and feelings. Then partner B facilitates partner A for five minutes in exploring his or her concern by using skills such as showing attention and receptiveness, giving a permission to talk, and sending body and verbal continuation messages in a relaxed and unpressurized way. Partner A has total responsibility for what material is presented. Partner B's role is to facilitate partner A in unfolding his or her internal frame of reference. Partner B can indicate if he or she fails to follow ('I'm not quite clear what you mean'), but can never introduce topics nor provide feedback. If partner A expresses getting stuck, partner B can say something like: 'Just take your time . . . let it come from within.' At the end of the session, discuss together, then reverse roles. This exercise can be done for progressively longer periods – ten minutes, fifteen minutes each way.

B   *In a training group*
The trainer introduces the concept of basic facilitation skills, presents the notion of body and verbal continuation messages, and stresses the importance of facilitating inner listening as well as outer expression. The trainer briefly demonstrates the exercise with a group member, playing each role if necessary. The group then does the exercise in pairs prior to coming together for a plenary sharing and discussion session. Group members are encouraged to observe their own and others' use of continuation messages in their everyday lives.

AVOIDING SENDING DISCOURAGING MESSAGES

An important set of choices that distinguishes helpers with good and poor facilitation skills relates to the extent to which they avoid sending discouraging messages. It involves risk for clients to talk about themselves and reveal personal information to you. They are offering something of themselves which may be rejected. The amount that they are likely to reveal relates to the level of safety, acceptance and trust in the relationship.

Clients require psychological space if they are going to talk openly to you and also to listen to themselves. Such space is both quantitative and qualitative. If you are not physically accessible or, when you are, you monopolize the conversation and keep interrupting, you are scarcely giving the client the *quantity* of space in which to talk. However, you can also preclude them from having the *quality* of psychological space they need by choosing to respond in ways that show a lack of respect for the importance of *their* thoughts and feelings. Below are some of the ways in which helpers can communicate to clients a lack of safety and freedom to be and to reveal themselves. I first cover vocal and body and then verbal discouraging messages. Discouraging is used in its literal sense of depriving clients of courage, or 'dis-couraging' them.

Discouraging Non-verbal Messages

You can freeze and threaten clients by using unaccepting body messages when they speak. The following is a patient–psychiatrist joke.

Patient: Doctor, why do you always look out of the window when I speak?

Psychiatrist: The reason that I always look out of the window when you speak is because you are such a boring person.

Here the psychiatrist, human after all, conveniently attributes his unprofessional behaviour to the client's shortcomings. However, the same situation might be seen from the patient's frame of reference. Here the psychiatrist's discouraging behaviour is viewed as both causing and also failing to reward the patient's disclosures.

Patient: Doctor, why do you always look out of the window when I speak?

Doctor: The reason that I always look out of the window when you speak is because you are such a boring person.

Patient: The reason I feel myself and seem to you such a boring person is because you always look out of the window when I speak.

Seeming not to be genuine when you listen breeds a feeling of insecurity in the client. Your clients may consciously or intuitively pick up more messages than you think. Assessing the matching of your words with your vocal and body messages is a major way in which they gauge your sincerity. If you say you are interested and look bored, the latter message will probably be the one that registers with them. If you say you are happy at their good news but seem to force a smile, they may receive the message that you can accept them more when they are depressed than when they are happy.

The damaging effects of poor body messages were highlighted in a study by Haase and Tepper, who asked counsellors to rate a number of ten-second videotaped interactions between a 'counsellor' and a 'client'.[2] They found that even good verbal empathy messages could be reduced to poor ones when the counsellor uttered the message without eye contact, in a backward trunk lean, rotated away from the client, and from a far distance. Another study, by Shapiro and his colleagues, found that judgements of counsellor empathy can reliably be made by both trained and untrained raters from photographs, with facial cues being particularly important.[3]

Exercise 3.2 looks at how you may be encouraging and discouraging clients from talking to you and listening to themselves through your vocal and body messages. Which of your behaviours are rewarding and give courage or confidence to clients and which might be viewed as put-downs?

Exercise 3.2   Encouraging and discouraging vocal and body messages

This exercise can be done on your own, in pairs or as part of a training group.

A   *On your own*
   1. Look at the non-verbal messages below. Imagine yourself in the client's role. Put an 'E' before all those messages on the part of your helper which you would find rewarding or encouraging, and a 'D' before all those messages which you would find unrewarding or discouraging.

____	1.	Picks nose	____ 16.	Looks alert
____	2.	Calm manner	____ 17.	Smiles
____	3.	Leans far back	____ 18.	Sits higher than you
____	4.	Head very close to yours	____ 19.	Shuts eyes
____	5.	Tugs at ear	____ 20.	High-pitched voice
____	6.	Looks towards you	____ 21.	Leans slightly towards you
____	7.	Sits on same level as you	____ 22.	Looks clean
____	8.	Bounces a leg	____ 23.	Comfortable speech pace
____	9.	Waves arms	____ 24.	Low-pitched voice
____	10.	Voice easy to hear	____ 25.	Body posture open to you
____	11.	Stares at you	____ 26.	Shuffles about
____	12.	Looks out of window	____ 27.	Has vacant look
____	13.	Relaxed seating position	____ 28.	Has warmth in voice
____	14.	Slouches	____ 29.	Whispers
____	15.	Raises eyebrow	____ 30.	Looks anxious

2. Assess whether you send any vocal and body messages that either discourage or might discourage clients from talking to you and listening to themselves.

B   *In pairs*
Independently answer the above questionnaire then discuss together, including assessing whether you send any vocal and body messages that either discourage or might discourage clients.

C   *In a training group*
The trainer divides the group into subgroups. Subgroup members answer the questionnaire and assess themselves independently, and then discuss and give feedback to each other. This is followed by a brief plenary sharing and discussion session. The trainer might highlight the emphasis of the exercise by showing video-recorded excerpts of helpers sending encouraging and discouraging vocal and body messages.

Discouraging Verbal Messages

> I was an insecure kid, anxious, unhappy.
> My parents told me I'd grow out of it.
> I was an insecure young man, frustrated, unhappy.
> My friends told me I'd grow out of it.
> I was an insecure husband, dissatisfied, unhappy.
> My wife told me I'd grow out of it.
> I'm an insecure father. My kids are anxious, unhappy.
> I tell them they'll grow out of it.
> Pass the word.

This Jules Feiffer joke is about an inadequate man who has both been sent and now sends verbal messages that discourage communication.

Below are some characteristic ways in which helpers may verbally communicate to their clients that they are not really safe and free to talk about themselves. Some of these are fairly common ways of responding in everyday conversations. To become an effective helper you may have to discipline yourself to give up bad habits. All of the following discouraging verbal messages come from a frame of reference external to the client. Almost all of them indicate difficulty accepting the client as a separate individual with responsibility for his or her own life. Most of the messages could be regarded as put-downs of the client, of varying degrees of subtlety. Consequently the emotional climate of helping becomes less conducive to client disclosure and inner listening than is desirable. Clients may block material from their own awareness and be more inclined to edit what they disclose to you so as not to risk disapproval.

● *Directing and leading.*   Taking control of what the client can talk about: for example, 'I would like you to talk about this today.'

- *Judging and evaluating.* Making evaluative statements, especially ones which imply that the client is not living up to your own standards: for example, 'You are overpossessive.'
- *Blaming.* Assigning responsibility for what happens to the client in a finger-pointing way: for example, 'It's all your fault.'
- *Moralizing, preaching and patronizing.* Telling clients how they ought to be leading their lives: for example, 'Sex is not everything in life.'
- *Labelling and diagnosing.* Placing a diagnostic categorization on the client or on some of his or her behaviour: for example, 'You have an inferiority complex.'
- *Reassuring and humouring.* Trying to make clients feel better, yet not really acknowledging their true feelings: for example, 'You'll be all right.'
- *Not accepting the client's feelings.* Telling the client that his or her positive and negative feelings should be different from what they are: for example, 'You shouldn't be so depressed, pull your socks up.'
- *Advising and teaching.* Not giving clients the space to arrive at their own solutions to their own concerns: for example, 'Why don't you have a coffee with her and talk things over?'
- *Interrogating.* Using questions in such a way that the client feels threatened by unwanted probing: for example, 'Do you masturbate? If so, when, how, and what are your fantasies?'
- *Over-interpreting.* Offering explanations of clients' behaviour which bear little relationship to what they might have thought of by themselves: for example, 'Your reluctance to socialize may indicate some unresolved conflicts, possibly sexual.'
- *Inappropriately talking about yourself.* Talking about yourself in ways that interfere with clients' disclosures: for example, 'You have troubles. Let me tell you mine.'
- *Putting on a professional facade.* Trying to make yourself seem an expert and thereby communicating in a defensive or otherwise inauthentic way: for example, 'I've had a lot of training and experience with problems such as yours.'
- *Faking attention.* Insincerely pretending to be more interested and involved in what is being said than you are: for example, 'That's so interesting.'
- *Placing time pressures.* Letting the client know that your available time for listening is very limited: for example, 'You had better be brief.'

Exercise 3.3 aims to get you exploring which of your present ways of responding may interfere with your being the sort of helper with whom others want to talk. What I am trying to do is to make you more aware of not only when you *choose to stay in* but also when you *choose to depart from* your client's frame of reference, so that you do it with good reason.

Exercise 3.3   How safe are you to talk to?

This exercise may be done on your own, in pairs or as part of a training group.

A   *On your own*
1.   Rate each of the following items according to how often you respond in this way when you help.

Very frequently	4
Frequently	3
Occasionally	2
Almost never	1
Never	0

Characteristic	*Your rating*
1. Directing and leading	_____
2. Judging and evaluating	_____
3. Blaming	_____
4. Moralizing, preaching and patronizing	_____
5. Labelling and diagnosing	_____
6. Reassuring and humouring	_____
7. Not accepting the client's feelings	_____
8. Advising and teaching	_____
9. Interrogating	_____
10. Over-interpreting	_____
11. Inappropriately talking about yourself	_____
12. Putting on a professional facade	_____
13. Faking attention	_____
14. Placing time pressures	_____

2.   Look at the items that you have rated 2, 3 or 4 and assess the impact of these messages on your clients.

B   *In pairs*
Either independently do the above exercise, then discuss;
or work through the above exercise together from the start.

C   *In a training group*
The trainer introduces the idea of being a safe person with whom to talk and avoiding sending discouraging messages. He or she ensures that group members understand what the items in the questionnaire mean. The trainer divides the group into pairs or subgroups who answer the questionnaire

independently and then discuss together. Afterwards, the trainer holds a brief plenary sharing and discussion session. Group members are encouraged to become aware of the times when they choose to send discouraging verbal and non-verbal messages, not only when they help, but also in their everyday lives.

EMPATHIC RESPONDING SKILLS

Empathic responding skills comprise the second phase of Barrett-Lennard's three main phases of 'facilitative relational empathy'.[4] Whereas the first phase was empathic resonation, the second phase focuses on communicating responsive understanding to the client. It is insufficient just to understand the client's frame of reference. You must also communicate accurate understanding. This increases the chances of the third phase of the empathy cycle being attained, namely the client's reception and awareness of your responsive understanding.

Defining Empathic Responding

The concept of empathy tends to get used in two main ways, reflecting the distinction between person- and task-orientations in helping. Carl Rogers' use of the term 'empathy' represents the person-orientation. Rogers views an empathic attitude and the creation of an empathic emotional climate on the part of the helper as freeing clients to listen to and get in touch with their own resources.[5]

Rogers is firmly against viewing empathic listening and responding as a non-directive technique whereby you repeat the last words a client has said. In 1975 he published an updating of his views on the process of being empathic.[6] What he termed his current definition of empathy includes the following:

> entering the private perceptual world of the other and becoming thoroughly at home in it. . . . being sensitive, moment to moment, to the changing felt meanings which flow in this other person . . . sensing meanings of which he/she is scarcely aware, but not trying to uncover feelings of which the person is totally unaware since this would be too threatening . . . communicating your sensings of his/her world as you look with fresh and unfrightened eyes at elements of which the individual is fearful . . . frequently checking with him/her as to the accuracy of your sensings, and being guided by the responses you receive . . . pointing to the possible meanings in the flow of his/her experiencing you help the person to focus on

this useful type of referent, to experience the meanings more fully and to move forward in the experiencing.

Rogers' use of empathy particularly focuses on the construct of experiencing. He attempts to improve the quantity and quality of his clients' inner listening to the ongoing 'psycho-physiological' flow of experiencings within them. This flow is a referent to which individuals can repeatedly turn to discover the 'felt meaning' of their experience. Rogers gives the example of a man in an encounter group not accepting the facilitator's reflection: 'It sounds as though you might be angry with your father', but strongly agreeing with the subsequent statement: 'Maybe you're disappointed in him.' Disappointment rather than anger was the word that described the client's experiencing. In his book on *Focusing*, Gendlin calls contact with this special kind of bodily awareness, awareness of a 'felt sense'.[7] Some clients who are very out of touch with their bodily flow of experiencing may benefit from a nurturing and healing person-oriented relationship prior to more task-oriented work.

In person-oriented helping, empathic reflections may be the major tool of the helper. In task-oriented helping this is not the case. Empathic responses are just one of the skills helpers use to help clients manage their problems or make decisions. For instance, one study showed over 53 per cent of Carl Rogers' verbal responses as falling in the reflection/restatement category. In the same study Arnold Lazarus, a more task-oriented therapist, had only 10 per cent of his responses in the reflection/restatement category. However he had 28, 22 and 19 per cent of his responses respectively in the direct guidance/advice, information providing, and information seeking categories.[8]

Some writers, such as Truax and Carkhuff,[9] Carkhuff,[10] and Egan[11] make a distinction between interchangeable or primary-level accurate empathy and advanced accurate empathy. In primary level accurate empathy, the helper's response is a reflection that matches what clients say and feel. In advanced level accurate empathy, the helper sensitively reflects the deeper or underlying nuances of what clients communicate or avoid communicating.

Client Perception of Empathic Responding

A further way of defining empathic responding is in terms of the extent to which it is perceived by clients. Client perception of empathy, or received empathy, represents the third phase of Barrett-Lennard's empathy cycle. Two ways of exploring the extent to which clients perceive the empathy of their helpers are from their behaviour in helping and by asking them how they view their helpers. There is some research evidence that clients vary in the depth of their self-exploration according to whether helpers offer high, medium or low levels of empathy. Thus it might be inferred that, by engaging in different degrees of self-exploration, clients show they perceive the different levels of empathy of their helpers, at least to some extent. Furthermore, there is again some research evidence that helpers offering high levels of empathy are more likely to be successful with their clients on various outcome measures than those offering low levels of empathy,[12] though this research seems to apply particularly to person-centred helpers. Another study found that clients, but not their helpers, may perceive a lower degree of helper-offered empathy in initial than in subsequent sessions.[13]

Barrett-Lennard has devised a relationship inventory which gives scales for how clients see the relationship offered to them by their helpers.[14] Again, this measure applies particularly to the work of person-centred helpers. The reason I mention it here is that one of the relationship inventory's scales measures the client's perception of the helper's level of empathic understanding. The scale is made up of both positive and negative items. Some illustrative positive items are:

'He/she wants to understand how I see things.'
'He/she nearly always knows exactly what I mean.'
'He/she usually senses or realizes what I am feeling.'
'He/she appreciated exactly how the things I experience feel to me.'

Some illustrative negative items are:

'He/she may understand my words but he/she does not see the way I feel.'
'Sometimes he/she thinks that *I* feel a certain way, because that's the way *he/she* feels.'
'He/she does not realize how sensitive I am about some of the things we discuss.'
'His/her response to me is usually so fixed and automatic that I don't really get through to him/her.'

Clients are likely to perceive helpers not only as they are, but also according to their own needs and wishes. Especially with more disturbed clients, there is a likelihood that their perception of their helpers and of their relationships with them gets distorted. However, this does not invalidate the importance of empathic responding, since the better it is the greater is the likelihood of empathy being perceived, in some measure, by clients.

Discriminating Empathic Responding

A useful distinction in thinking about the helping process is that between discrimination and communication. *Discrimination* involves you in *assessing* how well others or you yourself respond. *Communication* involves actually *responding*. The fact that you may have good skills at discriminating empathic responding does not guarantee that you have good skills at communicating it.

In this section my main emphasis is on interchangeable empathy, or communicating that you have understood the crux of your client's surface thoughts and emotions. Good empathic responding indicates a basic acceptance of clients as people. It avoids sending discouraging messages to clients that stop their flow of talk and emotions. These messages may make them feel inadequate, inferior, defensive or as though they are being talked down to. Good empathic responses are made in easily comprehensible language. They are accompanied by good vocal and body communication, something which the next exercise is unable to incorporate since it is in written form. Implicit in the notion of good empathic responding is the fact that helpers *work in collaboration with* their clients to understand their frame of reference and personal meanings. In such collaborative companionship, helpers always overtly or covertly check the accuracy of their understandings. Furthermore, clients feel secure enough to mention it if they are not being received accurately, and thus keep their helpers on track. The word 'tracking' is a colloquial way of describing making responses that stay within your client's frame of reference.

In discriminating empathic responding it is sometimes helpful to think of a three-link chain: statement–response–statement. The adequacy of an empathic response can partly be ascertained not just by relating it to the initial client statement but by imagining its impact on the next statement. Good empathic responses provide the opportunity for the next statement to be a continuation of the client's original train of thought and experiencing. Poor empathic responses do not.

In the light both of this discussion on good empathic responding and also of the previous discussion on avoiding sending discouraging messages, work through Exercise 3.4.

Exercise 3.4   Discriminating empathic responding

This exercise may be done in a number of ways. Some answers are suggested at the end of the chapter.

A   *On your own*
Empathic responding involves you in accurately listening to and under-standing what your client tells you and then sensitively communicating back your understanding in clear and easily comprehensible language. Take a piece of paper and rate the three responses to each of the client statements using the following scale:

Very good empathic response	4
Good empathic response	3
Moderate empathic response	2
Slight empathy in the response	1
No empathy at all	0

Write down your reason or reasons for each rating.

B   *In pairs*
With a partner either rate individual responses or segments of the exercise and then discuss, or go through the whole exercise making independent ratings and then discuss.

C   *In a training group*
The trainer gets group members to rate responses to one statement at a time. He or she facilitates a sharing and discussion of ratings of that statement before moving on to the next.

Example
Woman to marriage guidance counsellor
Client: I can't make up my mind whether to get a divorce or not. There are so many things to consider. Also I'm scared of being on my own.
Marriage guidance counsellor:
(a) Well, how long have you been married and are there any children involved?
(b) You're undecided about divorce since there are so many angles, including your fears of being alone.
(c) You're too frightened to get divorced at the moment.
Suggested ratings and comments:
(a) 0. External frame of reference, interrogating.
(b) 4. Communicates a very good understanding of her frame of reference.
(c) 1. Some understanding, but goes beyond what she has said. Too cut and dried.

Exercise
1.   Man to counselling psychologist in private practice
     Client: My firm is making me redundant. I'm forty-five and should be at the height of my career. It really hurts.
     Counselling psychologist in private practice:
     (a) You're angry at the way you've been treated.
     (b) You are wallowing in self-pity at the moment.
     (c) You're in a lot of pain because you've been made redundant when you should be at your peak.

2. Employee to manager

   Client: I've got three weeks' leave owing and I want to take it now. My wife's just had our first baby and I'd like to be at home to spend time with the family and do jobs around the house.

   Manager:

   (a) Congratulations. You're keen to take your back leave now for family reasons.

   (b) You've got a lot going on at home, but I'm afraid this is a busy time in the office, too.

   (c) Why didn't you give me advance warning of this request?

3. Young woman to drug counsellor

   Client: When things get on top of me I get this craving. It's like I simply must have a fix to get some happiness and relief.

   Drug counsellor:

   (a) Having a fix is your way of coping with psychological pain.

   (b) You feel compelled to have a fix when life gets too much for you.

   (c) When you feel vulnerable and overwhelmed drugs seem the only way out.

4. Final year secondary school pupil to teacher

   Client: As the year goes by I'm getting more and more tense. If I don't get good marks in the exams, I won't be able to become an engineer. That would be terrible.

   Teacher:

   (a) You have been doing reasonably well up to now. Just keep your head down and your courage up.

   (b) I used to get very tense over exams, but found that I was all right on the day.

   (c) You're increasingly anxious that, come the exams, you will blow your goal of becoming an engineer.

Reflection: Restating Content

'Mirroring' is another word for reflection. Though the two may overlap, a distinction is often made between reflection of content and reflection of feeling. In *reflection of content*, only the literal meaning of clients' words is mirrored. This is done by restating them in slightly different form. In *reflection of feeling*, there is a focus not only on picking up the literal meanings of clients' words, but also on mirroring the vocal and body messages that frame them.

To beginning helpers the notion of reflection may seem highly artificial. This feeling may be combined with the need for many of you to concentrate hard on the different choices you have to make, both in understanding your client and also in formulating your response, which may detract from your spontaneity and possibly add to your feelings of artificiality. A good analogy is with learning to drive a car. Initially you are highly aware of your choice processes as you learn the skill. However, once you are proficient, much of your choice process will take place beneath full awareness.

Even experienced helpers may have problems in making good reflections. A good reflection does not entail the mechanical repeating of what the client has just said. Clients require helping relationships with people, not parrots! A tongue-in-cheek example of such mechanical parroting is this story (probably apocryphal) about a prominent American therapist who was counselling a suicidal client in his office near the top of a tall building.

Client:	I feel terrible.
Counsellor:	You feel terrible.
Client:	I feel really terrible.
Counsellor:	You feel really terrible.
Client:	For two cents I would jump out of that window there.
Counsellor:	For two cents you would jump out of that window there.
Client:	Here I go.
Counsellor:	There you go.
Client:	(Lands on the pavement below with a thud.)
Counsellor:	Thud!

Many people falsely assume that, when they listen, they have an accurate and clear grasp of what has just been said. This may be the case in simple conversations, but is likely to become less true as conversations become more complex and personally involving. A relatively straightforward, but not absolutely foolproof, approach to getting some way into another person's frame of reference is to start your responses with 'you' or 'your'.

Exercise 3.5 aims to build up your skills at paraphrasing. You need the capacity to respond accurately and flexibly to your clients without being a parrot. Try to make your use of language simple and direct. A study I conducted on what terms lay people preferred in reading and learning about human relationships found numerous significant preferences regarding language.[15] For example, 'sexual problems' was preferred to 'sexual dysfunctions', and 'defensive thinking' to 'self-protective thinking'. Psychological jargon is definitely to be avoided. Colloquialisms, however, can add colour and freshness to your responses.

Exercise 3.5 Restating content

This exercise may be done in a number of ways. Some possible paraphrases of the client statements are given at the end of the chapter, but there are usually several ways of paraphrasing the same client statement.

A *On your own*
   Restate in different words the literal meaning of each of the following client statements in clear, simple and, where appropriate, colloquial language. Use 'you' or 'your' where the client uses 'I', 'me' or 'my'. You need not restate every part of the client's statement so long as your response accurately communicates its crux or central message(s).

B *In pairs*
   For each statement write out a restatement response independently, then discuss your responses together. Then counsel your partner for five minutes, focusing especially on restating content. Afterwards discuss and reverse roles. Using audio feedback may be helpful.

C *In a training group*
   The trainer gives group members time to formulate and write down restatement responses to one client statement at a time. The trainer then facilitates a sharing and discussion of the group's responses, including his or her own, before moving on to the next statement. The trainer may then demonstrate giving restatement responses in a brief counselling session with one of the group members. Afterwards the group may subdivide into pairs or triads in which members counsel each other by using paraphrasing.

Example
Client to rehabilitation counsellor
Client: 'Ever since my accident I've been depressed and feeling sorry for myself. At last I'm beginning to see that being disabled is not the end of my life.'
Rehabilitation counsellor's restatement of content: 'You've been feeling low and full of self-pity since your injury. You're now finally realizing that, despite not having full use of your legs, there is a lot left in life.'

Exercise TO P. 68
1. Widow to priest: 'My husband was a fine man. His unexpected death was a great shock. I still miss him terribly.'
2. Boss to employee: 'I'm delighted that you are doing so well. You are making a big difference.'
3. Mother to social worker: 'I seem to be getting on top of things. Before, just getting through the day was a big effort.'
4. Youth to probation officer: 'My mother says do this. My father says do that. I really don't know where I stand.'

Reflection: Focusing on Feelings

Reflecting feelings may be viewed as *feeling with* another's flow of emotions and experiencing and being able to communicate this back to the speaker. Beginning helpers often have trouble with the notion of reflecting feelings, since they just talk about feelings rather than offer an expressive emotional companionship which goes some way to mirroring their clients' feelings. Reflecting feelings can be seen as responding to your clients' music rather than just to their words. To do this properly, you need to be proficient in the following areas:

- Observing face and body movements.
- Hearing vocal communication.
- Listening to words.
- Allowing clients the space to listen to their own experiencing.
- Tuning in to the flow of your own emotional reactions.
- Sensing the meanings of your client's messages.
- Taking into account the client's degree of self-awareness.
- Responding in a way that focuses on feelings.
- Checking out the accuracy of your understanding.

Impressionists such as Rich Little in the United States, Max Gillies in Australia and Mike Yarwood in Britain are experts at mirroring the body and vocal characteristics of the people they impersonate. They mirror their subjects by *sending* information as their subjects do. Your job as a listener is to *receive* information in a way that shows emotional responsiveness to clients. To do this, you need to integrate the mirroring of emotional messages from clients into your responses. Much of this can be done by varying your vocal inflections and facial expressions. For instance, if a hypothetical suicide-prone client says 'I feel terrible', you could adjust your vocal and facial expression to mirror a sense of desperation. This does not prevent your voice and face also expressing warmth and sympathy.

Reflecting feelings entails expressive listening and responding. Thus reflection of feelings needs to be accurate in two ways. First, feelings need to be correctly identified. Second, their level of intensity needs to be correctly expressed. At one extreme there is the wooden helper who continuously subtracts from the level of intensity of the speaker. At the other extreme is the melodramatic helper who overemphasizes the speaker's intensity of feelings. If anything, in North American, Australian and British cultures, there is a tendency either to ignore or to subtract from the level of intensity of speakers' feelings rather than to overemphasize them.

Another consideration in reflecting feelings is whether and the degree to which clients acknowledge their feelings. For instance, as a helper you may infer that a parent is absolutely furious with a child. However, the parent may not be able to handle such an observation since it clashes with their self-image of being an ideal and loving parent. Thus you need to use your judgement in choosing how much of the client's feelings to reflect.

In the previous chapter I emphasized the importance of hearing vocal and observing body messages. Exercise 3.6 focuses on understanding feelings from voice and body messages. Children tend to express their emotions very openly, but as we grow up we receive and internalize numerous messages about which emotions it is appropriate for people of our cultural, social and family background and of our gender to express where and when. Consequently many emotional messages 'come out sideways' rather than being expressed loud and clear – they are encoded and need to be decoded. Even if they are decoded accurately, there is the further issue of whether your clients are sufficiently self-aware to acknowledge them if reflected back.

The first time you do the exercise, focus on the more obvious manifestations of anger, happiness, sadness and anxiety. Later on you may wish to list some of the ways an emotion like anger may be expressed when it 'comes out sideways' rather than gets expressed directly. For instance, clients may both smile and clench their fists. In other words, you receive a mixed message that requires decoding.

Exercise 3.6 Understanding feelings from voice and body messages

This exercise can be done on your own, in pairs or as part of a training group. Some answers are suggested at the end of the chapter.

A   *On your own*
   By filling in the blank spaces, write out what voice and body messages you might observe for each of the following feelings:

Non-verbal cue	Anger	Happiness	Sadness	Anxiety
Tone of voice				
Voice volume				

Non-verbal cue	Anger	Happiness	Sadness	Anxiety
Eye contact				
Facial expression				
Posture				
Gestures				

Assess your effectiveness at understanding other people's feelings from their voice and body messages.

B   *In pairs*
Either complete the above exercise independently, then discuss;
or work through the above exercise together from the start.

C   *In a training exercise*
The trainer gives each group member a copy of the exercise and gets them to fill it out independently, in pairs, or in triads. This is followed by a plenary session in which a master answer sheet for the exercise is drawn up.

What people actually say, the verbal messages, can also give you a considerable amount of information about their feelings. The ability to listen for another's 'feelings words' is an important subskill in reflecting feelings. The following is an example of feelings words being ignored.

Charles: I have my law exams coming up and its vital for my career to get a good grade. My whole future depends on it. I'm so worried.
Helper: Your exams are soon?
Charles: Yes, they are in the last half of March.

The focus of the helper's response has encouraged Charles to answer from his head rather than in terms of his feelings. The conversation has been steered towards facts rather than feelings.

Below is an example of how the reflection of his feelings might have helped Charles discuss them further.

Charles: I have my law exams coming up and it's vital for my career to get a good grade. My whole future depends on it. I'm so worried.
Helper: You're really anxious because you have these make-or-break exams imminent.
Charles: Yes. I can't sleep properly any more and I'm not eating well. I have a constant feeling of tension and wonder what I should do.

Here the helper's response has correctly identified Charles' worry and anxiety rather than blocked its discussion. Charles was able to use this reflection of feeling response not only to elaborate his feelings but also as a stepping stone to wondering about how he should handle them. Reflective responding *focusing on* Charles' *feelings* is helping him move on to *taking action* to cope with them.

There is, of course, a risk that constant reflection of feelings just encourages people to talk rather than to act. For instance, Sam may wallow in his feelings of hurt and self-pity when discussing his relationship with Bettina which is not going well. However, this does not invalidate the importance of reflecting feelings, but just means that judgement is needed in when and how much to use this skill.

Exercise 3.7 attempts to help you become more disciplined at listening for and picking up verbal messages about feelings. Having identified the feelings words, you are asked to provide alternative feelings words. The third part of the exercise asks you to formulate reflective responses focusing on feelings. For didactic purposes the format of this exercise requires you to respond to all the feelings expressed by the speaker. In real-life helping, your reflection of feelings may be much more selective. For instance, if a speaker mentioned three feelings, you might decide to respond only to the one felt most intensely. In formulating your reflective responses, try to match, rather than to add or subtract from, the level of intensity of the other's feelings.

Exercise 3.7   Listening to the music – reflecting feelings

This exercise may be done in a number of ways. Some suggestions for words, phrases and responses are provided at the end of the chapter.

A   *On your own*
   For each of the following statements: (a) identify the words or phrases the client has used to describe how he or she feels; (b) suggest other words or phrases to describe how the client feels; and (c) formulate a response focusing on and reflecting the client's feelings, starting with the words 'You feel . . .'. Write out your answers.

B   *In pairs*
   Either independently answer, and then discuss together, your answers to one statement at a time;
   or work through the exercise together from the start.
   Then counsel each other for a minimum of five minutes each way making sure to focus on and reflect feelings. Check your understanding when you are not altogether clear, so you make sure you describe your partner's feelings accurately.

C   *In a training group*
The trainer gives group members time to formulate answers to one statement at a time and then facilitates the sharing and discussion of them.
   The trainer may then demonstrate reflecting feelings in a brief interview
with a group member. Afterwards, the group divides into pairs or triads and
practises counselling each other, focusing on and reflecting feelings.
Example
Old man to priest: 'I feel that I've not long to go now. I'm grateful that I've
had such a good life. I've loved my family, who have meant more to me than
anything in the world. While I don't want to die, I am not frightened any more
of death.'

(a)   Client's words and phrases to describe his feelings: 'not long to go',
      'grateful', 'loved', 'have meant more to me', 'want to' and 'frightened'.
(b)   Other words and phrases to describe how the client feels: 'time is
      running out', 'thankful', 'adored', 'most important of all to me', 'wish to'
      and 'afraid'.
(c)   Possible response focusing on and reflecting the client's feelings: 'You
      feel that your time is nearly up. You are thankful for the blessings of life
      and especially for your family. The prospect of death, while unwel-
      come, no longer makes you afraid.'

Exercise
1.   Recent immigrant to community-relations worker: 'I'm glad that we've
     come here, since we're not nearly so poor as at home. I miss my
     homeland, though. There I was accepted and respected and enjoyed
     the closeness of village life.'
2.   Young male to youth worker: 'I wish that we could have a better club
     here. This town is very boring in the evenings and us young people
     need somewhere to go to meet each other and enjoy ourselves.'
3.   Female to student counsellor: 'I had a terrific row with one of my
     lecturers in a laboratory class the other day. I felt that he was putting me
     down. I've noticed in the past that I quickly get very irritable with people
     in authority.'
4.   Female to marriage counsellor: 'My husband seems to be losing his
     grip on his work as a painter and decorator. He does not get as much
     work as he used to and mopes round the house a lot. I'm getting fed up
     with living in such a depressing atmosphere.'

   One kind of reflective responding that is often helpful entails reflecting
back both feelings and reasons. For instance, in the examples of Charles
and his helper, Charles' main feeling, that of worry, came at the end of his
statement. When the helper replied the second time, he picked up
Charles' feelings and placed it at the start of his own response. After

reflecting the feeling, he used the word 'because' as a transition to reflecting Charles' reasons for the feeling. Exercise 3.8 requires you to reflect feelings and reasons in a standard 'You feel . . . because . . .' format. People starting listening training often have trouble both identifying feelings and stating them accurately. The exercise tries to make sure you do this first before moving on to reflect the reasons for the feeling.

Exercise 3.8   Reflecting feelings and reasons

This exercise may be done in a number of ways. Some possible responses are provided at the end of the chapter.

A   *On your own*
For each of the following statements formulate and write out a response which reflects both feeling and reasons, using the standard format: 'You feel . . . because . . ..'

B   *In pairs*
Either independently formulate a response reflecting feelings and reasons for each statement one at a time, then discuss;
or work through the exercise together from the start.

C   *In a training group*
The trainer gives group members time to formulate and write out their response, reflecting feelings and reasons, to one statement at a time and then facilitates the sharing and discussion of their answers, including his or her own versions.

Example
Sheila to her mother: 'I'm over the moon. I've got my exam results and they've surpassed my wildest hopes. I'm now sure to get into a good university.'
Possible response: 'You feel elated because you've done far better than you ever dreamed. Now you're certain to get a place in a good university.'
Exercise   — P. 65 —
1.   Brenda to teacher: 'I hate being teased. I just hate it. I'm really no different from the other girls and yet they seem to enjoy ganging up on me. It makes me feel so angry and lonely.'
2.   Merle to social worker: 'I've got this neighbour who wants her little boy to play with mine. I would like to please her and yet her boy is very naughty. I feel confused and wonder how best to handle her.'
3.   Sally to family welfare counsellor: 'Though it's not really what we planned, I'm pregnant. I'm surprised how strongly I feel about having the baby. Fortunately, John wants it too.'

4. Helmut to girlfriend: 'I get annoyed when people don't understand my relationship with Tom. Sure we are emotionally very close, but what's wrong with that? Some people can't understand intimate friendships between males.'

Making Empathic Responding Choices

In Chapter 1, I stressed that helpers are choosers who are required to make role, treatment and responding choices. Empathic responding is a complex skill.[16] Table 3.1 provides a checklist of some of the many choices you may need to make each time you want to respond empathically. Fuller guidelines on each choice are given after Table 3.1.

Table 3.1   *Formulating empathic responses: a checklist of choices*

Choices required in formulating an empathic response
1.   When do I respond?
2.   Am I understanding the client's internal frame of reference?
3.   How long should my response be?
4.   What should the pacing of my response be?
5.   How should my voice be?
6.   How should my body be?
7.   To what should I respond?
8.   What language should I use?
9.   How deep should I go?
10. Am I adequately checking the accuracy of my understandings?

1. *When do I respond?*   The choices here include: whether to keep silent, wait for a pause, interrupt, etc. The issue of when applies mainly to your verbal and vocal messages since you always send body messages. When a client initially shares their concern, you may choose not to speak too frequently until they have had time to tell their story. Other clients may need your empathic responses interjected from the start to help them feel more at ease. A simple rule of thumb is to respond sufficiently frequently to ensure that both you and your client know that you understand their frame of reference.

2. *Am I understanding the client's internal frame of reference?*   Here you need to be making good receiver choices entailing picking up and understanding, if possible, verbal, vocal and body cues. If you respond in a way that has implicit in it the question 'Have I understood you rightly?', your client is more likely to help you to

stay accurate. If you do not understand part of what your client has said, you can feed back the part that you did understand and ask them to say more about the part that you did not: for instance, 'You seem to be feeling . . . , but I'm not quite clear what you mean when you say . . ..' If you are totally unclear or have missed a passage, it might be as well to share this tactfully with your client: for instance, by indicating 'I am not clear' rather than saying or interferring 'You did not express yourself clearly.'

3. *How long should my response be?*   A rough guideline when the focus is on empathic listening is that the client-helper talk ratio should be about two to one. Sometimes a brief response may hit the nail on the head. On other occasions you may consider that a longer response is called for. What you are trying to do is to communicate that you have understood the crux of the client's message. It disrupts your client if you talk for too long or start repeating yourself.

4. *What should the pacing of my response be?*   You need to develop a relaxed interviewing style. Some beginning helpers communicate their own anxieties to clients by speaking too rapidly, being unwilling to allow any pauses or silences, and responding *at* clients rather than working in collaboration *with* them. Reasons for making your empathic responses relaxed, yet accurate, include the following: it may help to calm clients and also allow them more psychological space to get in touch with their deeper thoughts and feelings.

5. *How should my voice be?*   It is important that you respond clearly and reasonably loudly. Some beginning helpers have a tendency to mumble with certain clients. If you speak too softly you may appear weak. Also, you may reinforce lack of assertion in your clients. Of course, you can go too far in the other direction and dominate and overwhelm clients. Your vocal inflections should always express responsiveness to clients' thoughts and feelings.

6. *How should my body be?*   Mention has already been made of using your body to show attention and receptiveness, and of the importance of avoiding sending discouraging body messages. There is a possibility that matching some of your client's body messages may help. For instance, in one study, counsellors who mirrored a congruent arm and leg position were perceived as more empathic by their clients than those who did not.[17]

7. *To what should I respond?*   You may have to choose from a number of client messages those to reflect back in your response. Here are three guidelines for choosing what to focus on. First, try and communicate that you have understood the crux or most

important topic to the client. Second, if the client has been expressing a feeling of any significance, pick it up and place it at the front of
your response. Placing it towards the end may lose much of its
emotional impact. Third, if possible keep your responses focused on
the client. For example, if a client describes a row with his mother,
instead of helping him get into a description of her it is better to
reflect his own feelings and behaviour in relation to her. Try to
respond empathically in such a way that your clients stay self-
referent. Ivey and Authier corroborate this point when they write:
'Similarly for a client to talk about self, it is necessary that a
counselor focus on the client and use the client's name and/or the
pronoun "you". Examination of video and audiotapes of beginning
and advanced helpers revealed all too frequently an emphasis on the
content of the helping interview – the "war stories" of the patient –
rather than an emphasis on the client as an individual.'[18]

8. *What language should I use?*   Your language needs to be fresh,
clear and in tune with the client's. However, informal use of
language does not require you to be inauthentic. For instance, if
working with a delinquent teenager, terms like 'hey man' and
frequent swear words are uncalled for.

9. *How deep should I go?*   This is the interchangeable versus advanced empathy issue. To date I have mainly focused on interchangeable empathy. Advanced empathic responding expands or advances
clients' levels of awareness, yet still remains primarily within their
frame of reference. It tries to reflect thoughts, feelings and experiences at a deeper and possibly more threatening level than your
clients' current disclosures. In a sense you 'force' the issue by
making responses which offer clients the opportunity to go deeper
into their experiencing. The chances of being wrong are greater
since you may be responding on the basis of hunches. Consequently, making your responses in an exploratory manner is more
important in advanced than in interchangeable empathy. Normally
most of your empathic responses are likely to be interchangeable.
Factors which may affect your choosing to use advanced empathic
responding include: how well you understand your client, how safe
your client feels, how comfortable you are about the accuracy of
your hunches, and the level of awareness and of defensiveness of
your client. Needless to say, the *how* of your response (your vocal
and body messages) must be congruent to the *what* of your response
(your verbal message) in order to be received with minimal threat
by clients.

10. *Am I adequately checking the accuracy of my understandings?* The accuracy of your understanding should not be assumed. Ideally, you should develop a *working together* relationship with your clients. You need to create an emotional climate in which it is safe for your clients to correct you. Some clients may have a tendency to acquiesce even though their thoughts and feelings are not being picked up particularly sharply. Your empathic responses should always be delivered in a manner which contains the message that you are exploring and checking out their accuracy. Remember that it is the client's perception of your being empathic that is your goal.

Making a Succession of Empathic Responses

Person-centred helpers especially provide clients with a series of empathic responses. It is a useful skill to acquire even if the focus of your activities is likely to be more on problem management or decision making. For instance, when clients first share their concerns, you may use this skill to advantage. The following is an excerpt from an interview with a female college student. In it the helper makes empathic responding choices to one client statement after another. This is the skill that is the focus of Exercise 3.9. As you read the excerpt, remember that the helper does not know what the client is going to say next, but by means of empathic responding helps her to unfold her story in her own words and at her own pace. Furthermore, note that, as the short transcript progresses, the client talks in a more self-referent way and begins to explore the implications of the marital break-up for her. Often it is the case that when clients are responded to empathically, they shift from talking about more distant to talking about more personally relevant and emotionally tinged material.

Client: I went home last weekend and I was surprised to find that my mother was in the process of buying another house.
Helper: You hadn't expected her to be planning to move.
Client: No. She's only been married to Jack, my stepfather, for just over a year and this means she's leaving him.
Helper: So your mother's house move means that her marriage is breaking up.
Client: Yeah . . . and he doesn't even know what she's doing and I feel sad about it.
Helper: You're upset that your stepfather doesn't know what is going on behind his back.
Client: I can see that they haven't been getting on too well together, but

he's not a bad bloke and he's put an awful lot of time and money into our present house.

Helper: Their relationship hasn't been good, yet you quite like him and acknowledge the effort he has put into the house.

Client: I think it may be best for Mum to leave, but I wouldn't like him to feel that I had anything to do with persuading her. And I'll miss having a father-figure around.

Helper: Though the break-up may be the right thing for your Mum you don't want to be blamed for contributing to it. Also, you regret losing a father-figure.

Throughout the above transcript, the helper is trying to stay sensitively and accurately in the client's frame of reference and to give her the message: 'Please go on. I am interested.' The above client found it relatively easy to talk superficially about herself when she came for helping, but felt that she had no real identity of her own. She was always craving other people's affection, not least through promiscuous sex, which she found physically painful. As helping progressed she began to feel a greater sense of confidence in her own worth and opinions.

An issue in practising your empathic responding skills is whether it is better for those in the client role to be themselves and discuss their own concerns or to role-play actual clients. The main advantage of sharing your own concerns is that you each get practice at responding to genuine verbal, vocal and body cues. Furthermore, by discussing your own concerns you may get more of a feel for being the recipient of helpful and harmful responses than if you role-play another's concerns. Perhaps it is best viewed not as an either/or issue. You should have the opportunity both to work on your own concerns and to role-play representative clients and issues from your present or future client populations. Also, added realism is brought into skills training if, once you have acquired some basic facilitative skills, you are allowed to work with actual clients. This requires them to be carefully screened and for you to be closely supervised. Additionally, a useful way of acquiring skills resources and eliminating possible deficits is to have some sessions as a client with an effective helper.

Exercise 3.9   Making a succession of empathic responses

This exercise may be done on your own, in pairs or in a training group.

A   *On your own*
   Write out a two- or three-page transcript of an imaginary interview in which you are the client and your helper uses empathic responding to help you

explore and work on a personal issue, a decision, a work-related issue or an assessment of your helping skills.

B   *In pairs*

You counsel your partner for five, ten or fifteen minutes by giving a permission to talk, showing attention and receptiveness, giving appropriate continuation messages, avoiding giving discouraging non-verbal and verbal messages, and making a succession of empathic responses. Your partner should explore and work on a personal issue, a decision, a work-related issue or an assessment of his or her helping skills. If possible either audio- or video-record the session. Before playing back the recording, share how you each saw the session. Then play back the session with the 'client' indicating which 'helper' responses he or she found helpful and which harmful, and why. Afterwards, reverse roles. This exercise may be done for longer periods up to a complete interview of, say, forty-five to fifty minutes. With these longer sessions you may not wish to reverse roles until you have had a break. A variant of this exercise is to allow 'clients' to raise one finger if their 'helper' is slightly out of their frame of reference, and two fingers if badly out!

C   *In a training group*

The trainer demonstrates the exercise with a group member as client. The session is recorded and played back as above. The group then breaks up into triads (helper, client and observer) with each participant having the opportunity to play each role. The observer's tasks include: (1) providing feedback at the end of the session; (2) providing feedback during the playback; and (3) raising any socio-economic or cross-cultural issues that may have been pertinent to the interaction. The group may then meet as a whole, with excerpts from the audio- or video-recordings being played back and commented on. Group members are encouraged to practise together their empathic responding skills between training sessions, and also to use their skills in their outside lives.

CONCLUDING COMMENT

A quote from a client of Carl Rogers after about ten minutes of therapy: 'What's wrong with the way I've been saying it the first time?'

RESPONSES FOR EXERCISES

Exercise 3.4

1.   (a) 1.   Client talks about pain rather than anger.
     (b) 0.   External and judgemental.
     (c) 4.   Picks client up loud and clear.

2. (a) 4. Human and accurate.
   (b) 1. The first part shows some empathy, the latter part none.
   (c) 0. A defensive put-down.
3. (a) 2. Depending upon how said, this might be an external description.
   (b) 3. A good attempt.
   (c) 4. Picks up the client's feelings sharply.
4. (a) 0. Dreadful response, patronizing.
   (b) 0. Inappropriate self-disclosure and implicit reassurance.
   (c) 3. A reasonable effort.

Exercise 3.5
The following are suggestions. There is no single correct paraphrase response to each statement.
1. 'Your Bill was a good man. You were given a body blow by his untimely loss. You still pine for him.'
2. 'You're really pleased with my progress and contribution.'
3. 'You're coping much better than when each day was a struggle.'
4. 'You're confused . . . and getting mixed messages from your parents doesn't help.'

Exercise 3.6
Below are some illustrative voice and body messages. There are many others.

Non-verbal cue	*Anger*	*Happiness*	*Sadness*	*Anxiety*
Tone of voice	Harsh	Warm Excited	Soft	Timid Hesitant
Voice volume	Loud	Easy to hear Shouting for joy	Quiet	Quiet
Eye contact	Direct	Direct	Averted	Averted Very intermittent
Facial expression	Clenched teeth	Grinning Open	Tearful Mouth turned down	Forced smile

Non-verbal cue	*Anger*	*Happiness*	*Sadness*	*Anxiety*
Posture	Rigid	Relaxed	Slouched	Tense
Gestures	Fist clenched Finger pointing	Arms raised Jumping for joy	Holds head in hands	Finger tapping

Exercise 3.7
There are no single correct responses other than for (a).
1. (a) 'glad', 'miss', 'accepted', 'respected', 'enjoyed' and 'closeness'.
    (b) 'happy', 'pine for', 'regarded with favour', 'honoured', 'had the pleasure of' and 'intimacy'.
    (c) 'You feel happy to have immigrated here, since financially you are much better off. However, you still feel a sense of loss for back home where you used to enjoy acceptance, respect and the intimacy of village life.'
2. (a) 'wish that we could', 'boring' and 'enjoy ourselves'.
    (b) 'would like to', 'dull' and 'have some fun'.
    (c) 'You feel you would really like a better club here, since this is a dull place in the evenings and needs a place for young people to get to know each other and have some fun.'
3. (a) 'terrific', 'putting me down' and 'irritable'.
    (b) 'heated', 'disparaging me' and 'annoyed'.
    (c) 'You felt that one of your lecturers was putting you down and you had a heated argument with him recently in class. You are aware that you can quickly feel very angry with authority figures.'
4. (a) 'losing his grip on', 'mopes', 'getting fed up' and 'depressing'.
    (b) 'no longer on top of', 'moves aimlessly', 'becoming exasperated' and 'enervating'.
    (c) 'You feel that your husband is no longer on top of his painting and decorating work, not getting so many jobs as before, and mopes round the house a lot. You feel exasperated with living in such an uninspiring environment.'

Exercise 3.8
Again, there is no single correct response.
1. 'You feel enraged and isolated because you loathe being teased. Despite your being the same as the others, they take pleasure in joining forces against you.'

2. 'You feel confused and unsure of what to do because, though your neighbour would like her son to play with yours and you would like to please her, you have reservations about his bad behaviour.'
3. 'You're amazed at the strength of your feelings because you really want to have your baby, even though neither of you had planned it. Happily, John shares your feelings.'
4. 'You feel upset because people misunderstand your feelings for Tom. Though you have a deep sympathy for each other, some people read too much into such close male friendships.'

4 Further Facilitation Skills

This chapter presents some further skills of helping clients describe, explore and experience their frame of reference. The skills covered are: initial structuring, encouraging self-talk, helpful questioning, confronting, self-disclosing and summarizing. Though these skills may also involve a contribution from your frame of reference, I include them among facilitation skills so long as their main emphasis is on the client's frame of reference. Sometimes facilitation is caricatured as repeating the last words the client has said. I hope that this and the previous chapter demonstrate that there are numerous choices involved in being facilitative. Though facilitation in this context means making it easy for the client, demonstrating competence in these skills is not necessarily easy for helpers.

From early on in your contact with clients there are many ways to help them assume responsibility for their lives and problems. Though appropriate for some clients, an open discussion of the need to assume responsibility is not being advocated here. It may be perceived as moralistic and irrelevant. Instead there are a range of other skills that support the need for clients both to assume responsibility for themselves and also to avoid dependency on you. Sometimes well-meaning helpers collude in helping their clients stay stuck. They do not possess some of the skills of quietly and in non-threatening ways emphasizing client's responsibility to *make* their lives through the adequacy of their choices.

INITIAL STRUCTURING

'Structuring' is a term used to describe the behaviours by which helpers let their clients know their respective roles at various stages of the helping process. Structuring is conveyed by body and vocal, as well as by verbal, messages. It occurs throughout helping. However, here I emphasize making opening statements that establish expectancies conducive to your clients *working on* rather than just *talking about* their problems. This builds on the discussion in Chapter 2 regarding giving clients permission to talk.

The medical profession provides a common model of helping in our culture. Here the doctor is an expert who diagnoses, makes a prognosis, treats and hopefully cures patients of their ills. The patient is relatively passive, relying on the expertise of the doctor and the fruits of medical science to provide change. (I acknowledge the above overstates the case. Sometimes patients have to be active in working for change: for instance, a stroke patient may be required to perform exercises to recover lost functions.)

There are a number of reasons why, at least in its simplified version, the medical model is inappropriate for helping. There is no surgery and minimal use of drugs. There is no concept of cure. When people make progress with psychological concerns they still have to work to maintain and develop their gains. Additionally, clients have to assume responsibility for change. In the medical model the assumption is that doctors provide interventions that change patients. The assumption in helping is that clients are offered interventions that help them to change themselves.

The objective of initial structuring in helping is to facilitate the process of client self-help. An attempt is made to establish an alliance in which helpers collaborate with clients rather than do things to them. This holds true when helpers are task-oriented as well as when they are person-oriented. In the medical model, physicians might ask themselves: 'What can I do to cure my patients?' In a helping model, the appropriate question might be: 'How can I best collaborate with my clients to help them to help themselves?'

Below is an example of a possible opening statement that provides some structure to the first part of a session.

> Hello, Jim, my name is Julie Kent and I'm one of the student counsellors here. We have about forty minutes together and everything you say is confidential. Would you care to tell me what concerns you?

What the counsellor has done, in a friendly yet business-like way, is to state names, establish time parameters, reassure about confidentiality and give a permission to talk. What the counsellor has *not* done is set herself up as an expert, as though in the medical model, by means of a statement like 'What can I do for you?' This kind of statement invites dependence. Hopefully, as the session progresses, Julie Kent will not collude in any attempts by the client to place her in the role of an expert who will prescribe an effortless cure. She might counter any such attempt with a statement like: 'Though I appreciate your anxiety and concern, I see my role more as helping you work toward your own solution rather than as coming up with ready-made solutions for you.'

Sometimes the initial structuring of helpers is insufficiently task-oriented. If you intend to have a task-oriented session, there are times when you can build this into your early statements. For instance, instead of saying 'Are there any concerns you would like to *talk about* in this session?', you might say 'Are there any concerns you would like to *work on* in this session?'

Your initial structuring will vary with your theoretical orientation and the context in which you work. Also, much setting of expectancies may be done before clients come to see you, through the publicity you have provided and your reputation. Initial structuring is important. Exercise 4.1 provides you with the opportunity to think through some of the issues and to practise this skill.

Exercise 4.1   Initial structuring

This exercise may be done on your own, in pairs or as part of a training group.

A   *On your own*
  1.   Write down the main choices you need to consider when doing initial structuring.
  2.   Write down at least two initial structuring statements that might be appropriate for a helping setting where you either work now or might like to work in the future.
B   *In pairs*
  Either independently do the above exercise, then discuss;
  or work through the above exercise together from the start, including practising making initial structuring statements to each other.
C   *In a training group*
  The trainer discusses the issues involved in initial structuring and demonstrates the skill. The group is divided into pairs or triads to discuss and practise the skill. This is followed by a plenary sharing and discussion session.

ENCOURAGING SELF-TALK

In the previous chapter I mentioned, in choosing empathic responses, the desirability of keeping the focus on your client. Many clients have a tendency to avoid dealing with their concerns directly. Encouraging self-talk is an important way in which you can help them to stop distancing themselves from their experiencing of life. By *self-talk* I mean: keeping the focus on themselves; using the first person singular; owning their feelings, thoughts and actions; and owning their problems.

Keeping the Focus on the Client

Ultimately if clients are to change they have to assume responsibility for their own behaviour. They are unlikely to do this if they continuously focus on what others do, think and feel. Helpers are at risk of colluding in this process. Below is an example of a marital counsellor response that focuses *away from* the client.

Client: Jim and I had a terrible row last night. I've never seen him so angry. At one stage I was terrified that he was going to hit me. It's all his fault.

Counsellor: So Jim got really mad last night.

Now let us look at the same client statement, but with a marital counsellor response that keeps the focus *on* the client.

Client: Jim and I had a terrible row last night. I've never seen him so angry. At one stage I was terrified that he was going to hit me. It's all his fault.

Counsellor: You were terrified at the depth of Jim's anger and the possibility of being struck.

The first counsellor response focuses on Jim's anger. As a result of this the counsellor has increased the probability that, in a statement–response–statement chain, the client's next statement will focus on Jim rather than on herself. The second counsellor response focuses on her feelings in relation to Jim's anger. This increases the probability of her next statement being self-referent. Additionally, it may speed up the process of her examining her own behaviour in relation to Jim rather than keeping playing the injured victim. I do not wish to imply that clients should *never* focus on others to whom they relate, but rather that helpers should beware of colluding with clients who avoid the responsibility for their choices in life.

Encouraging 'I' Statements

Clients may distance themselves from their feelings, thoughts and actions by failing to make 'I' statements.[1] Such statements involve the use of the first person singular. Here clients clearly own their messages and speak for themselves. Ways in which clients avoid speaking for themselves include making statements starting with words like 'You', 'People', 'We', 'That', 'There' and 'It'. Also, sometimes clients dilute making an 'I' statement by asking a question and hoping that the answer is what they wish to express.

● *Owning a feeling:*

> Client non-'I' statement: He is the end when he behaves like that.
> Client 'I' statement: I feel hurt and angry at his behaviour.

● *Owning a thought:*

> Client non-'I' statement: People in our group sessions think that they are
> not going well.
> Client 'I' statement: I think that our group sessions are not going well, and
> I am not alone.

● *Owning an action:*

> Client non-'I' statement: The car crashed into the garage door.
> Client 'I' statement: I crashed the car into the garage door.

One way in which you can encourage your clients to make 'I' statements is to respond to them in ways that use the word 'you' as though they had made an 'I' statement, even when they have not. For instance, with the client who says: 'He is the end when he behaves like that', you could respond 'You feel hurt and angry at his behaviour.' Implicit in your response is an encouragement to your client to express feelings directly. If clients repeatedly fail to use 'I' statements, you might consider openly drawing this to their attention. However, you have to judge whether this intervention does not threaten clients prematurely and make them inhibited about how they express themselves subsequently. Each case must be judged on its merits. Another way of encouraging the use of 'I' statements is, where appropriate, to use them yourself.

Encouraging Clients to Own Problems

There are two levels of problem ownership for clients. One level is acknowledging that they may *have* certain problems. Another level is acknowledging that some of their behaviours *sustain* their problems. It is the former acknowledgement, of having a problem, to which I refer here. Accepting responsibility for sustaining problems is a theme developed later.

Often clients are quite clear about their problem areas: for instance, a student who is terrified about impending exams may have no difficulty acknowledging this. On other occasions, clients have difficulty in acknowledging problems: for instance, a mother may say she has a troublesome child and want to define her child as the problem. However, the mother has a problem too: namely, how to handle her feelings and behave towards a child whom she perceives as troublesome. In this instance, you may be more helpful in facilitating your client's understanding if you encourage her to focus more on *herself* in relation to her child than on her *child*.

Facilitating Acknowledging Choices

There are ways in which you can help your clients become more aware of themselves as choosers in their lives. One way to do this is to highlight their choice processes. For example, a wife might say about her relationship with her husband 'We are getting on better now.' When responding, the helper might emphasize the change in the wife's behaviour: 'You're now *choosing* to make much more effort to talk over problems calmly and to avoid nagging him and this seems to be paying off.' Another example is that of a middle-aged man who says of his mother: 'I resent having to visit her every weekend.' Here the response might both acknowledge the resentment and also avoid colluding in the client's sense of not being responsible for his actions: 'You feel resentful, but I wonder whether you sufficiently acknowledge that you *choose* to visit her every weekend.' Yet another way of emphasizing choice is to focus on the verbs that the client uses. For example, if a client says 'I *can't* do that', you may ask 'Can you say "I *won't* do that"?'[2]

Using Silence

Though, as with all skills, judgement is necessary, another way you can facilitate client self-talk is to use silence effectively. Obviously if you talk too much this acts as a barrier to your clients' talking. However, you may also need to learn when to keep silent as a way of giving clients space and encouragement to get more deeply in touch with their thoughts and feelings. For instance, it is often a good idea to pause after your clients speak to see whether they want to say something more before you respond. Whether longer silences are appropriate depends on what the client has been saying and on their body messages during the silence.

If your clients are silent this may mean a number of different things. It may be that you have generally uncommunicative clients. It may mean that the clients are struggling to get deeper into their experiencing. As Brammer observes: 'They may need some quiet time alone to pull their feelings together before they explore further. This is often a very productive time, and the most helpful thing to do is to wait quietly until the helpee is ready to go on.'[3] Other meanings of silence are that the client fears further disclosure or that they have come to the end of a thought or theme.

I have tried to show you some ways of helping clients, while staying predominantly in their frames of reference, to talk about themselves and move forward rather than stay stuck. If you use these interventions clumsily they may do more harm than good. Exercise 4.2 gives you the opportunity to practise responding to clients in ways that facilitate responsibility assumption and lessen your chances of colluding in responsibility avoidance.

Exercise 4.2   Encouraging self-talk

This exercise may be done in pairs or in a training group.

A   *In pairs*
  Counsel your partner for ten minutes by giving an initial structuring and then mainly using empathic responses. You should encourage self-talk by: keeping the focus on the client, encouraging 'I' statements, encouraging ownership of problems, facilitating acknowledging choices, and using silences appropriately. Afterwards, discuss, and then reverse roles. This exercise can be done for progressively longer periods.
B   *In a training group*
  The trainer discusses some of the choices that helpers can make to encourage client self-talk. The trainer demonstrates the above exercise. The group is then divided into pairs or triads to do the exercise. Audio- or video-recording and playback may be helpful. Afterwards the trainer conducts a plenary sharing and discussion session.

HELPFUL QUESTIONING

Viktor Frankl tells the following psychiatrist joke:

'Are you a psychiatrist?'
'Why do you ask?'
'You're a psychiatrist.'

Here, instead of unmasking, the psychiatrist has been unmasked.[4] Often, as in this instance, helpers ask questions inappropriately. Wrongly used, questions can lead to passive clients who implicitly or explicitly expect you to take responsibility for their lives and to solve their problems. Furthermore, you may put yourself in a spurious position of expertness and then not be able to deliver the goods. Effective questioning involves sensitivity to at least two major dimensions: the *type* of question and the *timing* of questions in the helping process.[5]

A major reservation about the use of questions is that they take clients out of their frame of reference. Sometimes it is said that questions are asked more to help the questioner feel secure than to help clients. However, judicious questioning can also help clients explore, clarify and understand their frame of reference better. As such, it can be regarded as facilitative. It is this use of questions with which I deal here.

There are a number of questioning errors to avoid.

- *Too many questions.* Conducting an interrogation that may lead to either defensiveness or dependence or both.
- *Leading questions.* Questions that put the answer into your client's mouth: for instance, 'You like coming to counselling, don't you?'.
- *Closed questions.* Closed questions curtail the other person's options for responding. They often give only two options, 'yes' or 'no'. For instance, a closed question is 'Do you like your parents?', whereas an open question might be 'What do you feel about your parents?' An outcome of closed questions is that, because they do not encourage clients to talk, they create silences in which the stage is set for further questions. Beginning trainees often put extra pressure on themselves through this mistake.
- *Too probing questions.* These questions are likely to create anxiety and resistance because they seek to elicit material that clients may be neither ready nor willing to disclose: for instance, asking an obviously shy teenager: 'Do you masturbate and what are your masturbation fantasies?'
- *Poorly timed questions.* As already mentioned, time is critical to asking good questions. For instance, a girl may be full of emotion as

she relates having a row with her mother, when the helper says: 'And what was your contribution to causing the row?' It is conceivable that, when she had calmed down, the girl might have been willing to explore the adequacy of her own behaviour in the situation, possibly without prompting from her helper. Another example of a poorly timed question would be if a client were to be asked 'What are your options for achieving your goals?' before he or she has even had time to share, explore and define a problem with the helper.

Though the use of questions differs according to the theoretical orientations of helpers, below are some types of question, albeit sometimes overlapping, that you might use. These questions are either virtually within or close to your client's frame of reference. They do not come from outer space or from what may be going on in your own head that is unrelated to what your client has just said.

- *Elaboration questions.* Elaboration questions are open questions that give your clients the opportunity to expand on what they have already started talking about. Illustrative elaboration questions or responses are: 'Would you care to elaborate?', 'Is there anything more you wish to add?', and 'Tell me more.'
- *Specification questions.* Specification questions, when used to facilitate client understanding, aim to elicit detail that helps them to clarify their concerns. For instance, a specification question to a client who says that her brother bothers her might be: 'Could you say what it is about your brother that bothers you?' Another type of specification question is: 'When you say you are not feeling quite yourself, what exactly do you mean?' Still another is 'Can you give a specific example?' Specification questions can have the effect of helping clients to work on their problems through understanding them more specifically and clearly
- *Eliciting personal reactions questions.* This type of question aims to elicit clients' feelings, thoughts and personal meanings. In general these questions should be open and tentative since the other person should, but not always will, know the answer better than anyone else. Illustrative personal reactions questions include: 'How do you feel about that?', 'Do you have any thoughts and feelings about . . .?', and 'I'm wondering about what the meaning of all this is for you.' Sometimes these questions can be used to help clients focus back on themselves rather than externalize about others.

Needless to say, *how* you ask questions is important alongside *what* questions you ask. Your voice and body messages should indicate support and interest at the same time as they minimize threat. It is usually desirable to intersperse empathic responses between questions. This disciplines you to listen to the answers, avoids putting you in the medical model, avoids creating a climate of interrogation, and allows your clients the psychological space to elaborate on their answers if they wish.

Exercise 4.3   Helpful questioning

This exercise may be performed in pairs or in a training group.

A   *In pairs*
Partner A presents a problem, to which he or she is having difficulty finding an adequate solution, to partner B. Partner B makes an initial structuring statement, uses empathic responding after *each* statement made by partner A, but may then ask questions designed to facilitate partner A (N.B. The main focus is on facilitating your partner's understanding rather than your own.)
Partner B's questions should be asked in the following sequence:
1. *Elaboration questions.* Spend a minimum of two minutes getting partner A to elaborate his or her problem by using elaboration questions interspersed with empathic responses.
2. *Specification questions.* Spend a minimum of two minutes getting partner A to clarify his or her problem by asking specification questions interspersed with empathic responses.
3. *Eliciting personal reactions questions.* Spend a minimum of two minutes helping partner A explore his or her feelings, thoughts and personal meanings in relation to the problem by asking personal reactions questions interspersed with empathic responses.
Allow partner A to give you feedback on whether and how your use of questions has helped/harmed him or her in clarifying and understanding the problem better. It may be useful to audio-record the session to illustrate this feedback. Afterwards, reverse roles.
B   *In a training group*
The trainer demonstrates the above exercise by using helpful questioning to enable a group member to understand his or her problem(s) better. The trainer then divides the group into pairs or triads and gets them to do the exercise. This is followed by a plenary sharing and discussion session.

CONFRONTING

Confrontation, sometimes called challenging, is a helper skill which aims to expand the client's awareness in some areas. Carkhuff and Berenson observe: 'Direct confrontation is an act, not a reaction. It is initiated by the therapist, based on his core understanding of the client. It brings the client into more direct contact with himself, his strengths and resources, as well as his self-destructive behaviour. The purpose of confrontation is to reduce the ambiguities and incongruities in the client's experiencing and communication.'[6] Berenson and his colleagues listed five major types of confrontation: *experiential,* confronting discrepancies (for instance, between helper experiencing of the client and client experiencing of self); *didactic,* clarifying information or lack of information; *strength,* focusing on the client's resources; *weakness,* focusing on the client's liabilities or pathology; and *encouragement to action,* encouraging an active and discouraging a passive stance toward life.[7,8] They found in their research that high-functioning helpers confronted clients more frequently than low-functioning helpers, with experiential confrontation being used most. Low-functioning helpers were much more likely to focus on client's weaknesses whereas, if anything, high-functioning helpers focused on strengths.

The *how* of confrontations is extremely important along with their *what* or verbal content. I propose three main categories of confrontation, partly based on this distinction.

● *Facilitative confrontation.*   Here helpers use their experience to help clients clarify and possibly expand their frames of reference. Two distinguishing features of facilitative confrontations are: first, they tend to be fairly close to the clients' existing frames of reference; and second, they are given in a relatively non-threatening manner.

● *Hot-seat confrontation.*   Whereas facilitative confrontations are slight challenges, hot-seat confrontations are direct and strong challenges. Here helpers indicate loud and clear that they are not prepared to collude in their client's fantasy worlds, illusions, defences and smoke screens. For instance, a member of an interactional group who uses humour as a distancing device might be confronted strongly with this tendency. Fritz Perls, the founder of gestalt therapy, worked in this category of confrontation when he used what he termed 'skillful frustration'.[9] Perls placed clients in the hot seat and confronted them until they communicated directly.

● *Didactic/interpretive confrontation.*   Here the focus of the challenge is on helping clients to understand how they sustain problems. For instance, the rational-emotive approach to helping heavily emphasizes challenging clients' irrational beliefs as a step toward helping them to think rationally.[10]

The above three categories of confrontation can overlap. Especially with hot-seat confrontation, helpers need to remember that, though a good challenge may accelerate helping, premature or clumsy challenges may retard the process or cause clients to end it. When confronting, you need to take into account both the strength of your relationship with the clients and their level of vulnerability. Because the focus of this chapter is on further facilitation skills, only the skill of facilitative confrontation gets reviewed here.

Facilitative Confrontation

Facilitative confrontations reflect and/or focus on discrepancies in thoughts, feelings and actions. Additionally, they sometimes offer alternative viewpoints. Areas for facilitative confronting include the following:

- *Discrepancy between verbal, vocal and body messages.* For example, Bella says that she is 'fine', but her helper catches a note of pain in her voice and sees her eyes moisten.
- *Discrepancy between words and actions.* For example, Stan says that he is committed to coming to counselling and working on his problems, but his time-keeping is poor.
- *Discrepancy between client self-image and helper's view of the client.* For instance, Laura sees herself as having few coping skills for handling her feelings of stress, but her helper points out and illustrates that she has already developed some coping strategies.
- *Discrepancy between present and past utterances.* For example, Julio now says that he hates his boss, whereas a couple of sessions ago he stressed how fair he thought he was.
- *Challenging failure to acknowledge choice.* For example, Diana had a row with her husband and says she had no choice in the matter.
- *Offering a different perception.* For example, Tim saw his mother as nagging him about doing household chores. A different perception was that his mother was a single parent who had to go out to work to support the family, and got very tired because she had more on her plate than she could handle.
- *Correcting misinformation.* For instance, Lois enjoyed dating boys and thought of herself as heterosexual, but when she found herself attracted to another girl she felt she was becoming a lesbian. The correction involves challenging Lois's simplification of her sexual orientation.

Below are some guidelines for if and when you choose to use facilitative confronting. Even though confrontations come from your frame of reference, their objective is to help your clients clarify and develop their frame of reference. Unlike that of hot-seat confronting, your aim is to avoid a direct collision with the client or to precipitate a crisis, however useful that might sometimes be. The facilitative confronting guidelines are as follows:

1. *Own your thoughts and feelings.* By this I mean you should make it clear that your confrontation is based on your frame of reference rather than representing the client's frame of reference or some objective viewpoint. Using 'I' statements can help with this. For instance, in the example in which Bella says she is fine you might first acknowledge her frame of reference prior to confronting her with your own: 'You say you are fine, but I catch some pain in your voice and your eyes are moistening.' Such a comment may enable Bella to drop her social mask and move more openly to discuss her experiencing.

2. *Do not talk down.* Keep your confrontations on a democratic level. A major risk in confronting another is that he or she may perceive what you say as a put-down rather than as helpful. For instance, if Bob thinks he is generous and implies that his friends think he is mean, you can reflect this as a discrepancy rather than make an accusation. For instance, you might say: 'I'm getting two messages. You say that you are generous, but the feedback from your friends seems to be that you are mean.' You are neutral in presenting both sides of the discrepancy.

3. *Leave the ultimate responsibility with your client.* Allow your clients to decide whether your confrontations actually help them to move forward in their exploration. Facilitative confronting involves slight challenges which, if well timed and tactfully given, are unlikely to elicit a high degree of defensiveness. In hot-seat confrontation part of the helper's skill is in learning to handle and persist in the confrontation, despite client resistance. However, in facilitative confronting, it is the client's choice whether or not to accept your challenge.

4. *Do not overdo it.* Facilitative confrontations help clients elaborate their frames of reference. However, persistent or clumsy confrontation, however well-intentioned, may direct the focus of the interview away from what the client thinks and feels on to the helper. Thus, while trying to encourage client responsibility, you risk undermining it. Furthermore, repeated confrontations may diminish the safety for clients of their contact with you.

Exercise 4.4 has been designed to give you practice at making slight challenges to your clients. When discussing empathic responding, I mentioned it can be helpful to think in terms of a three-link chain of statement–response–statement. Observe the effect that your confrontations have on your client's next statement. Are they helpful or harmful, and why?

Exercise 4.4   Facilitative confronting

This exercise may be done on your own, in pairs or in a training group.

A   *On your own*
Write down examples, either from your own helping experience or by making them up, of the following types of confrontation. Write out what you would actually say when confronting the client.
1. Discrepancy between verbal, vocal and body messages.
2. Discrepancy between words and actions.
3. Discrepancy between client self-image and your view of the client.
4. Discrepancy between present and past utterances.
5. Challenging failure to acknowledge choice.
6. Offering a different perception.
7. Correcting misinformation.

B   *In pairs*
Counsel your partner, who discusses his or her counselling/helping work or personal life for five to ten minutes. Your partner deliberately introduces some discrepancies into the session. Following the guidelines given in the text, use your facilitative confronting skills as appropriate. At the end of the session discuss with your partner your use of confronting. Afterwards, reverse roles.

C   *In a training group*
The trainer introduces the topic of confronting and demonstrates the pairs exercise with a group member acting as client. Afterwards, the group is broken up into pairs or triads to do the exercise, prior to coming together for a plenary sharing and discussion session. Alternatively, the trainer makes up a videocassette illustrating different types of facilitative confronting and shows it to the group before getting them to practise.

A final word here: confrontations in helping can go both ways. Some clients threaten and scare their helpers. When your clients confront you,

you require the skills of responding to challenges. These skills include empathic responses that acknowledge rather than deny what your clients seek to communicate. Another skill is the appropriate use of 'I' statements when and if sharing your thoughts and feelings in response to your clients' confrontations.

SELF-DISCLOSING

> Patient: Doctor, I've got a boil on my bottom. Let me show it to you.
> Doctor: Let me show you my bottom too.

As the above travesty indicates, helper self-disclosure can be for good or ill. Helper self-disclosure relates to the ways in which you let yourself be known to your clients. Usually it means intentional verbal disclosure. However, if you are not being genuine, what you do may speak louder than what you say. There are numerous ways in which helpers reveal themselves to clients: for example, by their verbal, vocal and body messages, their availability, the decor of their offices, their written communications, the way they handle themselves on the telephone and the size of their bills! The following discussion is focused on intentional verbal disclosure.

Reasons For and Against Self-disclosing

You may think that clients seek help to talk about themselves and their problems, and not to be burdened with their helpers' own disclosures. Undoubtedly you are right. There are risks to self-disclosing, which I deal with later. However, I start positively by suggesting some reasons why appropriate disclosure on the part of helpers may be beneficial.

- *Demonstrating a useful relationship skill.* Your disclosing something about yourself may help to free clients to talk about themselves, both inside and ouside their time with you, in a more spontaneous and intimate way.
- *Appearing genuine and involved.* Appropriate self-disclosures may prevent you from appearing wooden and uninterested. Also, they may contribute to your being perceived as a real human being rather than hiding behind a phoney or defensive facade. Carkhuff observes: 'Helper self-disclosure, in turn, is often, although not necessarily related to genuineness. That is, although a helper may be genuine and not self-disclosing or self-disclosing and not genuine, frequently, and particularly at the extremes, the two are related.'[11] Another way

of looking at self-disclosing is that it is a way of personalizing your
work with clients.

- *Sharing experiences.*   You may have had similar concerns to those of
  your clients. A possible advantage of such sharing is that it may
  provide them with different perceptions of their problems and of how
  to deal with them.
- *Providing feedback.*   There are times when it may be helpful to share
  your reactions to the client with him or her. Such feedback may be
  about the client as a person, about what the client says and does, or
  avoids saying and doing, and about your relationship and work
  together.
- *Being assertive.*   Sometimes you may choose to be firm and set
  limits. Such occasions may include: standing up to an aggressive
  client, not allowing time to be persistently wasted, and ending sessions on time.

There are, however, grave dangers in inappropriate helper self-
disclosure. Here I mention four of the main dangers:

- *Burdening the client.*   Clients usually have enough problems of their
  own without having to carry the burden of yours too.
- *Seeming weak and unstable.*   Clients may ask themselves 'Why is he
  or she telling me this?', and attribute negative reasons for the
  disclosure. Furthermore, vulnerable clients tend to need to perceive
  their helpers as strong people and may become anxious about evidence to the contrary.
- *Dominating the client.*   Inappropriate disclosure may shift the focus
  of the session from the client to you. Loughary and Ripley mention
  four types of 'helpers' who use self-disclosure in a dominating way:
  the 'You think you've got a problem! Let me tell you about mine!'
  type; the 'Let me tell you what to do' type; the 'I understand because I
  once had the same problem myself' type; and the 'I'll take charge and
  deal with it' type.[12]
- *Countertransference.*   Countertransference refers to negative and
  positive feelings toward your clients based on unresolved areas in
  your own life. Kennedy observes that: 'Anything that smacks of
  "going well out of one's way" for a client may indicate that this
  problem is present.'[13] Some helpers may, either intentionally or
  unintentionally, use self-disclosure to manipulate clients to meet their
  own needs for approval, intimacy and sex. This highlights the importance both of being aware of your motivation for self-disclosing and
  also of behaving ethically.

Showing Involvement

A distinction is sometimes made between self-involving statements and self-disclosing statements. Self-disclosing statements refer to 'the past history or personal experiences of the counselor, and self-involving responses are direct present expressions of a counselor's feelings about or reactions to client statements and/or behaviors.'[14] Another way of stating this is that there are at least two major dimensions of helper self-disclosure: showing involvement with clients and disclosing personal information and experiences.

There is a 'here-and-now' quality about showing involvement by disclosing your reactions toward clients. Three areas in which you can share your reactions are the following:

- *Reacting to client's disclosures.* Such comments might be: 'I'm delighted'; 'That's great'; 'That's terrible'; and 'I'm really sorry that you are going through such a bad patch.'
- *Reacting to clients as people.* Illustrative comments are: 'I enjoy working with you'; 'I'm really concerned about you'; and 'You seem to feel that you are a pretty unattractive person, but I certainly don't think of you that way.'
- *Reacting to the helping relationship.* For example, 'I have to make an effort to keep listening when you start repeating yourself'; and 'When you say your friends are suspicious about counsellors, I sense that you feel suspicious about me too.'

Showing involvement by reacting to clients' utterances can help them feel the companionship involved in your understanding of what they say. Disclosing reactions might appear judgemental, but the risk of this is lessened if your feelings and thoughts are communicated as being subjective rather than as objective evaluations. Also, even negative reactions can be used 'constructively as a basis for open-ended inquiry'.[15] At best, showing involvement can be a way of personalizing counselling and helping in a way that strengthens clients. It is important, of course, that your vocal and body messages match the feelings and thoughts that you express.

Exercise 4.5   Showing involvement

This exercise may be done on your own, in pairs or in a training group.

A   *On your own*
     With respect to either your present or future helping work, write down the
     sorts of situation in which it might be appropriate to show involvement by
     disclosing your reactions to client utterances and behaviours. Then, for
     each situation, formulate one or more appropriate self-disclosures.

B   *In pairs*
     You counsel a partner, who discusses a personal concern or role-plays a
     client. During the course of a five-, ten- or fifteen-minute session, try on a
     few occasions to show involvement by disclosing your subjective reac-
     tions. At the end of the session, discuss with your partner the impact of your
     attempts to show involvement. Afterwards, reverse roles.

C   *In a training group*
     The trainer introduces the topic of showing involvement by disclosing
     reactions. He or she then gives a demonstration of the pairs exercise.
     Afterwards, the group is broken up into pairs or triads to perform the
     exercise, prior to coming together for a plenary sharing and discussion
     session.

Disclosing Experiences

Disclosing experiences may help your clients feel that you understand what they are going through. For instance, unemployed people
might feel differently about helpers who disclose that they too have
been unemployed, and about those who have not. In some types of
helping, disclosure of shared experiences is an important part of the
process: for instance, disclosure of experiences by ex-alcoholics and
ex-addicts in Alcoholics Anonymous and certain kinds of drug
counselling.

There are many choices in disclosing experiences. First, whether to
mention them or not. Second, how honest to be. Third, whether to go
beyond disclosing facts to disclosing feelings: for instance, not only
having been unemployed but also then having had to struggle against
depression and feelings of uselessness. Fourth, how you coped with
your experience. Fifth, how you feel about it now.

Sharing of experiences can be a difficult area. Below are some
guidelines for *appropriate* disclosing of experience.

1. *Be self-referent.*   Do not disclose the experience of third parties.
2. *Be to the point.*   Do not slow down or defocus the interview
    through lack of relevance or talking too much.

3. *Be sensitive to your client.* Have sufficient awareness to realize when your disclosures might be helpful to your client and when they might be unwelcome or a burden.
4. *Do not do it too often.* Helpers who keep talking about their experiences risk switching the focus of their work from their clients to themselves.

Exercise 4.6   Disclosing experiences

This exercise may be done on your own, in pairs or in a training group.

A   *On your own*
   In respect of your present or future helping work, identify some experiences of yours which it might be helpful to disclose and share with certain of your clients. Write down what you might say to them.
B   *In pairs*
   You counsel your partner, who discusses a personal concern or role-plays a client. During the course of a five-, ten- or fifteen-minute session, try on one or more occasions to disclose an experience of yours which might 'help' your client. At the end of the session discuss with your partner the appropriateness of your attempts to disclose experiences. Afterwards, reverse roles.
C   *In a training group*
   The trainer introduces the topic of disclosing experiences. He or she then gives a demonstration of the pairs exercise. Afterwards, the group is broken up into pairs or triads to perform the exercise, prior to coming together for a plenary sharing and discussion session.

SUMMARIZING

One way of viewing a summary is that, instead of providing an empathic response to a single client statement, the helper responds empathically either to a series of client statements or to a whole interview. Summaries involve picking up the main feelings, themes and emerging directions in what the client says. They have a number of different purposes:

● *Acting as a bridge or stepping stone during a session.* The client may have mentioned a number of different thoughts and feelings in a rather random way. A good summary clarifies these disparate elements into a more coherent statement that the client may use to decide where to go next in the session.

● *Checking the accuracy of your understanding.*   Summarizing is a way of checking whether you are picking up the broader picture accurately.

● *Providing closure.*   One way to end a session is to indicate to clients that you would like to provide a summary; summarize; and then ask clients if they wish to add or alter anything in your summary. A summary at the end of a session can cover both where clients have been, but also where they may be going. For instance, a client may both have discussed a relationship problem and also have identified some possibilities for coping with it. The latter should be summarized along with the former. Also, you may use a summary as a way of providing closure to a theme during a session. In facilitative interviewing, the decision to move on would be left with the client.

● *As a bridge between sessions.*   At the start of a session you might provide a brief summary of the previous session. This may include checking on any pertinent happenings during the intervening time: for instance, how the client got on with enacting his or her coping strategies for the relationship problem discussed in the previous session. When using a summary as a bridge between sessions, you need to beware that what was important to clients last time may not be paramount now. There is a risk of backtracking clients rather than facilitating forward movement. In facilitative interviewing, clients should be given the freedom to develop another theme if they wish.

Below are examples of summaries. The first takes place fairly close to the beginning of an initial session. Here the helper summarizes the client's perception of why she has come for help.

> Helper: Let's feed back what you've said so far. You're depressed much of the time and find yourself crying and moping around. Along with the depression are spells of intense anger. Part of this anger is directed at yourself because you are not being more effective in your life. A lot is directed at your partner whom you think behaves like a selfish bastard much of the time. You would like not only to feel better about yourself, but also to cope better in the relationship.

The second summary provided here takes place at the end of the same session:

> Helper: Let's put the pieces together since we're coming towards the end of the session. You started by describing your feelings of depression and your intense anger both with yourself and with your

partner. You then proceeded to describe a whole range of Bill's behaviours that upset you: not doing household chores, complaining that you are too independent, and expecting sex on demand and then mainly paying attention to his own needs when making love. You then asked yourself whether you wished to stay in the relationship or not. You decided to give it another go for the time being partly because there is a lot about Bill that you like, and also because you wonder whether you haven't been colluding in his behaviour. You then went on to discuss your own difficulties in being assertive and tendencies to have very fixed ideas about how others should be. These were two areas that you wanted to think about before we meet again and possibly to work on next session. Is there anything that you would like to add to or alter in this summary?

In the above discussion on summarizing, I have focused on staying predominantly within the client's frame of reference. In more task-oriented interviewing, a summary of the client's frame of reference might precede a discussion of working goals and methods more from the helper's frame of reference. In Exercise 4.7 the emphasis is on summarizing to help your clients clarify, explore and develop *their* frame of reference.

Exercise 4.7 Developing your summarizing skills

This exercise can be done in pairs or as part of a training group.

A   *In pairs*
Counsel your partner, who either presents a concern from his or her work or personal life, or role-plays a client. This session should last at least ten to fifteen minutes. At one or more appropriate points during the session, provide a summary of what your client says. At the end, provide a summary to give closure to the session. Afterwards, get feedback from your partner on the quality and impact of your summaries. Then reverse roles. It may help to playback an audio- or video-recording of the session as a check on accuracy and on the highlighting of central themes and emerging directions.

B   *In a training group*
The trainer introduces the topic of facilitative summarizing. He or she then demonstrates the pairs exercise above. Afterwards, the group is broken up into pairs or triads to perform the exercise, prior to reconvening for a plenary sharing and discussion session.

FACILITATIVE SESSIONS

Termination

In this and the previous chapters I have suggested that there are a number of skills which can be classified as facilitative skills. To date I have not mentioned terminating a facilitative session. You may have gone some way towards structuring the timing of termination by an opening remark like: 'Well, we've got forty-five minutes together, and I would very much like to know what is concerning you.' It is the helper's responsibility to keep track of the time and, if it has not ended sooner, to draw the session to its close at the end of the allotted time. One option for closing a session is to say 'Well, we have about five minutes to go now, and perhaps I might summarize the main points covered in the session.' Some helpers dispense with summaries altogether and proceed straight to terminating the session, along the lines of: 'I'm afraid our time is drawing to a close', or 'We're going to have to end now.' If appropriate, arrangements for a subsequent session or sessions can be made. Alternatively, counsellors and helpers may ask their clients to summarize the main points of the session and to state what they learned from it. Further points and clarifications can be added if necessary.

Client Self-exploration

Rogers and his colleagues state that person-centred facilitation helps clients explore and experience themselves more fully.[16] Clients assume increasing responsibility for themselves and can communicate a rich self-awareness when desired. Partly based on Rogers' work, Truax and Carkhuff developed a nine-point scale to measure depth of client self-exploration.[17] At the lowest level, no personally significant feelings and material are discussed. The highest level, rarely attained, is an extension of stage eight of the scale, which is described as follows: '*Active intrapersonal exploration*. The patient is following a "connected" chain of thoughts in focusing upon himself and actively exploring himself. He may be discovering new feelings, new aspects of himself. He is actively exploring his feelings, his values, his perceptions of others, his relationships, his fears, his turmoil, and his life choices.' Though it is a tall order to achieve the above in a single session, I have included this description to give you an idea of the end product of successful facilitation.

Conducting a Session

The emphasis in the first part of this book has been on facilitative counselling and helping. I have endeavoured to help you develop good facilitation skills. This is both because they are useful in themselves and also because they provide a sound base for more focused interventions. Exercise 4.8 provides you with the opportunity to put all your facilitation skills together and to conduct a complete session. You may have to do this and similar exercises many times to develop fluency in the skills. Practice may not make perfect, but it undoubtedly increases the probability of improving your skills.

Exercise 4.8 Conducting a facilitative session

This is basically a pairs exercise but it may be done as part of a training group.

A *In pairs*
Conduct a complete session of, say, forty-five minutes with your partner. Your job is to facilitate your partner in exploring, clarifying and experiencing his or her concerns and frame of reference. The main skill you are to use is empathic responding. Other skills include: initial structuring, giving a permission to talk, sending continuation messages, avoiding sending discouraging messages, encouraging self-talk, helpful questioning, facilitative confronting, self-disclosing, summarizing and ending the session smoothly. It may help to audio- or video-record the session and play it back. Also, obtain feedback from your partner. Afterwards, reverse roles, though you should take a break between sessions.

B *In a training group*
The trainer may wish to ensure that, before doing it themselves, group members see one or more complete facilitative sessions performed by experienced helpers. Ways of doing this include: presentation of audio-recorded, video-recorded or filmed sessions; the trainer demonstrating a complete initial session; and making arrangements for group members either to observe behind a one-way screen, or to sit in on, the sessions of skilled facilitative helpers. Group members then do the pairs exercise above. If possible, the trainer goes over a recording of each session with the participants.

---

5 A Model for Managing Problems

Counsellor: Would you care to tell me what your problem is?
Client: My problem is that I have difficulty in remembering things.
Counsellor: When did your problem start?
Client: What problem?

Definition of having a problem: loving yourself more than your analyst.
Definition of overcoming a problem: loving your analyst more than yourself.

This chapter presents a five-stage framework or model for collaborating with clients to assist them in managing their problems better. As I mentioned in Chapter 1, focusing on clients' problems is not the only form of helping. Some may require nurturing and healing relationships to remedy previous emotional deprivation. However, this does not preclude a problem management focus being interspersed with facilitation, even though the emphasis may be more on facilitating the growth in confidence and emotional development of a *person* rather than on managing specific *problems*. Other foci for helping include managing crises, decision making and offering support. Here again problem management skills have relevance.

The term *managing* problems is preferable to that of *overcoming* or *mastering* problems for three main reasons. First, coping with problems is frequently a continuing process. For instance, an alcoholic may not drink for a month, but still has to continue managing a drinking problem. Second, some problems are realistic in their own right: for instance, a physical disability. Though clients can mitigate their adverse effects, they cannot totally overcome or master such problems. Third, the notion of mastering problems may cause both clients and helpers to set themselves unreasonably high goals.

A number of writers have presented problem management models. Perhaps the best known is Egan.[1] His model, now in its third version, has three stages: (1) problem definition, (2) goal development, and (3) action. Since each of these stages has three component steps, Egan's model contains nine steps and therefore arguably nine stages. Ivey has presented a five-stage structure for what he terms intentional interviewing and counselling.[2,3] His five stages are: (1) rapport/structuring, (2) defining the problem, (3) defining a goal, (4) explorations of alternatives and confronting incongruity, and (5) generalization to daily life. Additionally, Carkhuff has a model of helping consisting of four stages: (1) attending, (2) responding to clients, (3) personalizing their experience of where they are and where they want to be, and (4) initiating action.[4] Furthermore, all helping within either a behavioural or cognitive-behavioural framework is based on a problem management model. Thus there is nothing new about the notion of problem management models. Also, there is overlap between existing models. However, there are also significant differences between them in terms of both how they are stated and also the interventions to which they lead.

D'Zurilla and Goldfried define a problem as 'a specific situation or set of related situations to which a person must respond in order to function effectively in his environment'.[5] This definition requires elaboration. Clients' problems have the further characteristic that either the clients do not know how to deal with the situation at all or their attempted solutions have failed. Thus a problem is a combination both of the situation requiring a response and also of the clients' skills deficits in managing the problem. This position does not preclude realistic external factors such as poverty, unemployment and poor housing contributing to problems.

DOSIE: THE FIVE-STAGE MODEL

At the risk of simplification, I present DOSIE, a five-stage model for collaborative problem management. The model provides a framework or set of guidelines for your choices in helping your clients manage their problems more effectively. The use of an acronym is deliberate. I found that counsellor trainees with whom I worked at the Royal Melbourne Institute of Technology experienced difficulty remembering the five stages. This was not least because of the anxieties and pressures attached to working with clients for the first time. When I introduced the acronym DOSIE, they reported finding the model much easier to remember and hence to use. The five stages of the collaborative model are:

D   DESCRIBE and identify the problem(s)
O   OPERATIONALIZE the problem(s)
S   SET GOALS and negotiate interventions
I   INTERVENE
E   EXIT and consolidate self-help skills

Table 5.1 gives an overview of the central task, illustrative helper skills and desired client behaviours for each stage of the model. A more detailed description of the individual stages is provided in the remainder of the chapter.

Table 5.1   *DOSIE: a five-stage model for collaborative problem management*

Task	Illustrative helper skills	Client behaviours
Stage 1 DESCRIBE and identify the problem(s)		
Build a working alliance and help clients to reveal, identify and describe their problem(s)	Structuring, permission to talk, disciplined listening, continuation messages, emphatic responses, helpful questioning, encouraging self-talk, slight confrontations, summarizing	Identify problem areas Specify details Share thoughts, feelings and personal meanings
Stage 2 OPERATIONALIZE the problem(s)		
Elicit relevant information to define and state problem(s) operationally	Facilitation skills plus: focusing on accurately attributing responsibility, advanced empathic responding, didactic/interpretive confronting, developing different perceptions, focused information gathering, defining and stating problems operationally	Help identify and acknowledge skills deficits Relate to problem(s) more directly Develop new insights and perceptions
Stage 3 SET GOALS and negotiate interventions		
State working goals and negotiate interventions to attain them	Translating problem definitions into goal statements, choosing and negotiating treatment interventions, answering questions, aiding the generation and execution of alternative courses of action	Help set goals Acknowledge the need to work actively on problems Contribute to realistic discussion of interventions and to action planning

Table 5.1 (*contd.*)

Stage 4 INTERVENE		
Work to lessen skills deficits and to build skills resources in problem area(s)	Basic facilitation skills plus implementing appropriate interventions focused on client's feelings, thoughts and actions; establishing session agendas, negotiating homework, monitoring and evaluating progress, encouraging and supporting self-help, reverting to earlier stages of model as necessary	Work to acquire skills resources and to lessen skills deficits Discuss difficulties and successes in implementing approaches Help evaluate problem management process Acquire knowledge and skills for self-help

Stage 5 EXIT and consolidate self-help skills		
Terminate helping contact and consolidate self-help skills	Anticipatory structuring for termination, contributing to review of progress and of attainment of goals, facilitating consolidation of learning and self-help skills, getting feedback, handling affective and relationship issues, saying goodbye	Share in review of progress Present any personal termination issues Consolidate learning Strive to implement problem management self-help skills in daily living

DOSIE (describe–operationalize–set goals–intervene–exit) is intended to provide some guidelines rather than to be a straitjacket. Though your behaviours differ, the assumption is that you and your client collaborate to attain the goals for each stage. However, problem management helping rarely proceeds according to such neatly ordered stages. The stages tend to overlap: for instance, your clients' descriptions of problems contribute to clarifying and operationally defining them. Also, there may be reversion to earlier stages: for example, as more information emerges during the intervention stage, problems may be redefined and different goals set. Helping can be 'messy'. You work on the basis of hypotheses about your client, yourself and the helping process. You require flexibility in incorporating either new or previously overlooked information into your hypothesis making and testing. A further point is that the five-stage model needs to be adjusted not only to individual clients, but also to the setting and social context in which you work. For example, a priest helping a parishioner is likely to operate in a much more informal way than a counselling psychologist in private practice.

STAGE 1   DESCRIBE AND IDENTIFY THE PROBLEM(S)

Client: My problem is that everyone thinks I'm a liar.
Helper: Go on . . . I don't believe you.

Client: My problem is that I have an inferiority complex.
Helper: Lots of people have *important* problems and you come and bother
          me with your inferiority complex.

Unlike the helpers in the above exchanges, you need to help your
clients give their reasons for seeing you. A preliminary phase of the
describing stage is the introductions phase, the purpose of which can be
summarized as meeting, greeting and seating. The session starts with the
moment of first contact with the client. When meeting clients in a waiting
area, it may be perceived as more friendly if, as well as calling out their
names, you go over to them and show them into your office rather than
just stand at the door. You should politely show them to a seat and help
them feel safe. At an appropriate moment, possibly even in the waiting
area, you may greet them, along the lines of: 'Hello, I'm . . ., a helper
here.' The issue of what you and your clients call each other can be
handled during the initial or subsequent sessions according to the wishes
of both parties. From this initial moment of contact, you observe and
listen to your client's verbal, vocal and body messages so that you can
respond appropriately, and also start formulating your working model
about what sustains the client's problems.

The main work of the describing stage involves helping your clients first
to identify their problems and then to describe them more fully. You may
perform some initial structuring regarding such matters as how much time
you have together and any limitations on confidentiality. You may then
give a permission to talk and encourage clients to share with you their
frame of reference concerning their problem areas. You use your facilitative skills both to build your relationship with them so that *they* feel
understood and also to get them to elaborate their problems so that *you*
understand them better. Though you are likely to use other skills, the
main ones used at this stage are probably empathic responses interspersed with questions that help your clients describe their frame of
reference. In the previous chapter, I described elaboration questions,
specification questions and eliciting personal reactions questions. All of
these are appropriate here.

Facilitating Description of Problems

The case of Judy: a cautionary tale

It has been facetiously said about some people that the only exercise they
take is jumping to conclusions. The following is a cautionary tale about
resisting the impulse to label clients prematurely. Judy is a twenty-year-

old student who comes to helping as a client. In the following highly hypothetical excerpt, each time she says something more about herself, the helper labels her problem differently. Imagine a cartoon format, with each 'client says – helper thinks' pair representing captions in a box.

Judy:	I'm very tense about my upcoming exams.
Helper thinks:	This is an examination anxiety problem.
Judy:	I have not been studying effectively for some time now.
Helper thinks:	Aha. The exam anxiety is caused by poor study skills. This is a study skills problem.
Judy:	I wonder if I'm doing the right subject.
Helper thinks:	Perhaps this is really an educational choice problem.
Judy:	My parents are always pressurizing me to achieve on their terms. I just want to be my own person.
Helper thinks:	This is a late adolescent identity problem. Also, she needs to learn to assert herself more with her parents.
Judy:	I was doing all right until my relationship with Bill broke up. Since then I've been feeling very depressed.
Helper thinks:	This must be a reactive depression problem.
Judy:	I think I drove Bill away through my constant nagging.
Helper thinks:	This is now a managing anger problem. Help, I've got a problem too. I'm confused!

The message in the above tongue-in-cheek excerpt is the same that porcupine parents give to their offspring when advising them on how to make love: namely, 'proceed carefully'. There are risks in going firm on one problem area too soon. The problem initially presented may only be a safe 'calling card', to be followed by the real agenda if the client trusts you.[6] Sometimes clients have a number of different areas they want to discuss with you. On occasion, you may need to help them order their priorities concerning which problem is most important or which should be dealt with first. In all the above instances, if you overemphasize the problem stated at the beginning, you may block your client from revealing another. Furthermore, you may fail to create a working together relationship in which you and your clients collaborate in building their skills resources. You need to make the choices that enable your clients to do much of the work, rather than to do it for them. For instance, if you interrogate your clients, they are likely to wait for your next question rather than to explore relevant aspects of their problems for themselves. Though overlapping, a distinction may be made between a descriptive and an operational understanding or definition of a problem. A *descriptive* understanding provides basic information about the problem area. An *operational* understanding goes beyond description to identify and state what the client either does, or fails to do, or a mixture of the two, that helps sustain the problem.

Basic descriptive information may include the following:

- What do you perceive as the problem?
- When did it start?
- How long has it been going on?
- How frequent is it?
- What precipitates it?
- What are its negative and positive consequences?
- What feelings are associated with it?
- What physical reactions do you have?
- What thoughts accompany the problem?
- How do you actually behave?
- How have you attempted to cope with it in the past?

Open-ended questions are of value when getting started. For instance, if a client says she is depressed, you can respond 'You say you are depressed. Could you tell me more?'. Such a question allows her to choose the salient aspects of what bothers her. Always you show sensitivity to what is important to the client. This you may discover from what is said, the way it is said and from what is left unsaid or only partially said.

The describing stage focuses on client self-report. Though helpers vary in their use of them, questionnaires are another way in which clients can report their feelings and behaviour. Two examples are Wolpe's use of a fear inventory to identify anxiety-evoking stimuli, and Beck's use of the Beck Depression Inventory.[7,8] Also, clients can be encouraged to monitor and report on their behaviour.

Exercise 5.1 focuses on helping clients describe their problems. Remember to intersperse empathic responses with questions. The following is what you should avoid:

Client: I'm getting very anxious over my exams.
Helper: What makes you so anxious?
Client: The fact that I may fail.
Helper: Why are you so afraid of failing?
Client: Because then it may be harder to get a job.
Helper: What sort of job do you want?

Below is a more facilitative approach to the same presenting problem.

Client: I'm getting very anxious over my exams.
Helper: You're getting very anxious . . . Would you care to say a bit more about it?
Client: Yes. I have an important test in three weeks time for which I feel unprepared.
Helper: So you feel unready to take this vital test?
Client: My whole future depends on it.
Helper   You feel it is make-or-break. Could you explain this further?

Though the above are only short excerpts, in the first the helper controls and dominates the client whereas in the second the helper facilitates the client's description of his or her frame of reference in relation to the problem area. The emotional climate in the first excerpt is likely to be 'in the head'. The second excerpt encourages the expression of feelings as well as of thoughts.

Exercise 5.1   Facilitating a client in presenting and describing a problem

This exercise can be done on your own, in pairs or as part of a training group.

A   *On your own*
Write out a transcript in which you attempt to help a hypothetical client present and describe a problem. In your transcript include structuring, a permission to talk, continuation messages, empathic responses, helpful questioning and slight confrontations, and finish with a summary which you check for accuracy with your client.

B   *In pairs*
Partner A facilitates partner B's presentation and description of a problem along the above lines. This lasts for at least fifteen minutes and should be audio-recorded or video-recorded. The cassette is then played back with partner B identifying which of partner A's statements were helpful or harmful and why. Afterwards, reverse roles.

C   *In a training group*
The trainer introduces the topic of facilitating presentation and description of problem(s). He or she then demonstrates the pairs exercise. The group is then broken up into twos or threes (helper, client and observer) to perform the pairs exercise. Again, audio- or video-recording playback is recommended. Afterwards, the trainer convenes a plenary sharing and discussion session.

STAGE 2   OPERATIONALIZE THE PROBLEM(S)

The objective of this stage is to build a definitional bridge between *describing* and *actively working* on a problem. What you seek to do is to identify the choices that clients make in the areas of feeling, thinking and action that sustain their problems or at least their share of them. Operationalizing problems entails identifying and stating the operations that sustain them.

Problems can have many different layers and ramifications. For instance, Marie, a woman in her early forties, says: 'I'm bored at home.' Possible areas of relevant information here include: how good Marie is at helping herself rather than waiting for others to do so; the expectations that she, her husband and children have of each other; the work, educational, social and leisure opportunities that she has available both at and away from home, and so on. In short, Marie needs assistance in moving from a *descriptive* statement or definition of her problem to an *operational* definition of it. Such an operational definition identifies and states her current skills deficits in being able to solve the problem. In this hypothetical example, Marie's current deficits may include: an inability to tell her family that she wants some space for herself; failure in adequately accepting personal responsibility for owning and actively working on her problem; and an absence of information-seeking behaviour that has resulted in her being unaware of many of the available work, educational, leisure and social opportunities.

In stage 1, describing, you were facilitating your clients to describe and elaborate their problems largely from their frame of reference. In stage 2, you collaborate with them in the detective work of uncovering what sustains the problem or problems they have described. Here you are likely to operate as much, if not more, from your frame of reference as theirs. During this stage you endeavour to take them beyond their current perception of their problem to a new perception that allows them the opportunity to work for change. You bring to bear your theoretical knowledge and practical experience to elicit the relevant information that allows for an operational definition of their problem. Part of this process involves the capacity to separate relevant from irrelevant information and also to focus in on the crux of how clients contribute to sustaining their problems.

Prior to presenting some of the skills of further clarifying and operationalizing problems, I mention three broader considerations that can contribute to your effectiveness in stage 2.

● *An adequate theoretical framework.* You require a theoretical framework that offers adequate explanations of how your client's dysfunctional behaviours were acquired, have been and are sustained and can be changed. The theoretical position adopted here, implicitly if not always explicitly, is the integrative approach described in my book, *Personal Responsibility Counselling and Therapy*.[9] Some textbooks are listed in notes 10–14 for those of you wishing to do further reading in counselling and helping theory.[10,11,12,13,14] These textbooks indicate primary sources written by the theorists themselves.

● *A repertoire of practical interventions.* Your operationalization of problems should ideally be related not only to theory but also to interventions or skills that you can use to help your clients manage their problems more effectively. Many beginning helpers have very restricted repertoires of practical interventions. Consequently, they are limited in their capacity both to define operationally and to work with clients' problems. Some interventions that you may choose to use are described later in the book. Your knowledge of these interventions will contribute to your ability to operationally define problems.

● *Knowledge of medical considerations.*   I use the term 'medical considerations' to indicate some areas of helping that require biological and medical as well as psychological knowledge. Sometimes you may work in conjunction with your clients' doctors: for instance, with a client on medication or when you want to check whether your clients' problems have medical implications. When assessing clients, the helper as hypothesis-maker should not ignore medically related hypotheses: for example, thought blocking might be caused by brain damage and lowered interest in sex could have a physiological explanation. Also, helpers must be alert for symptoms of severe disturbance and for indications of psychophysiological disorders (formerly called psychosomatic disorders).

The main source book on psychiatric classification is the American Psychiatric Association's *Diagnostic and Statistical Manual of Mental Disorders* (third edition),[15] which is summarized in the *DSM-III Training Guide*.[16] Those wishing for further information about medical considerations are referred to *DSM-III*, introductory psychiatry textbooks like those by Trethowan and Sims and by Willis,[17,18] and to abnormal psychology textbooks such as those by Coleman and Butcher and by Davison and Neale.[19,20]

Focusing on Accurately Attributing Responsibility

Earlier I made a distinction between helping clients to own that they had a problem and helping them to acknowledge that certain of their behaviours may sustain it. In stage 2, you go beyond helping your clients to own that they have a problem by assisting them in acknowledging personal responsibility for what they do or fail to do that perpetuates it. Implicit in a problem management approach is the assumption that clients need to develop the skills of coping better with their problem area(s). By adopting a *problem management orientation* yourself, you are likely to help them adopt this too.

Clients can err in the directions of attributing too much of the responsibility and cause for their problems either outside of or to themselves. Accurate attribution is desirable. For example, Jim tends to externalize his problems. He comes to you saying he has marriage difficulties. He then plays the victim and launches into a long description of what Mary does to him without mentioning how he behaves towards Mary. Getting Jim to provide this further information may help him acknowledge his responsibility more accurately. Sometimes helpers may need to confront their clients strongly. On other occasions, they may ask *personal responsibility questions* that help clients to confront themselves with their role in sustaining their problems. Such questions include: 'How is this behaviour helping you?', 'How do you see your own behaviour contributing to the problem?', and 'Are there any ways in which you could be helping yourself more?'

Cindy is an example of someone who attributes too much responsibility to herself. Everything that goes wrong is 'her fault'. She contributes to her anxiety and depression through doing this.[21] She is in just as much need as Jim of help in the area of attributing responsibility accurately. Some clients, on the other hand, need help in overcoming a passive stance to life. For instance, Marie, the bored housewife described earlier, may have been waiting for change to come from outside herself rather than acknowledging her own responsibility for *making* changes occur. This observation could be shared with her.

Advanced Empathic Responding

In Chapter 3, a distinction was made between interchangeable empathy and advanced empathy. Interchangeable empathy involves making *reflective* responses that stay close to the surface of what clients say. Advanced empathy entails making *exploratory* responses that help clients articulate and explore more personally relevant, emotionally tinged and threatening areas of their experiencing. There is some evidence that, in person-centred counselling, client perception of helper empathy is positively associated with responses that go beyond surface reflection, yet are not so distant from the client's frame of reference as to constitute interpretations or explanations solely from the helper's frame of reference.[22] There are many ways that advanced empathic responses may help in operationalizing problems. Egan views them as bridging responses that help clients move to more goal-directed perspectives.[23] However, if inaccurate, clumsily worded, badly timed and with inadequate checking of clients' reactions to them, such responses can do more harm than good.

Pinpointing feelings more accurately

Frequently clients fail either to label their feelings accurately or to acknowledge their intensity accurately.

Client: I'm not really that keen on Sara, but I would like to see more of her.
Helper: I get the impression that you're very taken with Sara, but are afraid to acknowledge it.
Client: I think about her all the time.

Here, by not colluding in the client's dilution of his feeling, the helper may have helped the client operationalize his problems in terms of the skills he needs to maximize his chances with Sara.

Articulating skills deficits

Sometimes clients talk around their problem areas and require help in stating them succinctly.

Client: I'm rushing around trying to do a job, entertain for my husband and spend time with the kids.
Helper: You seem to be finding it difficult to set limits among the various pressures of kids, husband and work.
Client: That's exactly it.

In the above example, helper empathy helped the client move from describing her problem as though she were the victim of it towards stating it in terms of a skills deficit. Identification of a skills deficit, namely difficulty setting limits, is a bridge for her towards working on her problem.

Clarifying hidden agendas

Sometimes a surface agenda masks a more important agenda for the client.

Client: Vic and I got engaged two months ago. Ever since then we've been fighting like cats and dogs. Previously we got on very well.
Helper: You're concerned about the deterioration in your relationship. As you've been talking I've got the impression that underneath you're panicking about giving up your autonomy. What do you think about that?
Client: Yes, I feel very scared about being trapped.

In this greatly shortened example, the helper's sensitivity to an underlying agenda may have contributed to a reformation of the problem. For instance, previously the client may have defined the problem in terms of whether or not she should break her engagement to Vic. Now she defines it in terms of how she and Vic can best cope with her fears about losing her autonomy once married.

Identifying themes

This involves helpers in putting together the pieces of what clients say so that themes can be identified. These themes reflect skills deficits that sustain clients' problems.

> Helper: You describe yourself as a 'leaf in the breeze'. As I listen to you, there is a fairly consistent theme that you judge yourself in ways that put you down. For instance, you only compare yourself with those who do better, you can't stand the thought of making a mistake, and you back off from situations where there is any chance of rejection. Consequently, much of the time you seem to seek the safe or easy option.

Exercise 5.2   Advanced empathic responding

This exercise may be done on your own, in pairs or in a training group.

A   *On your own*
   1.   Try to identify and write down situations in your own life where *other people listen to you* on a surface level. What responses on their part might help you to pinpoint feelings more accurately, articulate skills deficits, clarify hidden agendas and identify themes?
   2.   Try to identify and write down situations where *you listen to others* on a surface level. What responses on your part might help them to pinpoint feelings more accurately, articulate skills deficits, clarify hidden agendas, and identify themes?
B   *In pairs*
   Partner A counsels partner B, who discusses and explores a problem for at least ten minutes. This session is audio- or video-recorded. During the session, partner A tries to make at least one or two advanced empathic responses. Afterwards, replay the cassette and discuss the helpfulness or harmfulness of these responses. Then reverse roles.
C   *In a training group*
   The trainer discusses using advanced empathic responses to help clients clarify problem areas. The trainer demonstrates the pairs exercise above.

Then the group is broken down into pairs or triads to do the exercise. This is followed by a plenary sharing and discussion session.

Didactic/Interpretive Confronting

In Chapter 4, a distinction was made between facilitative, hot-seat and didactic/interpretive confronting. In facilitative confrontation, you use your experiencing of your clients to help them clarify and possibly expand their frame of reference. In didactic/interpretive confrontation, you use your knowledge of how people sustain their problems to confront your client. Didactic/interpretive confrontations contain within them explanations of how clients perpetuate their difficulties. They constitute a form of helper feedback that helps specify areas in which clients need to work. Perhaps the main focus of didactic/interpretive confrontations is the ways in which clients sustain problems through *ineffective thought patterns*. This topic is covered in greater detail in Chapter 7. It may suffice for now to indicate two thinking-related areas in which you may choose to confront your clients.

● *Unrealistic inner rules.* Unrealistic inner rules are standards that clients have for their own and others' behaviour that are dysfunctional in that they generate self-defeating emotions and behaviour.[24] For example, Debbie gets anxious every time she meets a stranger. She becomes very quiet and diffident. Here a helper may confront Debbie with the possibility that she has an unrealistic inner rule concerning needing to be liked and approved of by everyone all the time. This unrealistic rule constitutes one of her skills deficits. What the helper does is offer Debbie an explanation of one aspect of her functioning that perpetuates the behaviour she wants to change.

● *Misattributing responsibility and cause.* This topic was mentioned earlier in the chapter. The example given was of Jim, who lengthily complained about his wife's behaviour without talking about his own. The assumption was that he was a reactive victim rather than possibly an active persecutor. Jim was playing the blame game. A helper may need to confront Jim with the need to look at his own behaviour if he wants to change anything at home. Furthermore, the helper may need to identify specific instances of Jim's tendency to externalize all his marital difficulties on to his wife. Jim could then be confronted with the observation that these are manifestations of a skills deficit that probably contributes to keeping him unhappy.

Didactic/interpretive confrontations may also focus on the *ineffective ways in which clients behave* as well as on their self-defeating thought patterns. Though there is a close relationship between what people think and what they do, below is an example of an area of didactic/interpretive confrontation that is more focused on behaviour.

● *Lack of assertion skills.* Sometimes clients do not see that they contribute to staying stuck in a problem through lack of assertion skills. Donna is a secretary. She gets extremely angry with her boss, Mike, who continuously asks her to stay late. She also gets angry with herself for not doing anything about Mike. Donna may need to be confronted with the possibility that, through her inability or unwillingness to talk to Mike and negotiate some limits, she colludes in perpetuating her own anger and unhappiness. If, despite her attempts at assertion, Mike persists in his behaviour, then Donna has the choice either to assert herself more forcibly or, if his behaviour upsets her enough, to look for another job. However, defining it as a job decision problem before viewing it as a lack of assertion skills problem is premature. Also, this prevents Donna from acquiring the self-help skills she may require to survive in other situations. In the above illustration a didactic/interpretive confrontation to Donna might be:

> Donna, you've been saying how angry you get both with yourself and your boss over these constant requests for you to work late. You've indicated that, to date, you have always acquiesced in these requests and never told Mike that you do not want to stay late so often. I think that part of the problem may be your lack of assertive behaviour towards Mike in which you try to convey to him realistic limits on your working late. What do you think about this way of viewing the problem?

Exercise 5.3 is designed to give you some practice at making didactic/interpretive confrontations. These confrontations identify possible skills deficits that sustain problems. When presenting didactic/interpretive confrontations, you may need to offer further explanations, if requested by your client. For example, Donna might request you to spell out what you mean by her lack of assertive behaviour in setting limits with Mike. You are negotiating explanations of your client's problems to provide a basis for later work. Consequently, it is important for the client to understand and own the relevance of your explanations.

Exercise 5.3 Didactic/interpretive confronting

This exercise can be done on your own, in pairs or in a training group.

A   *On your own*
Think of situations in either your personal life or counselling/helping work where didactive/interpretive confronting might be useful. Choose one situation where a thinking-focused confrontation and another where a behaviour-focused confrontation might help. For each, write out a description of the presenting situation and the wording of your didactic/interpretive confrontation.

B   *In pairs*
Partner A counsels partner B in relation to a problem in his or her personal or work life. Partner A starts by using basic facilitation skills, but then uses more focused problem definition skills, including trying to provide at least one didactic/interpretive confrontation and allowing his or her client to respond to it. Afterwards, discuss and reverse roles. Audio- or video-recording and playback may be helpful.

C   *In a training group*
The trainer discusses the topic of didactic/interpretive confrontations. He or she then models the pairs exercises. Afterwards, the group is divided into pairs or triads to do the exercise. This is followed by a plenary sharing and discussion session.

Developing Different Perceptions

A man with a duck on his head walks into a psychiatrist's office.

Psychiatrist: What is your problem?
Duck: Would you please help me get this man off my bottom?

As this joke illustrates, there are different ways of perceiving problems. Clients are often locked into fairly rigid ways of perceiving themselves, others and their problems. Sometimes, as in the case of a heavily defended mother whose egotistical behaviour has damaged the emotional development of her children, it may be too threatening to explore alternatives to her present perception that she is the perfect mother who has the misfortune to have ungrateful children. In many other instances, clients may gain greater insight into their problems if they explore different perceptions. The outcome of this may be that they reconceptualize their problems.

There are a number of ways in which you can help your clients explore different ways of choosing to perceive themselves and their problems. Some of these are listed below.

● *Exploring different perceptions questions.* The following are some questions that you can use to help your clients to explore different perceptions: 'What are your options?'; 'Is there any other way of viewing your problem?'; 'How do you think he or she views the matter?'; 'Could you have behaved differently?'; 'What do you really want in the situation?'; 'Is there any other interpretation?'; and 'What skills do you need to be able to manage the problem?'

- *Helping clients test their perceptions.*   Much of helping involves enabling clients to perceive themselves, others and the world more accurately. You can ask clients to supply evidence to corroborate their perceptions, especially if you suspect they may be distorted. For example, if Dale says that his boss does not like him, you can ask Dale to provide evidence to support this assertion. Again, if Farida says she is a weak person, you can help her explore the evidence for this judgement. Part of this process may also entail encouraging Farida to examine instances where she may have been a strong person.
- *Suggesting different perceptions.*   Though, in general, you should encourage clients to do their own work, at times it may be appropriate for you to suggest alternatives. For example, Gene is very hard on himself because he was made redundant. He keeps referring to it as a personal failure. Different perceptions that may be relevant to Gene's situation include these: broader economic forces and poor management contributed to his redundancy; his current lack of skills works against his getting re-employed; and his failure to keep occupied may contribute to his feelings of helplessness and depression.
- *Either providing or facilitating access to relevant information.*   Egan observes: 'Sometimes clients are not able to explore their problems fully and proceed to action because they lack information of one kind or another. In such cases helpers can provide the needed information or help clients get it from some other source.'[25] For example, Edna has a different perception of her chances of training to be a nurse when she obtains information on financial assistance. Dave has a different perception of his bisexual feelings when he is provided with information on the proportion of males with varying degrees of bisexual orientation. Ellie, a mother whose recent baby has been diagnosed as mentally retarded, has a changed perception of her situation when she receives valid information on the probability of her next baby being retarded.

Exercise 5.4   Helping clients develop different perceptions

The following exercise may be done on your own, in pairs or in a training group.

A   *On your own*
Pick a problem either in your own or in one of your clients' lives and write out as many different perceptions of the problem as you can think of in ten to fifteen minutes. Assess whether any of these perceptions might be helpful in operationally defining the problem.

B   *In pairs*
Partner A counsels partner B about a problem in his or her personal or professional life for at least ten minutes. Partner A endeavours to help partner B develop different perceptions of the problem by:
1.   asking exploring different perceptions questions;
2.   helping the 'client' test his or her perceptions;
3.   suggesting different perceptions; and
4.   either providing or facilitating access to relevant information.
      Afterwards, discuss, and then reverse roles.

C   *In a training group*
The trainer introduces the topic of developing different perceptions. He or she demonstrates the pairs exercise and then gets the group to do the exercise in pairs or triads. Alternatively, one of the group members presents a problem and the whole group joins in helping the 'client' develop different perceptions of the problem. Then another group member presents a problem, and so on.

Exercise 5.5   Providing and facilitating access to relevant information

The following exercise may be done on your own, in pairs or as part of a training group.

For all formats
In the following vignettes, state what information might help the client gain a more realistic perception of his or her problem.
(a)   Eric, aged twenty-three, says that he fears he is schizophrenic. However, he reports none of the major characteristics of schizophrenics.
(b)   Eunice, aged sixteen, is eight weeks pregnant and wonders whether or not to have an abortion.
(c)   Tina, aged eighteen, rarely has an orgasm during intercourse and wonders if she is frigid.
(d)   Julie, aged twenty-seven, is a single parent and has just lost her job. She is desperately worried about making ends meet.
(e)   Ian, aged thirty-two, is contemplating a divorce, but wants to keep a close relationship with his children (aged two and five).
(f)   Kim, aged fifty-nine, has been told he has cancer. He is reeling from the news.
(g)   Hazel, aged forty-two, has discovered that her fifteen-year-old daughter Lynn is addicted to drugs. She blames herself for this.

Focused Information Gathering

Generally an assumption in problem management helping is that your contact with clients will be relatively brief, say not more than ten sessions. This is not to deny that many problems are more deep-rooted and require longer attention. However, circumstances, including your own availability and the client's wishes, often preclude this. In relatively brief contact with clients you may have adequate time to work with their problems. If not, you are faced with making the most of the time available.

As you gather information with your clients, you try to formulate valid hypotheses about what sustains their difficulties. Sue, aged twenty-two, says she is extremely anxious about her final exams, which start in six weeks time. There are numerous choices you can make concerning what information you gather. Sue indicates that, though she may have other problems, getting through her exams is the problem upon which she wishes to focus. You have gathered an important piece of information: namely, your client's priorities.

Focused information gathering in stage 2 overlaps with getting the client to describe their problem more fully in stage 1. Below are some of the kinds of information that you may need to collect in order to operationalize Sue's problem adequately. It is important that you collect this information in a collaborative and supportive way. You attempt to increase Sue's understanding of her problem as well as your own. Empathic responses should be interspersed with questions.

- Basic details on what she means by the term extremely anxious, in terms of feelings and physical reactions.
- How her current functioning is being affected: for instance, her studying.
- The degree to which her anxiety relates to the period either *before* her exams and/or *during* them.
- Details of which exams trigger anxiety and why.
- Details of the timing of her exams.
- Whether or not she has suffered from exam anxiety in the past and if so, how has she coped.
- Whether she has a suitable location for studying.
- The extent to which her problems stem from inadequate preparation: for instance, is she far behind?
- Whether she is repeating all or part of the course.
- Whether she has any assessed work outstanding.
- Whether or not she feels she has been doing the right course.

- The adequacy of her revision and exam-taking techniques.
- The realism of her expectations concerning achievement.
- The reasons why she attaches so much importance to these exams.
- What she is telling herself may happen to her if she fails.
- The degree of support and understanding or lack of it she can expect from her academic, college and home environments.
- Whether she is taking adequate recreation or has allowed herself to become stale.
- Whether or not she is on medication.
- Whether or not she is under any other stresses.
- The degree to which she is an anxious person in other areas of her life.

Though the above may seem a long list, a competent interviewer should have little difficulty eliciting this information within less than an hour. Focused information gathering has two main emphases: further clarifying what the problem is and collecting data to test a series of preliminary hypotheses about what sustains it. The helper now has much more information with which to identify the hypotheses that best seem to fit Sue's problem. Focused information gathering entails choosing what information is important and discarding that which is not. The quality of the relationship between Sue and her helper during this process is again stressed. Talking about her problem and being understood and supported by the helper is likely to calm her.

Defining and Stating Problems Operationally

The desired outcome of the second stage is a clear statement of the skills deficits on which helper and client need to work if the client is to manage his or her problem better. Put another way, the client may have been making some poor choices. An operational formulation of the problem breaks it down and identifies the areas in which the client needs to make better choices. During later working sessions the problem may be broken down even more specifically. However, such detail may be inappropriate for an initial operational definition of a problem. This essentially pinpoints the areas in which later work is likely to be done.

An operational definition of a problem is a set of hypotheses about the skills deficits sustaining the client's problems. Though it forms the basis for goal setting and working on the problem, it should be open to modification in the light of new information and circumstances. In short, your initial operational definition of your client's problem is likely to be subject both to continuous testing and also to major or minor reformulations as you work with your client.

Some characteristics of a good operational statement of a problem are as follows:

- It bears a clear relationship to the information that the client has provided.
- It is formulated in collaboration with the client.
- It relates to a problem on which the client sets a high priority.
- As far as possible, it clearly identifies the skills deficits on which the client needs to work.
- It can be clearly and succinctly stated to the client.
- The client is likely to perceive it as relevant and to own it as a basis for working on the problem.
- It is stated as a hypothesis.
- It lends itself to setting helpful and realistic goals.

To revert to the example of Sue, whose presenting problem was that she was extremely anxious about her final exams in six weeks time: depending on what you discovered as together you explored her problem, you might operationally define and state her problem in different ways. Here are some options:

- *Option 1*   Together you decide that the focus of her anxiety centres on her fear of losing control of herself in the exam room. Here an operational definition of her problem would emphasize her lack of anxiety management skills in exam settings. You further identify her skills deficits as: using anxiety-engendering inner speech; not allocating her time well and then panicking when she does not have time to finish all the questions; and not knowing how to slow down physically, relax her body, and regulate her breathing to calm herself down.
- *Option 2*   Together you decide that she feels overwhelmed by what she needs to do in the time available before her exams. You further identify her skills deficits as: not gathering information about what is required in her exams; not having identified a suitable location for studying; not being able to break her revision task down and set herself priorities; and having poor skills of setting time aside for study and sticking to it.
- *Option 3*   Together you decide that she treats herself like a machine, works far too hard, has perfectionist standards, and is always physically tense. You operationally define her skills deficits as: having unrealistic standards for achievement; insufficiently understanding that how productive she is is more important than how many hours

she works; not setting aside some time for recreation and consequently becoming stale; and not having the skills of physically relaxing herself.

In the above example, I have tried to show how making valid operational definitions and statements of problems is based on gathering relevant information. These statements are both formulated in collaboration with your clients and then further checked with them to see if they 'fit'. If your client has reservations about your operational statement, you should explore these reservations further. Assuming that the reservations are not based on misunderstanding, you may then choose either to clarify further the reasoning behind your statement or to modify it.

I have dealt with stage 2 of the collaborative problem management model at some length. Operationally defining problems can be difficult. Mistakes in definition not only lead to time and effort being wasted, but may contribute to clients being even less able to manage their problems. For example, Lee was a Chinese-Malayan overseas student who was repeating the first year of his production engineering course and was obviously going to fail. He was afraid of how his parents would react to his failure and also undecided about whether or not he wanted to be a production engineer. Instead of helping Lee deal with these areas, his helper, who was a beginning counselling trainee, defined his problem as lack of assertive skills in seeking help from the college staff. Lee himself expressed reservations about this way of viewing his situation. Despite this, the helper persisted in spending time on trying to build up Lee's academic help-seeking skills. This blocked Lee from dealing with the more pertinent skills deficits.

Exercise 5.6 Operationally defining and stating problems

This exercise may be done in pairs or in a training group.

A   *In pairs*
    Partner A counsels partner B for as long as it takes to explore and clarify a problem to the point where it can be operationally defined and stated. Partner A works with partner B to operationally define and state the problem. Afterwards, reverse roles. Audio- or video-recording and playback may be helpful.

B   *In a training group*
    The trainer introduces the topic of operationally defining and stating problems. He or she demonstrates the pairs exercise. The group is then

broken up into pairs or triads to do the exercise. Since the exercise may last for some time, part or all of it may be done as homework. Afterwards, the trainer conducts a plenary session in which operational statements of the presenting problems are reviewed and discussed.

STAGE 3   SET GOALS AND NEGOTIATE INTERVENTIONS

In stages 1 and 2, you and your clients were moving from a description to an operational definition and statement of a problem. Thus in these stages you were attempting to answer the question 'What is the problem?' Given the operational definition of the problem arrived at in stage 2, stage 3 focuses on the question 'What is the best way of managing the problem?' It consists of two phases: stating goals and negotiating interventions.

Stating Goals

Goals can be stated in general terms such as: 'I want to feel less depressed'; 'I want to improve my relationships with my husband and children'; and 'I want to come to terms with my disability.' General statements of goals have value in giving clients visions of what they want out of helping. However, such general statements refer more to ends than to means. Here I focus on statements of goals that focus on means rather than ends.

Assuming you have been successful in operationally defining the problem, stating goals is a relatively simple matter. As Carkhuff observes: 'The goal, then, is simply the "flip side" of the problem. That is, when you turn the problem over you have the goal.'[26] Your operational definition states your client's skills deficits in relation to the problem. Your statement of goals identifies these as skills resources in need of development. For instance, lack of assertive skills is a problem, acquiring assertion skills is a goal.

To revert again to the earlier example of exam-anxious Sue. In one operational definition of her problem (Option 2), her skills deficits were identified as: (a) not gathering information about what is required in her exams; (b) not having identified a suitable location for studying; (c) not being able to break her revision tasks down and set herself priorities; and (d) having poor skills for setting time aside for study and sticking to it.

Sue's goals now become the reverse side of the skills she lacks: (a) gathering information about what is required in her exams; (b) finding a suitable location for studying; (c) improving her revision skills by breaking tasks down and ordering priorities; and (d) planning her time for study better and sticking to her plan.

Exercise 5.7 has been designed to give you practice at translating operational definitions of problems into statements of goals.

Exercise 5.7 Translating operational definitions of problems into statements of goals

This exercise may be performed either on your own, in pairs or in a training group.

A   *On your own*
   Take a problem in your own or in one of your clients' lives and write out:
   1.   a description of the problem in everyday terms;
   2.   an operational definition of the problem; and
   3.   a translation of the operational definition into a statement of goals.
B   *In pairs*
   Partner A counsels partner B, who presents a problem. Together you work through the above exercise. Afterwards, reverse roles.
C   *In a training group*
   The trainer demonstrates translating operational definitions of problems into statements of goals. The group is broken up into pairs or triads to perform the exercise. This is followed by a plenary sharing and discussion session.

Negotiating Interventions

Having stated goals, your next set of choices concerns how best to help clients attain them. An important issue here is the extent to which you either facilitate your clients in generating and assessing the courses of action they might take to attaining their goals, or whether together you decide that they should be recipients of one or more specific interventions provided by you. The next three chapters cover helping interventions focused on clients' feelings, thoughts and actions. In actual fact, the distinction between facilitating clients in managing their problems and your providing interventions for them is not clear cut. As you facilitate your clients' problem management, you may provide further interventions that develop their self-help skills.

I use the term *negotiating interventions* to cover both helping clients solve their problems and also providing helping interventions for them. Since later chapters deal with specific interventions, at this stage of the book it is difficult to discuss in detail how best to present these to clients. Some obvious guidelines are that your interventions should be: tailored to attaining the client's goals; discussed, with any questions being answered as clearly as possible; and agreed upon by clients.

Exercise 5.8 focuses on assisting clients' problem management rather than on providing interventions for them. You aid them in generating and assessing alternative courses of action they might take to attain their goals. Together you may discover that there are many more possibilities in difficult areas of their lives than they imagine. As well as empathic responding, judicious use of exploring alternatives questions may help. For instance, the following are some questions that you might use to aid clients in generating and evaluation alternatives: 'What are your options?', 'Are there any other ways in which you might attain your goals?', 'What might the positive and negative consequences bc of ———— course of action?', and 'Is that the behaviour that is going to be of most help to you?' Though you may suggest some alternatives yourself in a neutral way, possibly this should wait until you have provided your clients with a good chance to generate their own alternatives. Here it is important that not only your verbal but your vocal and body messages leave the decision to them. Use empathic responding each time your clients suggest or assess an alternative, before asking any questions. This helps keep the emphasis on their generating and owning their *own* solutions and courses of action for their problems.

Exercise 5.8 concludes by asking you to help your client develop a step-by-step plan to attain his or her goals. The idea here is that you help your client choose the most appropriate course of action. Then you aid him or her in specifying the steps that are necessary to implement the action. It can also be helpful to anticipate potential difficulties and setbacks and then to include ways of surmounting them in the plan. Remember to make your clients do most of the work when you aid their problem management. In most instances, the most effective way you can help others is to help them to help themselves.

Exercise 5.8   Aiding the generation and evaluation of alternative courses of action

This exercise may be done on your own, in pairs or in a training group.

A   *On your own*
In Exercise 5.7 you made a statement of goals based on an operational definition of a problem either in your own or in one of your clients' lives. Write out:
1.   as many different ways of attaining the goals as you can think of in ten to fifteen minutes,
2.   an assessment of the degree to which the better of these courses of action are realistic and useful; and
3.   a step-by-step plan, including a time schedule, for attaining your own or the client's goals.
B   *In pairs*
Either with the statement of goals made in Exercise 5.7 or with a statement of goals derived from an operational definition of another problem, facilitate your partner, who acts as 'client', in:
1.   thinking of as many different ways of attaining the goals as he or she can in ten to fifteen minutes;
2.   assessing the degree to which any of these courses of action are realistic and useful; and
3.   developing a step-by-step plan, including a time schedule, for attaining the goals.
Afterwards, reverse roles.
C   *In a training group*
The trainer demonstrates aiding the exploration and evaluation of alternative courses of action in relation to a group member's problem. The group is subdivided to perform the pairs exercise. Afterwards, the trainer conducts a plenary sharing and discussion session. Alternatively, the trainer can get the whole group to suggest alternative courses of action for attaining one or more members' goals. The trainer then helps members evaluate the suggestions and develop step-by-step plans to attain goals.

STAGE 4   INTERVENE

The task of the intervention stage is to lessen skills deficits and to build skills resources in problem areas. The aim is to help clients help themselves both to make better choices and to become better choosers. This stage is dealt with briefly here, since much of the remainder of the book covers interventions for working with clients.

The emotional climate throughout the intervention stage should be collaborative. Within the context of understanding relationships, helpers assist their clients to assume responsibility for building the self-help skills they require to manage their problems. The place of basic facilitation skills during the working phase should not be underestimated. Such skills enable you to: offer clients support as they try out new behaviours, give them a sounding board for understanding their new experiences, understand yourself what they go through and what work still remains to be done, and make knowledgeable choices concerning when and how to intervene.

Apart from the various interventions discussed later, there are a number of skills pertinent to the working stage. These include the following.

Sensitivity to your client's current experiencing

There is a risk in the intervention stage of becoming too task-oriented. For instance, a client comes to a session after a very difficult week. If you are sensitive to the messages they send and possibly check how they feel, you may decide that it is premature to work directly in their problem area. Instead, it may be better to help them share and process their thoughts and feelings concerning what currently bothers them. There is, of course, a risk in the other direction; namely, becoming too person-oriented and not task-oriented enough.

Beginning a session

One option is to ask a fairly open-ended question, such as, 'How have things been going for you the past week?', 'Where would you like to start today?', or 'What would you like to work on today?' These sorts of question allow clients to bring up pressing concerns other than the problem with which you have been working. Another option is to be more direct and ask a more specific question related to the problem area, such as: 'To what extent have you been anxious about your exams in the past week?' or 'How did you get on with ———— homework assignment?' Another option is a combination of the above, such as 'Before we focus on your ———— problem, is there anything pressing that you would like to discuss first?' My preference is to give clients the opportunity to indicate first 'where they are at.' Helpers are not omniscient. Without checking, they risk missing significant information.

Establishing session agendas

Session agendas can be both implicit and explicit. For instance, without necessarily verbalizing that you have a session agenda, you may go from checking how your client feels, to reviewing the past week's homework, to continuing to work on a specific aspect of the problem. On the other occasions it may help to negotiate with your client a session agenda. This can still be flexible. If, between sessions, you have developed a plan or had some thoughts about how best to approach the client's problem, you may wish to bring this up. Similarly, your client may also have ideas about what aspects of his or her problem to focus on. Once a session agenda is established, it can still be altered if an existing focus fades out or if a new focus emerges.

Broadly speaking, each session has three phases: (1) introductions and checking, (2) working, and (3) consolidating and terminating. Session agendas are likely to be verbalized at the start of the working phase. They identify which aspects of the problem are to be worked on in what order. Establishing a session agenda provides structure. This helps avoid the problem many beginning helping trainees have of allowing their sessions to drift aimlessly.

Negotiating homework

Much of the work in problem management helping can be achieved by judicious use of between-session time. I use the term 'negotiating homework' in preference to 'setting homework', because it is essential that the client sees the relevance of the homework and is prepared to do it. In the early stages of the model, homework may have been used to collect baseline data on the problem. During the intervention stage, sessions may draw to a close with a summary of the significant self-help points covered during the session. Helpers may either do this themselves or ask their clients to do it. The latter option has the advantage of helping you check whether the client really understands the learnings from the session.

During the intervention stage, homework is used for practising both the subtasks and also, ultimately, the overall skills required to manage the problem. Helpers need the skills of: choosing what homework if any, is appropriate; presenting it clearly; getting reactions from their clients; and coming to an agreement or contract with them about doing it. In the subsequent session, helpers require the skill of reviewing homework with clients in a constructive way.

Monitoring and evaluating progress

Reviewing homework is one way of checking on progress. Sometimes clients review progress of their own accord. On other occasions, you may wish to suggest that time be set aside for a review of progress. If you have defined the problem operationally and stated goals clearly, both you and your clients have a basis for monitoring and evaluating progress. Earlier, I mentioned that your operational definitions of problems should be viewed as hypotheses. The information that emerges during the working stage may confirm your and your client's initial hypotheses. However, if it does not, you and your client will need to go back and redefine part or even all of the problem.

STAGE 5   EXIT AND CONSOLIDATE SELF-HELP SKILLS

Problem management helping is based on the notion of relatively brief contact. Consequently, termination is part of the process from the start. Sometimes this termination is formalized into fixed-term 'contracts'. Such fixed-term contracts are considered by some to motivate clients. Also, they may assist helpers to share their time amongst more clients. In most instances, termination is more open-ended. Ideally, it is based on both parties perceiving that clients have made some demonstrable and appreciable gains in their ability to manage their problems, and furthermore, that they have consolidated their gains into self-help skills for use afterwards.

Most often the topic of termination is introduced by either party in sessions before the final one. This allows both parties to work through the various issues connected with ending the relationship. These issues include: any further review of progress necessary; finishing any outstanding work; helping clients to consolidate their skills for use afterwards; getting feedback; and allowing time for handling any affective issues connected with termination. A recent study conducted in an American university counselling centre found that, from clients' perspectives, it was important for counsellors to help them explore their feelings about ending, and that this usually occurred.[27] A useful option for some clients is to fade the contact by seeing them progressively less often. Thus support is gradually withdrawn as, hopefully, clients gain greater confidence and ability at managing their problems. Some clients may appreciate the opportunity for a follow-up session three to six months later. This provides both client and helper with the chance to review progress and to consolidate self-help skills.

There are a number of further strategies that you may choose to use during the 'exit and consolidate self-help skills' stage. For instance, you may encourage your clients to assume the primary responsibility for reviewing their progress.[28] Also, you can get them to recite for you the self-help skills they have acquired for managing their problem. It may be desirable for them to write this out or put it on a cassette for revision purposes. A strategy with some clients who have difficulty acknowledging their gains is to encourage them to go back and listen to a recording, if one exists, of an early session. For those clients who are fearful of what may happen without your support, you can encourage them to anticipate future difficulties and work with them to develop ways of coping.

Problem management helping, with its limited focus, may be insufficient for some clients. Here you may choose to indicate your availability for future contact of a more broad-based nature. Alternatively, you may bring up the topic of further individual or group work with another helper. Additionally, you can let your clients know that you are available to see them again should they experience future difficulties in managing their problems. As Shakespeare wrote in *Julius Caesar*:

If we do meet again, why, we shall smile!
If not, why then, this parting was well made.

6 Focusing on Feeling

In the next three chapters, I focus on helper interventions in the areas of feelings, thoughts and actions. As Figure 6.1 shows, it is hard to view feelings independently from thoughts and actions. For instance, your thoughts are often the expression of your feelings at varying levels of awareness. Also, you may choose to regulate your feelings by altering the way in which you think about yourself, people and the environment. The connection between thoughts and actions is also two-way: thoughts influence actions and actions in turn influence thoughts. Likewise, feelings and actions affect each other. Consequently, the next three chapters are heavily interrelated.

All clients' problems involve their feelings in some way or another. Five areas in which helpers can work with their clients in the area of feelings are: acknowledging, accepting, managing, appropriately expressing feelings, and not being overwhelmed by their strength. The three main foci of this chapter are: helping clients become more responsive to their feelings, management of troublesome feelings and coping with crises.

AIDING RESPONSIVENESS

Question: How many social workers does it take to change a light bulb?
Answer: One, but the light bulb has to feel like changing.

Many clients are out of touch with their feelings. I present here some interventions that helpers can use to help their clients acknowledge and experience their feelings more fully. I use the term 'interventions', to describe skills focused on clients' feelings, thinking, and actions, for two main reasons. First, these skills imply a conscious choice to intervene. As I attempted to show in Chapter 3, even empathic responding involves a range of choices as to how best to intervene. So long as you are with a client you cannot not intervene. However, effective helpers do so in ways that assist their clients in developing self-help skills. Second, using the term 'intervention' makes it easier to draw skills from a variety of different theoretical positions. For instance, when you intervene either with empathic responding or by disputing a faulty inner rule, you need not label yourself as being client-centred or rational-emotive respectively. Instead, you use interventions which allow you access to the strengths of each position without necessarily imposing their constraints.

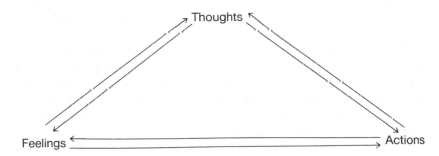

Figure 6.1   Relationship between feelings, thoughts and actions

The interventions presented in the next three chapters are not mutually exclusive. However, you have to consider carefully which intervention to use when and with which client. Also, *how* you intervene is critical.

Empathic Responding

In Chapters 2 and 3, I presented the skills of being a good listener and responding with empathic understanding. I now re-emphasize the importance of empathy. This is partly as a corrective to those who may be tempted to engage in a mechanistic and superficial problem management approach. In his 1975 article on empathy, Rogers discussed the respective merits of genuineness, caring and an empathic stance.[1] He wrote that an empathic way of being is the most precious gift one can give when 'the other person is hurting, confused, troubled, anxious, alienated, terrified; or when she is doubtful of self-worth, uncertain as to identity.' Here I particularly emphasize the role of empathy in helping to thaw clients whose experiencing of their feelings is being or has been significantly frozen by adverse family environments.

What are some of the reasons why helper empathy can help clients get in touch with and experience their feelings? It gives clients permission to experience themselves as separate and unique individuals rather than in terms of the way others want them to be. The affirmation provided by the helper's time, attention and understanding increases clients' sense of worth and is likely to lower their anxiety and defensiveness. Being sensitively listened to, they gain practice at listening to themselves, valuing their own experience, and being increasingly able to identify and label it accurately. They are given the psychological space to explore and delve deeper into understanding the meanings and implications of their feelings. They are encouraged to identify their wants and wishes and to recognize what comes from them and what comes from others. Furthermore, empathic helpers provide clients with secure bases from which they can act out on to the world, get new experiences, and come back and discuss them, knowing that they will be understood. Though helper empathy is not always sufficient nor sufficiently expeditious for helping clients get in touch with their feelings, it is invariably necessary. Also, there is a limit to which the pace can be forced with clients out of touch with their feelings. Consequently, another facet of empathy is showing sensitivity to the pace at which clients are best able to work.

Some exercises on listening with understanding and empathic responding were provided in Chapters 2 and 3. Since the above section focuses on provision of empathy to vulnerable clients over a series of sessions, it does not lend itself to brief exercises. Hence a further exercise is not provided here.

Providing a Rationale for Acknowledging and Focusing on Feelings

It can help some clients if their helpers legitimize the importance of focusing on their feelings. The precise way in which this is done depends upon the needs of the individual client. Below are some clients, all of whom require a tailor-made rationale for acknowledging their feelings more fully.

> Lisa, a sixteen-year-old school student, talks about her educational and career choices in terms more of what her parents want than in terms of her own wishes.

> Andrew, aged twenty-four, has difficulty acknowledging the extent of his hurt and anger with his partner Sandra. Instead his feelings 'come out

sideways' in frustrating her needs and in gossiping about her.

Gina, aged forty, comes from a family with a history of heart problems. She feels tense much of the time, takes tranquillizers and smokes a lot. She still persists with an extremely punishing work schedule.

Sam, aged sixty-seven, has recently lost his beloved wife Alice. Sam has been brought up to control his feelings and to keep a stiff upper lip. He has bottled up his feelings of grief, pain and anger and wonders if he can go on.

In each of the above vignettes, clients inadequately acknowledge their feelings: Lisa, her own wants and wishes about her future; Andrew, the nature of his hurt as a basis for managing it; Gina, the messages from her body to prevent a heart attack; and Sam, his need to share his grief rather than withdraw. In different ways, all the above clients demonstrate a skills deficit in their ability adequately to assume responsibility for their feelings.

Let us look at some possible helper choices, albeit overlapping, in the case of Lisa. First, you could keep on empathizing with her in the hope that she becomes more inner than outer directed. Second, you could make a facilitative confrontation along the lines of: 'Lisa, you seem to be saying a lot about what your parents want for you, but I'm wondering what *you yourself* feel that you would like to do. What do you feel are your choices?' Third, you might suggest to Lisa that she takes an occupational interest inventory to assist her self-exploration. Fourth, you might provide her with a rationale for acknowledging her *own* feelings more fully:

> Lisa, you seem to be saying a lot about what your parents want for you. However, I think you may be inadequately attending to your own feelings about what *you* want to do. Though not the only source, your feelings can provide you with a rich source of information about what may be the right choices for you. Learning to acknowledge and listen to your feelings is a skill. If you do not adequately listen to your feelings you risk making choices that lead to lowered fulfilment and may later have to be unravelled. I think it would help if you focused more on your *own* feelings. What do you think?

Providing a rationale for acknowledging and focusing on feelings is intended to make certain clients more aware of the importance of attending to their feelings. It may lead to a discussion with clients about how well they think they currently handle their feelings and what the consequences are for them. As an intervention for aiding responsiveness, it needs to be accompanied by other interventions. However, it may accelerate some clients in taking their feelings more seriously as a basis for further work involving them.

Exercise 6.1   Providing a rationale for acknowledging and focusing on feelings

This exercise can be done on your own, in pairs or in a training group.

A   *On your own*
1.   Explore how good you are at acknowledging your own feelings. If you have identified a skills deficit in this area, write out a rationale for your acknowledging and focusing on your own feelings more. Make this statement in the first person singular.
2.   In terms of a counselling or helping setting in which you work or would like to work, write out a rationale for a client to acknowledge and focus on his or her feelings more. Your rationale should be in the form that you would communicate it to a client.
B   *In pairs*
Either do the above exercise independently, then discuss;
or verbally work through the above exercise together from the start.
C   *In a training group*
The trainer introduces the topic of providing a rationale for clients for acknowledging and focusing more on their feelings. He or she demonstrates the skill. The group is then encouraged to perform the above exercise either singly, in pairs or in threes, prior to coming together for a plenary sharing and discussion session.

Facilitating Body Awareness

Some clients may have a very inadequate sense of both their bodies and also of their body sensations. Though not wishing to go so far as the founder of gestalt therapy, Fritz Perls, in denying the role of mind, there is nevertheless much truth in his aphorism 'Lose your mind and come to your senses.'[2] Perls saw most humans as being in a state of low grade vitality because they blocked their animal capacity for responsiveness with unnecessary intervening thoughts. Helpers may choose to intervene to facilitate their clients' becoming more aware of the flow of their body sensations, and also more in touch with and able to express their sensuality.

Getting clients to focus on every verbal, vocal and body aspect of their experiencing can be a useful way of heightening their self-understanding and responsiveness. For instance, gestalt therapy demands that clients experience themselves as fully as possible in the here and now. Perls wrote: 'The basic sentence with which we ask our patients to begin therapy and which we retain throughout its course – not only in words, but in spirit – is the simple phrase: "Now I am aware".'[3] Clients are asked to become aware of their body language, their breathing, their voice quality and their emotions as much as of any pressing thoughts. This awareness technique, sometimes called focal awareness, involves much concentration. Clients learn to experience and to be responsive to each role and each need. Perls aimed to make clients aware not only of the fact that they were interrupting their contact with themselves and the world, but also of what they were interrupting and how they were doing it. Exercise 6.2 is designed to give you some ideas on how you might facilitate the body awareness of your clients.

Exercise 6.2   Facilitating body awareness

This exercise may be done on your own, in pairs or in a training group.

A   *On your own*
1.   Sit in a quiet place, close your eyes for about five minutes and try to tune into your body sensations. Focus on the flow of what your body feels rather than on what you think. In other words, focus on physical sensations.
2.   Sitting in a quiet place with your eyes closed, focus on the physical sensations in the following parts of your body for about a minute each:
        your arms,
        your head,
        the trunk of your body, and
        your legs and feet.
3.   Sit in a quiet place with your eyes closed and for the next three to five minutes focus on the sensations of your breathing.
4.   Write down the body sensations attached to your experiencing the following emotions:
        anger,
        grief,
        joy, and
        fear.

B   *In pairs*
    Partner A acts as helper and gets partner B to do each part of the exercise above (Question 4 can be done verbally), and then facilitates partner B in discussing his or her thoughts and feelings about it. Afterwards, reverse roles.

C   *In a training group*
    The trainer discusses the idea of how clients are grounded in their bodies

and the importance of helping them listen to their body sensations. The trainer then takes the whole group through the exercise described above, either stopping for disucssion after each part or leaving discussion to the end. Alternatively, the trainer may get the group to do the exercise in pairs, prior to coming together for a plenary sharing and discussion session.

___

Sensate Focus

Relatively few counsellors and helpers specialize in sexual problems. Nevertheless, a number of you may have occasion to try to assist your clients in being more in touch with and able to express their sensuality. Lack of sexual responsiveness may take different forms and have multiple causes. Often it is part of a broader pattern of inadequate relationship skills. However, some clients may function moderately well in other areas of their life and yet require specific assistance in acknowledging and exploring their sensuality. This may be independent of having a more specific sexual dysfunction, for instance, premature ejaculation.

Masters and Johnson developed the technique of sensate focus to help couples to think and feel sensuously.[4] Sensate focus acknowledges the importance of touch in stimulating and experiencing sexual responsiveness. Partners are asked to time their periods of sensate focus for when they feel a natural sense of warmth and compatibility. They should continue for so long as it is pleasurable. Both partners should be unclothed with a minimum of physical fatigue and tension. Avoiding specifically sexual stimulation, including genitals and breasts, the 'giving' partner is instructed to trace, massage or fondle the 'getting' partner with the intention of giving sensate pleasure and discovering the receiving partner's individual levels of sensate focus. The rules of sensate focus for receiving partners are that they have to protect 'pleasuring' partners from causing discomfort or initiation. There is no requirement on them, verbally or nonverbally, to comment on their experiencing, unless such expression is completely spontaneous. Giving partners are committed not only to giving pleasure, but also to acknowledging their sensations in giving pleasure, exploring another's body by touch, and receiving pleasurable reactions. After a reasonable time, partners exchange roles. Sensate focus tends to give couples time, space and permission to respond sensually without feeling that they have to perform intercourse. Kaplan observes that, though most couples experience positive reactions to sensate focus, some people experience very little reaction and others negative reactions.[5] She indicates that these negative reactions may be indicative of deeper inhibitions concerning sexual responsiveness and makes suggestions for treating them. Helpers require sensitivity in following up clients' reactions to their sensate focus experience.

Role-play Methods

There are many variations in the use of dramatic or role-play methods that can be used in individual helping. These role-play methods tend not to be ends in themselves but include ways of allowing clients expression of feelings and catharsis. This in turn may generate further self-exploring and developing new perspectives. Thus after a role play you may either use empathic responding to help clients explore the meaning of the feelings released, or focus on specific aspects of their thinking, or a mixture of the two.

Role-play methods can be a powerful way of releasing and exploring the emotions invested in various kinds of personal relationship, be they past, present or future. Clients may play both parts of a relationship either with eyes closed in imagination or by switching chairs as they play each part. Alternatively, the helper may play one of the parts in the relationship, for example, a parent, spouse, boyfriend or girlfriend. Indeed, the helper may switch roles and be the client as the client plays the other person in the relationship. This is known as *role-reversal*. Additionally, the helper may mirror both verbal and nonverbal aspects of the client's behaviour in an enactment. Nowadays it is also possible to video-record and play back the enactment. This allows clients to see for themselves how they come across.

Exercise 6.3   Using role-play methods

This exercise may be done on your own, in pairs or in a training group.

A   *On your own*
Imagine a recent encounter with another person in which you felt strongly, but did not show the full extent of your emotions. Role-play in your imagination first how the encounter was and then how you would have felt and behaved without your inhibitions. Concentrate on vocal and body as well as verbal expression of emotion.

B   *In pairs*
Partner A encourages partner B to describe a two-person encounter in which he or she felt strongly but did not express the full extent of his or her emotions. Partner A and partner B then re-enact the scene, first as it was

and then with partner B being encouraged to express verbally, vocally and bodily what was being left unsaid. Then partner A facilitates partner B in processing his or her thoughts and feelings concerning the role play. Afterwards, reverse roles.

C   *In a training group*
The trainer introduces the topic of using role-play methods to release clients' emotional responsiveness. One possibility is for the trainer to demonstrate the pairs exercise and then get the group to do it, prior to coming together for a plenary sharing and discussion session. Another possibility is for the trainer to conduct one or more psychodramas, with group members playing all roles other than that of director.

Teaching Inner Empathy

The importance of helper empathic responding has been stressed on a number of occasions. However, another intervention is to train clients in innner empathy. By *inner empathy* I mean the skills of listening to, experiencing, understanding and exploring their own feelings. Assuming that they have a moderate degree of insight, clients can be taught inner listening and empathy as a self-help skill. In their regular work with clients, helpers indirectly impart some of this skill. However, the skill may be more fully understood and developed given a direct approach to training in it.[6]

Elements of inner empathy training include the following:

● *Presenting a rationale for the importance of inner empathy.*   Clients need to be helped to understand that this is a useful skill for understanding themselves and others.

● *Stressing both the setting aside of sufficient time and also the creation of psychological space for inner listening.*   To practise the skill, clients must give it sufficient priority in their lives. This may mean either that they spend a certain amount of time with themselves each day or make sure to clear a space when something bothers them or needs deciding.

● *Explaining and demonstrating the skill.*   Much of the material in Chapters 2 and 3 is relevant here, but with modifications. For instance, the concept of internal frame of reference in this context becomes that of getting inside one's own frame of reference rather than another's. In inner empathy it is vital that you tune into your feelings. You flow with them, try and understand their messages and label them accurately. It may be beneficial if helpers demonstrate inner listening by verbalizing their experiences as they attempt it.

● *Coaching.* Clients should be given coaching as they practise the skill.

● *Setting and checking up on homework.* Homework is an important part of learning any self-help skill. Furthermore, it acts as a bridge between training and relying on one's own resources.

Eugene Gendlin has developed a method he terms *focusing* to help people change and live from a deeper place than just their thoughts and feelings.[7,8] Focusing is a process in which people make contact with a special kind of internal bodily awareness which he terms a 'felt sense'. The process of focusing consists of six movements: making a space, the felt sense, finding a handle, resonating, asking and receiving. Gendlin writes: 'When these are successful, there is a physical change in the body, a felt shift. Then the problem seems different.' I do not develop Gendlin's ideas in detail here. They are briefly mentioned for two reasons. First, he has developed empathy into a self-help skill rather than a listening to others skill. Second, some may wish to read his work in greater depth.

Exercise 6.4 encourages you to think about whether and how you might train clients in inner empathy. For instance, if you frequently use empathic responding with a client, before terminating it might be beneficial to train that person in inner empathy as a self-help skill for afterwards.

Exercise 6.4   Teaching inner empathy

This exercise may be done in pairs or in a training group.

A   *In pairs*
Partner A attempts to teach partner B inner empathy as a self-help skill. Partner A goes through the following steps with partner B:
1. presenting a rationale;
2. stressing both the setting aside of time and also the creation of psychological space;
3. explaining and demonstrating;
4. coaching; and
5. setting homework.
Afterwards, reverse roles.
B   *In a training group*
The trainer introduces the topic of teaching inner empathy as a self-help

skill. He or she attempts to demonstrate the skill by training the group in it. Afterwards, the group may be given the opportunity to become trainers to each other.

Encouraging Action

Clients frequently cannot fully experience and explore their feelings until they act. For example, there is a limit to which a male college student can explore his emotional and sexual responsiveness to women by talking inside counselling and fantasizing outside. The role of empathic responding in enabling clients to feel that their helpers are secure bases from which to engage in exploratory behaviour and in personal experiments has already been mentioned. Specific interventions focused on getting clients to alter their behaviour are covered in Chapter 8. Suffice it for now that the link between aiding responsiveness and helping clients to act differently has been clearly acknowledged.

ASSISTING MANAGEMENT OF FEELINGS

> Client: I don't know whether I am a wigwam or a teepee.
> Counsellor: Don't worry, either way you are too tense.

The previous section focused on helping clients release and experience their feelings. In this section I present some ways of assisting clients contain or manage feelings that are unpleasant and impair their effectiveness. The interventions presented here are *progressive muscular relaxation* and *systematic desensitization*. However, many of the choices helpers make when assisting clients in managing their feelings involve helping them to discipline their thinking. This is the topic of Chapter 7. Additionally, by helping them to act differently, you can help clients manage their feelings more effectively.

Helpers may use relaxation procedures when dealing with such problems as tension headaches, insomnia and general feelings of tension. Furthermore, relaxation training comprises a significant part of Wolpe's systematic desensitization technique. Systematic desensitization is a behavioural technique used to help clients cope with specific fears and phobias.

Progressive Muscular Relaxation

The acknowledged pioneer of relaxation training is Edmund Jacobson, the first edition of whose major work, *Progressive Relaxation*, appeared in 1929.[9] His term 'progressive relaxation' refers to the progressive cultivation of the relaxation response. There are many variants to Jacobson's original progressive muscular relaxation procedures, including those described by Wolpe and by Bernstein and Borkovec.[10,11] Although the latter's manual, *Progressive Relaxation Training*, provides a particularly clear introduction to the subject, the following description is drawn from a number of sources, including the author's counselling experience.

The physical setting of your room should be conducive to relaxation. This involves absence of disruptive noise, interior decoration that is restful, and lighting which may be dimmed. The client may be taught to relax in a recliner chair, or on a mattress or, at the very least, in a comfortable upright chair with a headrest. At an early stage you explain that much tension is learned. By training and practice it can be unlearned. From the beginning you endeavour to see that clients view relaxation training as learning a coping skill for use in daily life. You do not just treat them as passive persons.[12] Furthermore, clients should understand that success at learning relaxation, just like success at learning any other skill, requires practice. Relaxation homework will be required. Before starting relaxation, you might suggest that the client wear loose-fitting, comfortable clothing both during interviews and when doing relaxation homework. Furthermore, it is helpful to remove items such as glasses and shoes.

Bernstein and Borkovec observe that in teaching muscular relaxation there is a succession of events which must be observed with each muscle group. This tension–relax cycle has five elements: (1) *focus*, by which is meant focusing attention on the muscle group; (2) *tense*, that is, tensing the muscle group; (3) *hold*, maintaining the tension for five to seven seconds; (4) *release*, releasing the tension in the muscle group; and (5) *relax*, focusing attention on the letting go of tension and further relaxation of the muscle group. Clients need to learn this *focus–tense–hold–release–relax* cycle so that they may apply it in their homework.

Having explained the basic tension–relax cycle, you may then demonstrate it by going through the cycle in relation to your own right hand and forearm and at each stage asking clients to do the same. Thus, 'I'm *focusing* all my attention on my right hand and forearm and I'd like you to do the same' progresses to 'I'm *clenching* my right fist and *tensing* the muscles in my lower arm . . .' then on to 'I'm *holding* my right fist clenched and keeping the muscles in my lower arm tensed . . .', followed by 'I'm now *releasing* as quickly as I can the tension from my right fist and lower arm . . .', ending with 'I'm *relaxing* my right hand and forearm, letting the tension go further and further and letting these muscles become more and more relaxed . . .'. The final relaxation phase tends to last from thirty to sixty seconds, frequently accompanied by 'patter' about letting the tension go and acknowledging and experiencing feelings of deeper and deeper relaxation as they occur. Having been through the tension–relax cycle once, especially in the initial sessions the client may be instructed to go through it again, thus tensing and relaxing each muscle grouping twice. You may then take the client through the muscle groups, modelling them as necessary. Table 6.1 shows sixteen muscle groups and suggested tensing instructions. The arms tend to come at the beginning, since they are easy to demonstrate. For most clients the face is particularly important.

Table 6.1   *Muscle groups and tensing instructions for muscular relaxation training*

Muscle group	Tensing instructions*
Right hand and forearm	Clench your right fist and tense the muscles in your lower arm.
Right biceps	Bend your right arm at the elbow and flex your biceps by tensing the muscles of your upper right arm.
Left hand and forearm	Clench your left fist and tense the muscles in your lower arm.
Left biceps	Bend your left arm at the elbow and flex your biceps by tensing the muscles of your upper left arm.
Forehead	Lift your eyebrows as high as possible.
Eyes, nose and upper cheeks	Squeeze your eyes tightly shut and wrinkle your nose.
Jaw and lower cheeks	Clench your teeth and pull the corners of your mouth firmly back.
Neck and throat	Pull your chin down hard towards your chest yet resist having it touch your chest.
Chest and shoulders	Pull your shoulder blades together and take a deep breath.
Stomach	Tighten the muscles in your stomach as though someone was about to hit you there.
Right thigh	Tense the muscles of your right upper leg by pressing the upper muscle down and the lower muscles up.
Right calf	Stretch your right leg and pull your toes towards you head.
Right foot	Point and curl the toes of your right foot and turn it inwards.
Left thigh	Tense the muscles of your left upper leg by pressing the upper muscle down and the lower muscles up.
Left calf	Stretch your leg and pull your toes towards your head.
Left foot	Point and curl the toes of your left foot and turn it inwards.

*With left-handed people, tensing instructions for the left side of the body should come before those for the right.

Once clients have learned how to tense the various muscle groups, they are instructed to keep their eyes closed during relaxation training and practice. After a tension–relax cycle, you may ask whether the client has been completely relaxed and indicate that, if this has not been the case, they should raise the index finger of the hand nearest to you. To facilitate genuine relaxation, ensure that clients feel safe to share any feelings of residual tension. Furthermore, observe clients' body posture and breathing as a check on the extent of their relaxation. Complete relaxation is not to be expected immediately. Consequently, you use judgement about whether to repeat the tension–relax cycle. Given persistent failure to relax a muscle group, another approach is to alter the muscle group strategy. For instance, in the neck and throat muscle group, shrugging the shoulders by pulling the head down and the shoulders up may be an alternative to pulling the chin down hard towards the chest and resisting having it touch the chest. Clients differ in the muscle groups in which they experience much of their tension and you may pay special attention to these.

Towards the end of a relaxation session, you ask clients for a summary of their relaxation, along the lines of 'Well, how was your relaxation today?', and discuss any issues that have arisen. Termination of a relaxation session may be achieved by counting from five to one and, when you get to one, asking your clients to wake up pleasantly relaxed as though from a peaceful sleep. Bernstein and Borkovec advocate relaxation sessions ending with an 'enjoyment period' of a minute or two. They suggest that the client focus on the very pleasant state of relaxation prior to the counting procedure for terminating relaxation.

The importance of practising muscular relaxation may be further stressed at the end of the initial relaxation session. Clients are likely to be given the homework assignment of practising muscular relaxation for one or two fifteen-minute periods a day. You might ask clients whether they anticipate any obstacles to such practice, such as finding a quiet place, and help them to devise strategies for ensuring good homework. There is some evidence that clients who monitor their relaxation practice are much more likely to continue doing it.[13] Consequently, clients can be asked to keep a log monitoring their relaxation homework. An example of an entry in such a log is provided in Table 6.2.

Brief relaxation procedures

When the full muscular relaxation procedures have been learned and the client is able to attain deep relaxation, briefer muscular relaxation procedures may be introduced. The idea here is to learn to attain deep

Table 6.2   *Monitoring log for relaxation homework*

Date	Time, place, length	Comments
3 Oct.	6 p.m., living room at home, 15 minutes	Started off feeling tense after day at work. Tensed and relaxed the sixteen muscle groups. Distracting thoughts about work interfered with relaxation. Nevertheless, ended feeling considerably better.

relaxation with less time and effort. This skill may be useful both within and outside interviews. Brief muscular relaxation procedures may involve sequential or simultaneous application of the tension–relax cycle to various muscle groups, albeit interrelated. Bernstein and Borkovec provide examples of sequential brief muscular relaxation procedures. One variation is to tense four muscle groups; arm muscles; face, neck and throat muscles; chest, shoulder and stomach muscles; and leg and foot muscles.

Simultaneous muscular relaxation involves tensing virtually all muscles at once. An introductory statement might be 'When I give the signal, I would like you to close your eyes tightly, take a deep breath and simultaneously clench your fists and flex your biceps, frown very deeply, pull your shoulder blades together and tense your legs and feet. Now take a deep breath and tense everything . . . hold for five seconds . . . now release and relax as quickly and deeply as you can.' Simultaneous muscular relaxation may provide useful economies in interview time when using systematic desensitization procedures. When ready, brief muscular relaxation procedures should be incorporated into the client's relaxation homework.

Mental relaxation

Usually in conjunction with other relaxation procedures, clients may be encouraged to engage in mental relaxation. Such relaxation involves instructions to imagine a peaceful scene, such as 'lying in a meadow on a nice warm summer's day, feeling a gentle breeze, watching the clouds'. Counsellors and helpers can discover from clients which scenes are most conducive to their relaxing. Mental relaxation is used frequently at the end of a muscular relaxation procedure.

Use of cassettes

Frequently cassettes of relaxation instructions are provided for clients to play back during home practice. A risk here is that inadequate attention may be paid to muscle groupings which the client finds difficult to relax. One approach to this problem is to alert clients and ask them, if necessary, temporarily to switch off the cassette recorder and spend extra time relaxing a particular muscle grouping. The extent to which home relaxation cassettes enhance treatment outcome is open to question.[14]

Exercise 6.5 Progressive muscular relaxation

This exercise may be done on your own, in pairs or in a training group.

A *On your own*
  1. Make up a progressive muscular relaxation cassette using the instructions in Table 6.1. Include a mental relaxation instruction at the end.
  2. Practise relaxing yourself for at least fifteen minutes a day for a week, and keep a log monitoring your relaxation homework.

B *In pairs*
  1. Partner A makes up a progressive muscular relaxation cassette as he or she relaxes partner B using the instructions in Table 6.1. Afterwards, reverse roles.
  2. Each of you practises relaxing yourself for at least fifteen minutes a day for a week, and you each keep a log to monitor your relaxation homework.

C *In a training group*
  The trainer demonstrates and teaches the group progressive muscular relaxation as though they were clients. Then the group is subdivided to do the first part of the pairs exercise, prior to coming together for a discussion. Group members are also encouraged to do the homework part of the exercise. This should be followed by a further session or sessions with the trainer to obtain feedback and to work through problems.

Systematic Desensitization

Systematic desensitization is an intervention in which relaxation forms an important component. When your assessment indicates that the client has certain specific areas of anxiety or phobic areas, rather than just general tension, systematic desensitization may be the preferred method of treatment. However, an adequate, operational definition of the problem is essential. For instance, anxiety about tests or about occupational decisions may be the consequence of inadequate revision or poor decision-making skills. In such instances the anxiety is likely to be more effectively diminished by skills training than by systematic desensitization.

Joseph Wolpe was the originator of systematic desensitization.[15] As he formulated it, systematic desensitization involved three elements: (1) training in deep muscular relaxation; (2) the construction of hierarchies of anxiety-evoking stimuli; and (3) asking the client, when relaxed, to imagine items from the anxiety-evoking hierarchies. The idea is that the pairing of the anxiety-evoking stimuli with the relaxation response brings about a lessening or suppression of the anxiety responses, in effect weakening the bond between the anxiety-evoking stimuli and the anxiety response. Thus Wolpe provides a counter-conditioning explanation. However, there are numerous other theoretical explanations for the efficacy of systematic desensitization. If anything there is a trend towards viewing systematic desensitization not just as a helper offered skill, but also as a client self-help skill.

Rationale

When negotiating goals and approaches you present a rationale, related to your operational definition of the problem, for using systematic desensitization. Presumably your client has some form of anxiety management skills deficit for which this appears the preferred mode of treatment. You may briefly explain all three elements of desensitization. Additionally, you may stress learning desensitization as a coping skill for anxiety-evoking situations. Having already discussed relaxation training, I now turn to the construction of hierarchies.

Constructing hierarchies

Wolpe writes: 'An anxiety hierarchy is a list of stimuli on a theme, ranked according to the amount of anxiety they evoke.'[16] There are a number of considerations in the construction of desensitization hierarchies. First, suitable themes have to be identified around which anxiety-evoking stimuli can be clustered. Needless to say, precedence needs to be given to themes or areas which are proving most debilitating to the client's functioning. Such themes are likely to emerge from your assessment and may concern any one of a number of stimulus situations: for example, public speaking, examinations, eating in public, being with a member of the opposite sex, and sexual intercourse.

Second, the client has to be introduced to the notion of a subjective scale of anxiety or fear. A common way of checking on the anxiety-evoking potential of an item in a hierarchy is to say that 0 is a feeling of no anxiety at all and 100 is the maximum anxiety possible in relation to a particular theme. Thus individual items can be rated according to their positions on this subjective anxiety continuum or scale.

Third, appropriate hierarchy items need to be generated around each theme. Since clients are going to be asked to imagine the items, the situations need to be specifically and graphically described. You indicate the appropriate way for items to be formulated. Sources of hierarchy items may include data gathered in assessment, homework involving self-monitoring, suggestions from your client or you, and questionnaire responses.

Fourth, the items generated around a particular theme need to be ordered into a hierarchy (see Table 6.3). This involves rating the items on a subjective anxiety scale and ordering them accordingly. Some of this work may be done as a homework assignment, but you need to check any hierarchy before starting treatment. Also, during treatment, hierarchy items may need to be re-ordered or reworded, or additional items

Table 6.3 *Hierarchy for a client with fear of examinations*

Ranking/rating	Item
1. (Rated 5)	Thinking about exams while revising at my desk three months before the exams.
2. (Rated 10)	Thinking about exams while revising at my desk two months before the exams.
3. (Rated 15)	Thinking about exams while revising at my desk one month before the exams.
4. (Rated 20)	Thinking about exams while revising at my desk one week before the exams.
5. (Rated 25)	Thinking about exams while revising at my desk on the night before the exams.
6. (Rated 30)	Being driven in a car on the way to the exams.
7. (Rated 35)	Waking up on the morning of an exam.
8. (Rated 40)	Going up to the notice board to have a look at the exam results.
9. (Rated 50)	Waiting outside the exam room.
10. (Rated 60)	Going into the exam room.
11. (Rated 70)	Looking at the exam paper for the first time.
12. (Rated 80)	Sitting down in the exam room.
13. (Rated 90)	Sitting in the exam room thinking of the inescapability of three hours in a hall full of people.
14. (Rated 95)	Experiencing a panic attack during the exam with the feeling of wanting to leave.
15. (Rated 100)	Having to leave the exam room due to panic.

introduced. You may write, or ask your clients to write, items on index cards to facilitate ordering. In general, gaps of over ten units on the subjective anxiety scale are to be avoided. Where they occur, you and your client may spend additional time formulating an intervening item or items.

Exercise 6.6   Hierarchy construction

This exercise may be done on your own, in pairs or in a training group.

A   *On your own*
Identify one or more themes of anxiety-evoking stimuli in your life. Construct a hierarchy for each theme as demonstrated in Table 6.3.

B   *In pairs*
Partner A helps partner B to identify a theme for hierarchy construction in his or her life. He or she then works with partner B to construct an appropriate hierarchy centred on that theme. Afterwards, reverse roles.

C   *In a training group*
The trainer describes hierarchy construction. He or she then demonstrates the skill by working with a group member as 'client' to develop a hierarchy. Alternatively, the trainer plays a demonstration video constructing a hierarchy around an anxiety-evoking theme. The group is then subdivided to do the pairs exercise. If possible the trainer checks and makes comments on all hierarchies. Either as part of this checking process or after it, the trainer conducts a plenary sharing and discussion session.

Presenting hierarchy items

During desensitization sessions you relax your clients and then get them to imagine scenes from their hierarchies. A basic assumption is that the client is capable of imagining the scene so that it represents the real-life situation. It is essential that you check whether a client can become anxious from an image before using this intervention. Clients' imaginal capacities can be tested by asking them, when not relaxed, to imagine a situation which causes them anxiety in real life. Sometimes clients can be helped to imagine scenes by being asked to verbalize what they see in the situation. Also, you yourself may provide fuller verbal descriptions of scenes.

A desensitization session starts with relaxing your client. After you are assured that the client has attained a state of deep relaxation, you present scenes along the lines of 'Now I want you to imagine what you think about exams while revising at your desk three months before exams . . .' You start with the least anxiety-evoking scene on a hierarchy and ask the client to raise an index finger if any anxiety is experienced. If no anxiety is experienced, after five to ten seconds you ask the client to stop imagining the scene and go back to being pleasantly relaxed. After thirty to fifty seconds, the client may be asked to imagine the same scene again. If this causes no anxiety, withdraw the scene, possibly spend time further relaxing the client, and move on to the next item in the hierarchy. In instances where the client's index finger is raised to indicate anxiety, the scene is immediately withdrawn and the client is encouraged to relax more deeply before one or more further presentations of the scene. If a scene repeatedly causes anxiety, you may present a less anxiety-evoking item instead.

An important assumption underlying systematic desensitization is that once a low anxiety-evoking item, for example ten units, has ceased to cause anxiety, all the other items in the hierarchy become less anxiety-evoking by ten units. Thus the 100-unit item becomes a 90-unit item, and so on. Only weak anxiety-evoking stimuli are intentionally presented to clients during desensitization sessions.

Helpers may work from more than one hierarchy during a desensitization session. Indeed, time spent on desensitization may form only part of a longer interview in which you focus on other problems and use other interventions. A record is kept of all scene presentations and their outcomes. Wolpe's desensitization sessions last fifteen to thirty minutes, and he observes that 'whereas at an early stage 8 or 10 presentations may be the total at a session, at an advanced stage the number may be 30 or even 50.'[17] Goldfried and Davison indicate that it is more useful to cover from two to five items in a given session.[18]

Exercise 6.7   Presenting hierarchy items

This exercise can be done on your own, in pairs or in a training group.

A   *On your own*
   Cassette record the items on your Exercise 6.6 hierarchy. Relax yourself. Present the cassette-recorded scenes to yourself but do not move on to a

more anxiety-evoking item until comfortable with the earlier ones. If you find yourself getting very tense, keep the cassette switched off while you relax yourself more deeply.

B   *In pairs*
Partner A relaxes partner B and presents scenes, as described in the text, from partner B's Exercise 6.6 hierarchy. Afterwards discuss, then reverse roles.

C   *In a training group*
The trainer demonstrates presenting hierarchy items. He or she then subdivides the group into pairs. If possible, each of the pairs goes into a separate quiet and suitably furnished room to perform the exercise. The trainer visits as many pairs as possible. Afterwards, the trainer conducts a plenary sharing and discussion session.

In vivo *desensitization*

Two kinds of considerations may make *in vivo* or real-life, rather than imaginal, desensitization the method of choice. First, clients may have difficulty in imagining scenes, and second, the stimuli in clients' hierarchies may lend themselves to real-life presentation. Even using imaginal desensitization, it helps to encourage clients to try out in reality the situations for which they have been desensitized in imagination. Relaxation may be used as part of *in vivo* desensitization. For instance, a client with a fear of public speaking may be relaxed at the start of each session, then over a number of sessions be asked to give a short talk in front of increasingly large numbers of people, who may also ask increasingly demanding questions. The intervention differs from imaginal desensitization mainly in that the hierarchies are constructed out of real-life situations. Otherwise, many of the imaginal desensitization considerations apply; such as the level of anxiety within which to present items.

Self-help variations of desensitization

Goldfried has presented a view of systematic desensitization as self-control training in coping with anxiety-evoking situations.[19] This anxiety-management approach focuses on increasing the client's feelings of being able to cope with these situations. Procedural changes from traditional systematic desensitization include: (1) presenting a rationale which views desensitization as the learning and application of an active coping skill;

(2) learning to recognize the physical sensations associated with tension so that relaxation may be applied as a coping skill; (3) only constructing a single hierarchy composed of situations involving increasing amounts of anxiety rather than focusing on hierarchies constructed around a number of different themes; (4) encouraging clients both to continue imagining scenes, even though experiencing anxiety, and also to learn to relax away their tension; and (5) possibly greater encouragement for clients to practise their anxiety-management skill *in vivo*.

Meichenbaum has suggested a further self-help variation of desensitization.[20] First, an attempt is made to make subjects aware of their self-defeating thoughts, self-verbalizations and instructions in relation to their area of difficulty. Next, a coping imagery procedure is added to the presentation of desensitization scenes, in which subjects are asked to visualize themselves becoming anxious and tense and then coping with these feelings by means of relaxation behaviours, slow deep breaths and both calming and task-orientated self-instructions.

CRISIS MANAGEMENT

In crisis management, helpers are faced with making immediate choices that help clients get through their sense of being overwhelmed. Some of these choices may also help clients manage better any underlying problems contributing to the crisis. I define crises prior to discussing some skills of crisis management.

Defining Crises

Crises may be defined as situations of excessive stress. Stress tends to have a negative connotation in our culture. This is unjustified if one thinks of stress in terms of adjustive demands or, more colloquially, challenges in life. Each person has an optimal stress level or a particular level of stimulation at which they feel most comfortable. At this level the person may experience what Hans Selye, a noted writer on stress, has termed 'stress without distress'.[21] Beneath this level they may feel insufficiently stimulated and bored. Above this level they are likely to experience physiological and psychological distress. If the heightened stress is prolonged or perceived as extremely severe, clients may feel that their coping resources are inadequate to meet the adjustive demands being made on them. In such circumstances they are in a situation of excessive stress or a state of crisis.

This section, on handling crises, relates mainly to clients who are in a fairly acute state of crisis. At this stage clients may be experiencing heightened or maladaptive reactions in a number of different, though interrelated, areas:

- *Body.*   Body reactions may include hypertension and proneness to heart attacks, gastric or duodenal ulcers, etc. The weakest parts of different clients' bodies tend to be most adversely affected by stress.
- *Feelings.*   The feelings associated with excessive stress may include shock, depression, frustration, anger, anxiety, disorientation and fears of insanity or nervous breakdown.
- *Thoughts.*   Some of the main thoughts associated with excessive stress are that clients are powerless to make a positive impact on their situations, that things are getting out of control, and despair or lack of hope for the future. The notion of excessive stress implies that clients' thought processes have become somewhat irrational. They think ineffectively: for example, with 'tunnel vision', which involves focusing on only a few factors in a situation.
- *Actions.*   Avoidance and overactivity are two of the main ways in which clients handle excessive stress. Their behaviour may range from giving up and not making an effort to rigid and repetitive attempts to deal with their problems. Violence, either turned outwards or inwards, is more possible at times of excessive stress than when clients' stress levels are lower.

Below are two examples of people who are finding that life is currently getting them down to the point where they are in a state of crisis.

Janis is a nineteen-year-old hairdresser who recently broke up with her boyfriend. She said he found her too moody and irritable. Janis came from a home in which she felt she was repeatedly being 'put down' by her parents who, in turn, did not get on well with each other. She was never able to show any feelings of anger with them. She thinks that they will see her breaking up with her boyfriend as further evidence that she is a difficult person. She feels agitated, restless, tense and depressed.

Rob is a fifty-two-year-old single steelworker who was made redundant a year ago and has remained unemployed ever since, despite looking hard for work. Recently his mother, with whom he lived, died. He feels that life has lost all meaning for him now that he has companionship neither at home nor at work. He says he has been feeling depressed, disoriented and weepy.

It is very important to realize that crises, however large or small they may appear from an outsider's frame of reference, tend to seem overwhelming from the client's frame of reference. Some crises have been simmering in the background for some time and then erupt, whereas others are more clearly a reaction to an immediate precipitating event:

for example, a bereavement or loss of employment. Perhaps many stressful situations only really turn into psychological crises at the point where clients feel that their efforts to adapt and cope are totally insufficient, at which stage they become most prone to despair, disorientation, breakdown and suicide.

There are numerous situations which may cause clients to feel that they are at the limit of their coping resources, though there are wide differences in people's ability to tolerate these various stressors. Resilience in the face of stress depends partly on personal resources. However, it may also be heavily influenced by the amount of family, social and community support available. Table 6.4 lists many of the stressors which may cause clients to reach states of crisis. Whereas on some occasions one stressor may be enough to precipitate a crisis, on other occasions stressors may have a multiple, concurrent and/or cumulative impact. A common theme is that of changes which challenge the adequacy of clients' existing conceptions of themselves.

Table 6.4   *Illustrative stressors which may contribute to crises**

Marriage and family

Living in a state of continuous conflict
Having a row with a spouse/parent/child
Marital infidelity
Interfering in-laws
Problems in sex life
Not being adequately listened to
Unreasonable/angry/dishonest people
Pressure to meet others' expectations
Pressure to collude against others
Being financially dependent
Separation or divorce
Death of partner/spouse/child
Birth of a baby
Financial problems
Concern over homosexual tendencies
Moving house
Poor health
Alcoholism and drug abuse

Occupational/educational

Unemployment
Threat of or actual redundancy
Obtaining a job
Changing a job
Reorganization at work
Poor relations with a boss
Continuous office in-fighting
Overwork

Difficulty in controlling subordinates
Lack of opportunity for mobility/
   promotion
Retirement
Impending exams
Failing an exam
Public speaking difficulties
Lack of leisure outlets

Adverse social conditions

Poverty
Poor housing
Lack of social/community support

Intrapersonal

Loss of meaning in life
Feeling of guilt and worthlessness
Breakdown in defensive thinking
Severe depression
Psychotic tendencies

Body harm

Being mugged
Being raped
Being battered by a spouse
Being diagnosed as having a severe or
   terminal illness
Being disfigured or disabled in an
   accident

* The categories may overlap.

Some Guidelines for Crisis Management

At times of crisis many people will have the support of family and friends. Others may not be so fortunate or may feel that, despite the support they get, they need the assistance of someone not personally involved in their problems. Sometimes helping itself may contribute to clients' crises. At worst this is because it is incompetent and insensitive. On other occasions, clients may feel under great stress as they start both acknowledging aspects of themselves that previously they have denied and also trying out new behaviours. Crises for clients can be crises for you too. You may feel under great pressure to relieve a client's distress at the same time as being threatened by the strength of their emotions. As indicated in the preceding section, there are many reasons why people may feel that their coping resources are being overwhelmed. Furthermore, there are considerable individual differences in the ways in which people react to excessive stress. Nevertheless, below I suggest some guidelines for crisis management.

- *Be prepared.*   You can relieve much of your own stress regarding crises if you realize that, since these events are likely to be part of any helper's life, you should be prepared. One means of preparation is to ensure that you have identified and can quickly mobilize a good support system: for example, a competent physician or a bed in a psychiatric hospital (hopefully not for yourself!). You can also prepare for crises if you think through the limits of your responsibility for clients. I consider that, so long as you have provided a sincere and competent service to the best of your ability, you have fulfilled your side of the 'contract'.
- *Act calmly.*   Even though it may seem a limitation on being genuine if you do not really feel calm inside, it is important that you act calmly. Do not add your own anxieties to the client's agitation and distress. Responding in a warm yet firm and measured way may both give the client the security of feeling that you are a strong person and also help calm their heightened emotions.
- *Listen and observe.*   One of the main reasons that stressful situations became crises for many clients is that they feel that they have no-one to whom they can turn who will listen to and understand their difficulties. Clients may become calmer and feel less isolated and despairing simply by being able to share their problems and air the related emotions. Catharsis is another word for this process of letting out bottled-up or pent-up feelings and emotions. Listening, observing and empathic responding help you to understand the clients' world as well as contributing to their feeling of being heard and accepted.

● *Assess severity of disturbance and risk of damage to self or to others.* One area of assessing severity concerns the degree to which clients are in contact with reality. Assessing client risk may also mean assessing the damage the client may do to other people. However, it is more likely to involve assessing the damage that clients may do to themselves, including committing suicide. A high proportion of suicidal people talk about the possibility before making an attempt. Helpers need to be sensitive at picking up 'cries for help' and not allowing their anxieties to block their listening skills. Suicidal people tend to be ambivalent about it. A caring question about whether or not they are suicidal may be very appropriate. Avoidance of the topic on your part may increase rather than diminish risk.

   Demographic indications of suicide risk include the following: (1) gender – although more women attempt suicide, more men succeed; (2) marital status – single, separated, divorced and widowed people are much more likely than married people to commit suicide; (3) age – despite the fact that the suicide risk is greater for those over fifty, quite a few people in late adolescence and early adulthood commit suicide; and (4) socio-economic status – suicide risk and socio-economic status are inversely correlated.

   Helpers working with suicidal clients need to assess their suicide potential or lethality. Fujimura and her colleagues cite the following as *characteristics of lethality*[22]: previous suicide attempts: sleep disruption; definitiveness of plan; degree of irreversibility of plan; absence of proximity of others; a history of severe alcohol or drug abuse; a history of previous psychiatric treatment or hospitalization; perceived absence of resource and support systems; and unwillingness to use resource and support systems.

● *Assess client strengths and coping capacities.* You can both assess, and help your clients to explore and assess, their strengths and coping resources. Often, in a crisis, clients are so overwhelmed by negative thinking that they allow themselves to get out of touch with their strengths. While not advocating superficial reassurance, the following remarks *may* be helpful with *some* clients in *some* situations: 'Well, we've explored your problems in some detail. I'm now wondering whether you feel that you have any strengths or resources for dealing with them?'; 'You've been telling me a lot about the negative aspects of your life. Can you tell me if there are some positive aspects as well?'; and 'As you talk you seem to be facing your problems very much on your own. I'm wondering whether there are any friends, relatives or other people who might be available to offer you some support.'

● *Assist exploration and clarification of problem(s).*   Clients in crises have often lost perspective on themselves and their problems. One of the reasons for this is that crises involve very intense feelings. Until some progress is made with relieving the intensity of these feelings, clients may lack the ability to be sufficiently rational about the factors generating these strong emotions. Skills during the work of exploring and clarifying problems are likely to include empathic responding, use of questions, summarizing and challenging those distortions in clients' thinking that are making their lives seem hopeless.

● *Assist problem-solving and planning.*   The primary focus in crisis management helping is to help clients regain a sense of control over their lives. For some clients the opportunity to talk with an understanding person may give them enough confidence in their ability to cope with life for them to move out of the 'danger zone'. With other clients, your role will include helping them to develop strategies for coping with their immediate distress and, if appropriate, for initiating ways of dealing with their longer-term problems. If the client is at any risk, plans for coping with the immediate situation should be formulated as specifically as possible. Indeed, you may feel some responsibility for seeing that they are implemented. For example:

> We have agreed that you will stay at your sister's for tonight and that we will meet again at 11 a.m. tomorrow. Do you think there is any reason why you cannot carry out this plan?

> I'm uneasy about your being on your own in such a distressed state. I know that Mr Smith, the warden of your college, is keen to help students in difficulty. Would you mind if I phoned him to tell him about your situation.

As in these examples, assisting problem-solving and planning may involve the mobilization of additional resources who may be either professional helpers (for example, doctors and chaplains) or friends and relatives. In some instances it may be better if the client takes the responsibility for making the contact, but not invariably. You always assess what is in the best interests of your client and, at a highly vulnerable time in their lives, act accordingly.

● *Be specific about your own availability.*   Part of your crisis management plan with certain clients may be to give them the security of another appointment in the near future. Also, you need to consider the matter of between-session contact. If such contact seems appropriate, you can say something along the lines of 'If you feel you need me in an emergency again, please don't hesitate to get in touch with me either here or at my home number, which is ————.' In most instances clients will not get in touch until the next session. However, they appreciate that you cared enough to be available if necessary. In other instances, you either may be genuinely unavailable or may consider it more appropriate for clients to make any between-session contact with another person or agency. For instance, you might refer a client to a specific crisis service, such as the Samaritans or Lifeline.

Apparently the Chinese use two symbols for the concept of crisis: those for danger and opportunity. Crises can be the impetus for certain clients to work on problems which have been simmering in the past, yet which have not been confronted. This may release a tremendous amount of constructive energy. The pain of crises may be so acute that these clients both are forced to face the fact that all is not well and also want to avoid future pain of such magnitude. As you work with clients who have been in crisis, their old ways may increasingly appear to be more threatening than the risks of change. At best, a crisis can give helper and client the opportunity to form an effective relationship. This lays the basis for the client to develop the confidence and skills either to prevent or to cope with future crises.[23]

Exercise 6.8   Crisis management

This exercise may be done in a number of ways.

A   *On your own*
   1. Identify crises in your past life. Who were the people that helped you to manage these crises, and how did they behave?
   2. Write down, regarding your present or future helping work, the kinds of stressors that bring or may in future bring clients in crisis to see you.
   3. How can you best prepare yourself to be effective in crisis management interviews and helping contacts?
B   *In pairs*
   1. Together identify, with regard to your present or future helping work, the kinds of stressors that bring or may in future bring clients in crisis to see you.
   2. You counsel your partner, who role-plays a client in a crisis. As much as possible, pay attention to the following eight guidelines for working with clients in crisis: be prepared; remain calm; listen and observe; assess client severity and risk; assess client strengths and coping capacities; assist exploration and clarification of problem(s); assist problem-solving and planning; and be specific about your own availability. Afterwards, reverse roles.

C   *In a training group*
The trainer identifies the kinds of stressors and client behaviours in crises that are most common in the helping setting for which the group is being trained. The trainer describes and demonstrates crisis management interventions with this client population, possibly getting group members to role-play clients in state of crisis. The trainer may also play prerecorded videos of crisis management interviews and helping contacts. The trainer sets either the individual or pairs parts of this exercise, and then holds a plenary sharing and discussion session.

FACILITATING SELF-HELP

I have tried to emphasize that, if possible, interventions focused on feelings should emphasize self-help. Gains made as a result of helping require maintenance and preferably development. Consequently, there is much to be said for offering interventions like empathy and relaxation as self-help as well as helper-offered skills.

Three further self-help interventions that you might consider for certain clients are suggesting that they: engage in co-counselling; develop a support network; or join a peer self-help group. They might undertake such activities either concurrently or after working with you.

Co-counselling

Clients may become and stay more in touch with their feelings if they engage in co-counselling with another person. This may be either on an ad hoc or on a regular basis. At its simplest, co-counselling involves each partner providing the other with listening time and space, say fifteen minutes each way. This can be followed by discussion of any points raised. Listening partners help talkers listen to their feelings. Consequently, they must not take talkers out of their frames of reference by interrupting, etc. Hopefully partners develop reasonable empathic responding skills: indeed, they may obtain training in them. Co-counselling need not be restricted to partners in existing relationships. Some may seek out either a congenial person or a congenial network, and experience, explore and discharge their feelings within these contexts.

Support networks

Some clients may need encouragement to develop support networks for themselves.[24] These may be especially useful in helping them experience, explore and handle feelings in transitions and crises. Clients' support networks may consist of their intimate relationships, their family unit, their friends, their workmates, their church and other people to whom they are able to entrust confidences: for example, social workers, priests or doctors. Knowing that they have supportive people to whom they can turn may make the feelings generated by crises and setbacks much more bearable. Also, good support networks are a way of preventing feelings such as loneliness and isolation.

Peer self-help groups

You may choose to bring up the topic of your client joining an appropriate peer self-help group, if available. The range of peer self-help groups is large, and they include: women's groups; men's groups; gay groups; groups for various categories of disabled people (for instance, those with multiple sclerosis); alcohol and drug abuse groups; groups for various categories of parents (for example, of the mentally handicapped); groups for spouses of senile people; groups for the bereaved, and so on. A major purpose of these groups is to offer mutual support by providing members with a chance to share feelings, experiences and coping strategies.

THE HELPER'S FEELINGS

Like clients, helpers need to learn to acknowledge, accept, manage, appropriately express and not be overwhelmed by the strength of their feelings. I deal with feelings of burn-out in Chapter 11. Meanwhile, I end this chapter with two jokes about sexuality and helping.

The first one is about the notorious Californian psychiatrist, Dr Randolph YAVIS. The good doctor was said to have acquired his surname because of his marked tendency to work only with female patients who were also *y*oung, *a*ttractive, *v*erbal, *i*ntelligent and *s*exy. No prizes for guessing Randolph's nickname! To what extent do you consider your selection of which clients you work with and for how long is influenced by their personal attractiveness for you?

The second joke is about a person-centred therapist being seduced by a client.

Client:	I quite like you.
Therapist:	You quite like me.
Client:	Yes, I think you're kinda cute.

Therapist:	Yes, you think I'm kinda cute.
Client:	I find you attractive.
Therapist:	You find me attractive.
Client:	I find you really attractive.
Therapist:	You find me really attractive.
Client:	I find you so attractive that I would like to go to bed with you.
Therapist:	You find me so attractive that you would like to go to bed with me.
Client:	Yes, why don't we go ahead and do it?
Therapist:	I can't go to bed with you, I'm your therapist.
Client:	Well, you're fired as my therapist. Let's go to bed.

Many a true word is said in jest. As helpers, your feelings can be both assets and liabilities. How you handle your sexual feelings constitutes an important area of professional ethics. I have personally known both a counsellor and a group leader who were unable to resist the temptation to turn helping into sexual relationships. This is a fertile area for self-deception. Helper, beware!

7 Focusing on Thinking

As helpers it can be useful to focus on how your clients think. An important area of defining and operationalizing problems involves identifying client thinking skills deficits that sustain them. Accordingly, much of the intervention stage in problem management helping can involve endeavouring to help clients correct their faulty thinking choices. Furthermore, realistic thinking is the cornerstone of effective self-help and of the maintenance of gains made in helping. The late Abraham Maslow is reported to have said that most clients were not sick, but just cognitively wrong. In other words, they made poor thinking choices. Below is an example of this.

> There was a young lady from York
> Whose life was increasingly fraught.
> Rather than thinking,
> She turned to hard drinking
> With aggressive self-pity for thought.

Thinking includes four components. First, there are the processes of thinking, such as memory, reasoning, generation of ideas, association, reflection, evaluation and defensive processes. Second, there are visual images. For instance, if you were asked to think of someone you loved, you would probably conjure up a visual image and not just words concerning them.[1] Third, there is the inner speech of thinking. During your waking hours you are in a more or less continual process of holding an inner dialogue. Much of this inner speech is at or just below the level of conscious awareness. A good deal of the work of helpers who focus on clients' thinking involves helping them to guide their thought processes more fruitfully through appropriate use of inner speech. This leads into the fourth component of thinking, that of metacognition. This involves thinking about how you monitor and regulate your thought processes.[2]

ASSESSING THINKING

Assessing your clients' thinking entails your having an underlying model concerning which aspects of thinking it is important to assess. The risk of such an underlying model or theoretical orientation is that it may lead you to look for only what you want to see. Consequently, your focus may be blinkered or partial. In this chapter, you are not presented with a comprehensive coverage of areas of poor thinking choices. Nevertheless, the coverage should be sufficient to help you guard against the kind of *confirmatory bias* that is likely to result from a narrow model.

Assessment of thinking is best viewed as a *collaborative* enterprise. Helpers have their own models and may suggest some areas for information gathering. However, ultimately much of the data has to come voluntarily from clients themselves. Consequently, the formation of an understanding relationship is stressed. This provides the necessary context for collaborative exploration and assessment.

Methods of assessing clients' thinking include the following:

- *Client self-report.*   Clients may have some insight into their own thought processes, for example, a tendency to self-downing, without quite knowing what to do about them.
- *Making inferences from what clients say and how they say it.*   For instance, Ellis's 'trained ear' detects irrational beliefs from what clients say about how they think and act, or avoid acting, in different situations.[3] Furthermore, focusing on the helper–client relationship may provide data.
- *Questions and confrontations.*   Clients can be asked what they think about themselves, others and particular situations. Additionally, they can be confronted with questions challenging their thinking: for example, 'Where is the evidence?'
- *Think aloud.*   This involves encouraging clients to speak aloud their thought processes in relation to a specific situation.[4] For instance, the client can be asked to imagine an anxiety-evoking scene, then to explore and talk through their thought processes about it. Additionally, clients can think aloud when confronting real or simulated situations.
- *Thought charting.*   Thought charting entails keeping a record of the

thoughts that are associated with specific scenes involving negative feelings. At its simplest it involves filling in two columns: one for negative scenes and feelings, and one for the thoughts that accompany them.

● *Questionnaires.* There are numerous self-report measures assessing thinking: for example, the Beck Depression Inventory and Seligman and his colleagues' Scale of Attributional Style.[5]

● *Acting differently.* Clients can be encouraged to act differently in relation to feared or difficult situations. Then their thoughts concerning the processes and outcomes of their changed behaviour can be shared and evaluated.

There are many issues of validity in regard to assessing clients' thinking. These concern both what are valid constructs and also accurate ways of measuring them. Furthermore, assessments of clients' thinking should be regarded as hypotheses which require monitoring by both helpers and clients. If necessary, these hypotheses should be altered. Additionally, monitoring and assessing thinking are useful self-help skills for after helping.

WHEN TO FOCUS ON THINKING

Apart from always being sensitive to it in initial assessments when problems are defined and formulated, there is no simple answer about when to focus on the way clients think. The timing will partly stem from the way problems are operationalized. Some approaches (perhaps rational-emotive therapy is the prime example) have as their central objective helping clients to become more rational. Consequently, there is a focus on teaching thinking skills from the initial session. On the other hand, providing an empathic client-centred relationship can also help clients change their thinking. However, this is likely to be at their own pace.

Another consideration relates to the level of vulnerability of clients. In choosing when to focus on vulnerable clients' thinking, helpers need to be mindful of the following points. First, such clients may wish to use the early phases of their contact to discuss and discharge their feelings of hurt and pain. Second, they may be so anxious and distorting information so badly that until they become less anxious they may not have sufficient insight to explore thinking difficulties. Third, it is likely to take time for vulnerable clients to learn to trust their helpers. Until a good relationship is established they may be too threatened to work on their own contribution to sustaining their distress. Fourth, some clients may require encouragement to action: for instance, some of Beck's depressed patients prior to interventions focused on thinking.[6] Having said all this, there are no easy generalizations. Many vulnerable clients will benefit from an early focus on their thinking, especially if sensitively conducted.

THINKING-FOCUSED INTERVENTIONS

A number of areas in which helpers can focus on their clients' thinking are mentioned below. There is some overlap between these areas. Helper interventions for thinking difficulties involve both facilitative and educational skills. When using them you are essentially teaching your clients the self-help skills of making realistic thinking choices in one or more areas. As well as to individual work, the interventions mentioned below are relevant to group work and to life skills training, especially if focused on thinking.

Attributing Responsibility Accurately

The underlying assumption of the scientific and applied work on attribution is that humans strive for a causal understanding of themselves, others and their environments in order to maximize their control over their lives. Helpers invariably, either implicitly or explicitly, work with their clients to increase their ability to make accurate causal inferences so that they may gain a greater degree of freedom of choice. Since the area of attributing cause is so bound up with that of assuming responsibility, I have called this section 'attributing responsibility'. Clients need to be able to attribute responsibility accurately for what has happened in the past, what is happening in the present, and what they might do in the future. This area was touched on in Chapter 5, where I mentioned that clients may require help both in owning that *they* have problems and also in acknowledging that certain of their behaviours contribute to sustaining them.

This section is not about clients' overall ability to respond to the existential mandate to make their lives through their choices. Rather, I focus here on accurately attributing responsibility in specific situations or series of situations. Table 7.1 illustrates some of the possibilities. Attributions of causal responsibility can be either accurate or inaccurate. Furthermore, they can be to self, to others or to the environment, or to any combination of these.

Table 7.1　*Possibilities for attributing responsibility in any specific situation*

	Accurate attribution to	*Inaccurate attribution to*
Self (internal)		
Others (external)		
Environment (external)		

Let me provide some examples. Jacobson and his colleagues conducted research into the attributional processes of distressed and non-distressed marital couples.[7] They found that distressed couples were particularly likely to offer internal attributions for their partner's *negative* behaviour, while non-distressed couples were particularly likely to attribute their partner's *positive* behaviour to internal factors. They inferred that distressed couples may have an inaccurate attributional style that maximizes the negative and minimizes the positive impact of the partner's behaviour. In these cases, the couples need to become aware of and strive to change their inaccurate attributional tendencies that put others down.

Attributions can also be inaccurate in regard to oneself. Beck and his colleagues observe that a common pattern in depression involves incorrectly assigning the responsibility for adverse events to oneself.[8] To counteract this, he advocates a 'reattribution' technique. Together with his patients he reviews the relevant evidence to make appropriate attributions of responsibility. Further evidence of an association between inaccurate attributional style and depression is provided by Seligman and his colleagues.[9] They found that depressed students, when contrasted with non-depressed students, attributed bad outcomes to internal and good outcomes to external causes.

Apart from ad hoc interventions during helping sessions, you can focus on attributions of responsibility in a number of ways.

- *Providing a rationale.* Discuss with your client why it can be important to focus in this area. Illustrate some of the problems that stem from inaccurate attribution.
- *Facilitating self-exploration.* Help your clients feel safe to examine their attributions.
- *Questions and confrontations.* Challenge clients to examine their behaviour and perceptual biases. Useful questions are: 'How is this behaviour helping you?' and 'Let's look at the evidence.' Where appropriate, confront 'smokescreens' and defences. Provide feedback.

● *Paying attention to the language of personal agency.* This involves encouraging the use of 'I' statements, verbs that acknowledge choice (for example, 'I won't' rather than 'I can't'), and avoiding static self-labelling (for example, 'I choose not to work hard' rather than 'I'm not a hard worker').

● *Reformulating attributions of responsibility.* Help clients see how they might reword attributions into more realistic inner speech.

Interventions in the area of attribution of responsibility have to be well timed and sensitively handled. The last think that certain clients may want from you is to hear that they contribute to their own and to other people's distress.

Exercise 7.1   Attributing responsibility accurately

This exercise may be done in a number of ways.

A   *On your own*
1.   Do you consider that you have any habitual distortions in your attributional style (for example, blaming, self-blame)?
2.   Write down for one or more problem areas in your life:
     (a)   the ways in which you may misattribute responsibility that may adversely affect your feelings and actions;
     (b)   what might be more accurate attributions of responsibility; and
     (c)   how attributing responsibility more accurately might alter your feelings and actions.
     Draw on your experience to identify typical misattributions of responsibility in any helping setting in which you are or have been.

B   *In pairs*
     Counsel your partner by:
1.   discussing the concepts of attributing responsibility and attributional style;
2.   facilitating your 'client's' exploration of possible misattributions of responsibility in any situation in his or her life, including, where appropriate, challenging perceptual distortions and biases;
3.   together formulating more accurate attributions of responsibility; and
4.   exploring how attributing responsibility more accurately might change feelings and actions.
     Afterwards, reverse roles.

C   *In a training group*
     The trainer can facilitate a discussion of attributing responsibility accurately, and of attributional style, by presenting the concept, getting trainees to

illustrate it from their personal and work experience, and illustrating it himself or herself with examples pertinent to the helping setting for which the group is being trained. The trainer might also break the group into pairs or threes to practise along the lines of Part B above. Furthermore, the trainer might set as homework the part of the exercise in Part A above.

Coping Inner Speech

Inner speech is an important element in thinking. Meichenbaum uses the term 'internal dialogue' to describe this private speech which is a process of both talking and listening to oneself in a self-communication system.[10] All interventions focusing on thinking aim to influence clients' inner speech so that they *discipline* their thinking in appropriate ways. Inner speech provides a mechanism for articulating your thinking about your thinking. It provides the means of instructing yourself in more realistic thinking skills, be they in the area of attributions, beliefs, conceptualizations or expectancies. Inner speech is also important when confronted with specific tasks, such as managing anxiety, stress, anger, conflict, shyness and impulsiveness.

In helping, a useful distinction is that between *coping* and *mastery*. For instance, when using inner speech with anxious clients, you strive to help them cope with or manage their anxiety rather than to feel no anxiety at all. Even the notion that they only need cope with rather than master their anxiety helps relieve some clients.

Just as clients can talk themselves into their problems, they can be helped to talk themselves out of them. Below is an example of anxiety-engendering and task-irrelevant speech.

> Kate is a shy person who is invited to a party. On arrival her inner speech is 'Oh, God. This is awful. I'm starting to feel anxious. People will see that I'm dull and uninteresting. I'm getting even more tense. Isn't it dreadful? Nobody is going to talk to me. I'd like to go home. I feel the situation is just too much for me.'

When working with Kate you might try not only to make her more aware of her self-defeating verbalizations, but also to train her to use coping inner speech. Additionally, you may use other interventions to build up her social confidence and skills. Coping inner speech has two main objectives: task-orientation and anxiety management. A *task-oriented* self-instruction is 'Just take one step at a time.' An *anxiety-management*

self-instruction is 'Now keep calm and breathe slowly and regularly.'
Task-orientation and anxiety management can be built into the same
self-instruction: for instance: 'Keep calm and take one step at a time.'

You may train your clients to use coping inner speech *before, during*
and *after* situations that give rise to negative feelings and actions. For
instance, imagine that Kate goes either to a party full of strangers or out
on a date. Your mutual objective is to get her helping herself to contain,
cope with and lessen any uncomfortable feelings of anxiety that she may
have; and also, to stop her behaving in ways that distance her from others.

Coping self-instructions that she might give herself *before* the stressful
social situation include:

'This anxiety is a signal for me to use my coping skills.'
'Now calm down. Develop a plan to manage the situation.'
'I'm a strong person who has coped with difficult situations like this in the
past.'

Coping self-instructions that she might give herself *during* the stressful
social situation include:

'Now calm down. Take your time. Breathe slowly and regularly.'
'Relax. I can manage it if I just take one step at a time.'
'As I acknowledge my anxiety and use my coping skills I can feel the tension
draining away.'

Coping self-instructions that she might give herself *after* the stressful
social situation include:

'Each time I cope it seems to get easier.'
'I'm proud of the way I'm learning to manage my fears.'
'Why did I get so uptight? It simply wasn't justified.'

Counsellors and helpers who use coping inner speech as an intervention can think of it in five phases.[11,12]

1. Educating clients to understand more about how thinking, feeling
    and behaving are related.
2. Helping them become aware of times when they produce negative
    self-statements, catastrophize and are task-irrelevant.
3. Assisting them in learning to approach problems in a step-by-step
    manner to avoid feeling overwhelmed.
4. Teaching and rehearsing them in inner speech as a coping skill, plus
    focusing on other skills as required.
5. Getting them systematically to experiment with, rehearse and prac-
    tise their inner speech on their own.

Helper skills that are useful in working in this area include: helping clients 'think aloud' their current internal dialogue; modelling more effective inner speech; coaching and rehearsing; and setting and monitoring appropriate homework assignments.

Exercise 7.2 Coping inner speech

This exercise may be done on your own, in pairs or as part of a training group.

A   *On your own*
Identify a situation in your life in which you experience difficulty in coping as effectively as you would like. Write down:
1.   a rationale for the relevance of coping inner speech for your problem;
2.   your current negative, catastrophizing and task-irrelevant self-statements;
3.   a step-by-step approach to the problem;
4.   at least two coping inner speech statements for each of before, during and after your difficult situation; and
5.   a systematic plan to experiment with and practise your coping inner speech.

B   *In pairs*
Counsel your partner in such a way that you train him or her to use coping inner speech in a situation where he or she experiences difficulty in coping as effectively as he or she would like. After your client has identified a suitable situation, work through the following five phases:
1.   providing a rationale;
2.   identifying self-defeating inner speech;
3.   teaching a step-by-step approach to the situation;
4.   teaching and rehearsing coping inner speech; and
5.   developing a plan for experimenting with and practising coping inner speech.
Afterwards, reverse roles.

C   *In a training group*
The trainer demonstrates how helpers can train clients to use coping inner speech. The trainer may then train the whole group to use coping inner speech in relation to their own problems. This could be followed by the group doing the pairs exercise above, prior to coming back for a plenary sharing and discussion session.

Realistic Inner Rules

To a greater or lesser degree all of us have a tendency to create our version of reality. Also, sometimes despite conflicting evidence, we may sustain our belief in it.

> There is a joke about a psychiatrist, Dr Parry Noid, who with some justification worked in a mental hospital. For three months he had as a patient a man who thought he was dead. Although the doctor deployed the full repertoire of his psychiatric skills, the patient held firm to his belief. Increasingly frustrated at this challenge to his self-esteem, one day Dr Noid decided that desperate measures were called for. He went up to the patient and asked, 'Do dead men bleed?'. The patient looked around himself and, seeing no blood, replied, 'No, dead men don't bleed.' The psychiatrist then grabbed hold of the patient's finger, took out a scalpel, slashed the finger and held it up in front of the patient's eyes. With amazement the patient exclaimed, 'Well, blow me, doc, dead men *do* bleed.'

Albert Ellis is the psychologist who has done most to get helpers to realize the importance of focusing on clients' irrational belief systems. He has developed a simple ABC framework for thinking about thinking difficulties.[13]

A   The activating event.
B   Your beliefs or thoughts about the activating event.
C   Your feelings and actions that are the consequence of the activating event.

Ellis reckons that much of the time people are only aware of what happens at points A and C. However, what happens at point C is mediated by the thoughts and beliefs at point B.

This section focuses on the largely implicit belief systems that constitute an important part of what happens at point B. Each of us has an inner rule book concerning appropriate standards for ourselves, others and the environment. Many clients have rules representing the internalization of others' standards rather than rules thought through by themselves. Inner rules can be beneficial so long as they help individuals to meet their needs. However, unrealistic rules can cause clients to be tyrannized by their 'shoulds', 'oughts' and 'musts'. Such unrealistic standards tend to generate negative emotions. Furthermore, these unrealistic rules and negative emotions sustain clients in behaving in ways that are less rational than desirable.

Ellis has identified three major clusters of irrational beliefs or inner rules that 'create' dysfunctional emotional and behavioural consequences.[14]

1.   I *must* do well and win approval for my performances, or else I rate as a rotten person.

2. Others *must* treat me considerately and kindly, in precisely the way I want them to treat me.
3. The conditions under which I live *must* be arranged so that I get practically everything I want comfortably, quickly, and easily, and get virtually nothing that I do not want.

Ellis calls these musts 'irrational beliefs' or 'musturbatory thinking'. Below are some examples of unrealistic or irrational inner rules set within the ABC framework; A is the event, B is the inner rule and C the consequences.

Val is a housewife in her early forties.
A. Her children are not as tidy as she would like.
B. Everything in the house *must* be neat and tidy or else I am less of a person.
C. Worry and anxiety that the house is not perfect. Unreasonable demands on her family to be perfectly tidy. Hesitation about having friends around because the house may not be perfectly tidy.

Geoff is a family man with two children.
A. His children do not overtly show appreciation for how hard he works to support them.
B. I *must* always have approval or else I am less of a person.
C. Hurt, self-pity and anger. Curtness with children that creates emotional distance.

Annie is a twenty-year-old nursing student.
A. Difficulty completing an assignment.
B. I *must* be perfectly competent all the time. Life *must* present no real obstacles to my achievement.
C. Anger with herself. Depression. Difficulty in concentrating.

Helper interventions in working with clients who have unrealistic inner rules may range from identifying and disputing them on an ad hoc basis to more systematic approaches. A systematic approach is likely to consist of three elements: (1) presenting a rationale; (2) detecting and disputing unrealistic rules; (3) formulating more realistic rules.

Presenting a rationale

Part of your presentation of a rationale is likely to focus on the relationship between people's beliefs and their emotional and behavioural consequences. The ABC framework provides a useful shorthand way of doing this. You may point out that many of these beliefs operate below the surface of conscious awareness and that clients may require help in learning to detect them. Additionally, you may indicate that you are teaching the self-help skills of detecting, disputing and reformulating unrealistic inner rules. Your work together has relevance not only for now but also for the future.

Detecting and disputing unrealistic inner rules

There are two main signals for detecting unrealistic inner rules.

● *Inappropriate negative emotions and behaviour.* For instance, in the above examples of Val, Geoff and Annie you might backtrack from their negative feelings and behaviour to explore the unrealistic inner rules that contribute to them.
● *Musturbatory language.* Being mindful of when clients rigidify their thinking by using 'shoulds', 'oughts' and 'musts'.

Helpers may discuss with their clients both how to identify unrealistic rules and also the characteristics of effective rules. Some of the main characteristics of unrealistic inner rules include:

● *Demandingness.* Thinking of wants and wishes as demands rather than preferences.
● *Perfectionism.* Nobody's perfect!
● *Overgeneralization.* Making rules for *all* situations rather than allowing flexibility for specific situations.
● *Self-rating.* Rating the person and not just the characteristic. For instance, Sally might say that she felt bad blushing, but also think that because she blushed *she* was bad.
● *Catastrophizing.* Thinking that it is or will be absolutely awful that you, others or the environment are not as they should be.

Some of the main characteristics of realistic inner rules include:

● *A coping emphasis.* Managing or coping with situations rather than being perfectionist in regard to them.
● *Being based on the client's own needs, preferences and values.* They are not just rigid internalizations from others.
● *Flexibility.* Where appropriate, being amenable to change.
● *Absence of self-rating.* A functional rating of specific characteristics according to whether they are useful for survival and fulfilment rather than anything that involves a global rating of personhood.

Helpers can both themselves question and also help their clients to question their unrealistic inner rules. Ellis observes: 'Disputing makes use of the scientific method of challenging and questioning shaky or untenable hypotheses that clients hold about themselves and about the world.'[15] For instance, he might say: 'Where is the evidence?'; 'Prove that it is awful.'; 'In what way can't you stand it?'; or 'How does this make you a worthless person?' Another type of question focuses on asking clients whether there are more realistic inner rules that could replace the existing self-defeating ones.

Formulating more realistic inner rules

It is insufficient to detect and dispute unrealistic inner rules. You then collaborate with your clients to develop more realistic reformulations that have meaning for them.

Let me illustrate some possible reformulations of the unrealistic rules in the three earlier examples of Val, Geoff and Annie.

Val   Unrealistic inner rule: Everything in the house *must* be neat and tidy or else I am less of a person.
More realistic reformulation: Though I would prefer the house to be tidy all the time, it is unrealistic to expect this with children. Nevertheless we can make a special effort when guests are expected.

Geoff: Unrealistic inner rule: I *must* always have approval or else I am less of a person.
More realistic reformulation: I would like to have the approval of my kids, though what is more important is that I approve of my own behaviour towards them. Their lack of appreciation may be a signal for me to re-examine my behaviour.

Annie: Unrealistic inner rule (the first one): I *must* be perfectly competent all the time.
More realistic reformulation: Nobody's perfect. To err is human and what is more important is that I learn from my mistakes.

Alongside their contact with you, clients can do homework exercises in which they explore the realism of their inner rules and reformulate them as necessary. Another element of homework may be getting them to listen to a cassette recording of your previous session before coming again. Additionally, you may make up a special cassette, in which their main unrealistic rules are stated and reformulated, for them to play regularly between sessions. A whiteboard is a useful tool for any thinking-focused interventions. It can help both you and your clients understand and work through their thinking difficulties. Visual presentation often increases the power of verbal presentation.

Exercise 7.3   Detecting, disputing and reformulating inner rules

This exercise can be done on your own, in pairs or in a training group.

A   *On your own*
Drawing either on your own personal life or on your experience with a client, analyse at least one situation in which you or your client could be feeling and acting more positively, by writing down for each situation:
1.   the relevant event(s), unrealistic inner rule(s), and emotional and be-havioural consequences, using an ABC framework;
2.   your disputation of your or your client's unrealistic inner rule(s);
3.   a more realistic reformulation of your or your client's inner rule(s);
4.   the likely emotional and behavioural consequences of the new inner rule(s); and
5.   any warning or danger signals which might in future cue you to the presence of your or your client's unrealistic inner rule(s).
B   *In pairs*
Counsel your partner in an area where he or she considers he or she could be feeling and acting more positively, by:
1.   presenting a rationale for focusing on inner rules mediating his or her negative feelings and actions;
2.   collaboratively formulating the ABCs of the situation;
3.   collaboratively disputing any unrealistic inner rules at B;
4.   collaboratively reformulating unrealistic into more realistic inner rules; and
5.   working out with your partner a suitable homework assignment for consolidating the learnings from your session. It may be helpful to cassette-record your session.
Afterwards, reverse roles.
C   *In a training group*
The trainer introduces the topic of helpers collaborating with their clients on detecting, disputing and reformulating their unrealistic inner rules. The trainer either presents a video- or audio-recorded demonstration or, acting as helper, models the above pairs exercise. He or she uses a whiteboard to highlight aspects of the 'client's' thinking. Furthermore, any live demonstra-tion is recorded so the 'client' may replay the cassette as homework. Afterwards, the group is broken into pairs or triads to perform the pairs exercise, prior to coming together again for a plenary sharing and discus-sion session.

Developing Different Perceptions

In Chapter 5, attention was paid to helping clients develop different perceptions of their problems. Here I focus on the skills of helping clients develop different perceptions of specific situations that trigger unwanted feelings such as depression, anger and anxiety.

There is usually more than one way of perceiving a situation. For example, the following is a joke based on the Freudian Oedipus complex in which the son, in love with his mother, competes with and has murderous fantasies about his father.

Mum: Oedipus, Oedipus, come back . . . all is forgiven.
Dad: Over my dead body.

Another joke that illustrates that situations can be perceived differently is the one about the psychiatrist, Dr Fritz Angst, who had been using the Rorschach test when treating a sex offender. The Rorschach is a projective test, presenting ten ink-blot pictures in succession, to each of which subjects are asked to respond by saying what they see. After a number of sessions the following dialogue took place.

Dr Angst: I am unable to help, but my assessment is that you are an inveterate sex pervert.
Sex offender: Come off it, doc. You're the one who's been showing me the dirty pictures.

Aaron Beck has focused on the intervening thoughts which precede negative feelings such as depression and pathological anxiety.[16,17,18] An important category of such intervening thoughts are what he terms *automatic thoughts*. Either his patients were not fully conscious of these thoughts and images or it did not occur to them that they warranted special scrutiny. Characteristics of these automatic thoughts include their being: specific; discrete and occurring in a kind of shorthand; autonomous, in that people make no effort to initiate them; regarded by those having them as plausible, even if they seem far-fetched to others; idiosyncratic; and generally involving more distortion of reality than other types of thinking.

Helpers working with clients on developing different perceptions need first to help them understand the relationship between their thoughts, feelings and actions. Sometimes a few simple examples based on the ABC framework can help.

A.   Greg goes to a party with Joan, but spends quite a lot of time there with other people.
B.   Joan thinks or perceives Greg doesn't really care for her.
C.   Joan gets angry and sulky with Greg.

However, if at B Joan had thought 'I'm glad he's enjoying himself', at C she would probably have felt more confident to enjoy the party herself.

Another example is:

A. Patricia sits at her desk doing homework.
B. Patricia thinks or perceives: 'I can't do this. What an idiot I am.'
C. Patricia gets frustrated and tense and stops working, but feels guilty about this and then gets depressed.

Again, if at B Patricia had thought 'This is a difficult assignment that I require time to work through. If necessary, I can get extra assistance', she would have stood more chance of working and feeling better at C.

Once they understand the notion of automatic thoughts, your clients need to become better at identifying them. Clients with poor vocabularies can be told to detect 'the things you say to yourself' immediately preceding negative emotions. In short, clients need to be taught to monitor and record the ABCs of their self-defeating feelings and actions. The Bs frequently are automatic thoughts containing unrealistic perceptions or interpretations. Ideally they should be monitored and recorded as they happen. However, setting aside some time each day to record upsetting thoughts provides an alternative.

Exercise 7.4   Monitoring and recording upsetting thoughts

This exercise can be done on your own, in pairs or in a training group.

A   *On your own*
Below is a format for monitoring and recording your upsetting thoughts:

A The events (include date and time)	B Your thoughts	C Your feelings

Make a chart similar to the above. Then, for the next twenty-four hours, monitor and record the ABCs either of a single category of upsetting feelings or of all significant upsetting feelings. In particular, focus on identifying at B the thoughts immediately preceding your negative feelings.

B   *In pairs*
Complete the Part A exercise individually. Afterwards partner A counsels partner B in relation to detecting his or her upsetting thoughts. Then reverse roles.

C   *In a training group*
The trainer demonstrates filling in an upsetting thoughts chart. Trainees
then do the Part A exercise individually. The trainer then demonstrates the
counselling part of the Part B exercise with one of the trainees as client. The
group then breaks into pairs or triads to do the Part B counselling exercise.
This is followed by a plenary sharing and discussion session.

The next step, once your clients build up their skills of detecting their
upsetting thoughts, is to teach them to challenge their own thinking at B
by developing different ways of perceiving A. The idea is not to force the
client into unrealistic different perceptions. Instead, you strive to help
them overcome distorted and narrow ways of thinking. They then can
have a greater range out of which to choose the perception that has the
best or most realistic 'fit'.

Your skills here include two main types of question. The first, 'What is
the evidence?', challenges clients to support their thinking with logic and
reason. The second, 'What are different ways of perceiving the situation?', encourages clients to develop greater flexibility in their thinking
and not to accept the first or automatic explanation out of habit. A
humorous illustration of this kind of questioning is that of the young lady
who says to her boyfriend: 'If you love me so much, why do you keep
asking me to marry you?' Clients can be encouraged to provide more
than one explanation for each situation. Though keeping a focus on
clients doing much of their own work, you may also choose to offer
different perceptions. Additionally, you help clients evaluate perceptions. As Beck observes: 'The therapist needs to ask repeatedly which
alternative way of thinking is most helpful for the patient.'[19]

Exercise 7.5   Generating and evaluating different perceptions

This exercise may be done either on your own, in pairs or in a training group.

A   *On your own*
Make a worksheet in the following format:

Situation	Upsetting thoughts	Different perceptions

Either work with fresh situations or take one or more situations from your Exercise 7.4 chart. For each situation, write down as many different perceptions of it as you can think of. Then evaluate which has the best 'fit' for explaining the situation.

B   *In pairs*
Either do the above exercise individually, then discuss;
or partner A acts as helper and works with partner B to identify one or more situations associated with upsetting thoughts, and to generate different perceptions of these situations. Partner A then facilitates Partner B in evaluating which perception has the best fit for explaining the situation. Work with one situation only at a time. Afterwards, reverse roles.

C   *In a training group*
The trainer demonstrates filling in the different perceptions worksheet. Also, he or she may demonstrate the helper–client pairs exercise with a group member as 'client'. Trainees then do either the individual or the helper–client pairs exercise above. The group then comes together for a plenary sharing and discussion session.

Accurately Anticipating Risk and Gain

People lead their lives into the future rather than into the past. Anticipations are thoughts and images regarding the future. People both think forward and look forward. However, past circumstances in people's lives often adversely colour their view of the future. Furthermore, many clients' *sense of competence* or anticipation of their competence to act successfully on their environments in order to meet their needs and preferences is lower than their *actual competence* might warrant. Sense of competence and anticipating risk and gain are closely related, in that people who do not own their competence are more likely to emphasize the risks of acting than those who do. Most clients are more pessimistic than optimistic in relation to their underlying abilities. However, there are some whose optimism leads to impulsiveness and excessive risk-taking. Consequently, helpers may need to help their clients think about and look at the future accurately.

The helping relationship assists many clients in viewing the future realistically. It both affirms their sense of worth and also provides the opportunity to explore and talk over specific situations. Additionally, as clients acquire other skills in relation to their feelings, thoughts and actions, they are likely to fear the future less.

Helpers can work with clients to explore not just why they avoid acting (*exploring risk*) but also, and perhaps more important, what the benefits of acting in a particular situation might be (*exploring gain*). For some clients obtaining the gain may be the risk. As one psychiatrist quipped: 'There is only one thing worse than not getting what you want, and that is getting it.' Furthermore, certain clients may be afraid to lose the secondary gains of their problems: for instance, they may get special treatment and privileges, not be expected to take risks, etc. Consequently, you may have to help them see that holding on to these secondary gains may result in impoverishing their future.

An initial step is to get your clients to verbalize and even visualize what they perceive to be the gains and risks of certain courses of action. An underlying question in exploring gain is 'What do you enjoy?' Relevant questions in exploring risk are: 'What are you afraid of that blocks you from getting what you want?'; 'Where is the evidence?'; 'Is there any other way of viewing it?'; 'What resources do you have?'; and 'What is the worst thing that could happen?'

Your role is to help clients obtain an accurate appraisal of the future. You encourage them to articulate gains and to explore the accuracy of their perception of risk. A further step, based on more realistic anticipations, is to think through appropriate ways of acting in situations. You may also focus on altering your clients' anticipation by helping them experience success. Both behavioural and imaginal ways of doing this are discussed in the next chapter.

Exercise 7.6 Anticipating risk and gain

This exercise may be done on your own, in pairs or in a training group.

A *On your own*
1. Identify a situation where you seem afraid to act to meet your needs.
2. In two columns, one for gains and the other for risks, write down what you perceive to be the gains and risks of acting. If you block on identifying gains, brainstorm and write down any conceivable gains, however far-fetched, that you can think of in five minutes.
3. Assess the gains versus the risks.
4. Write down what might be an appropriate course of action based on a realistic assessment of gains and risks.

B *In pairs*
Counsel your partner by:
1. discussing the concept of anticipating gain and risk accurately;
2. helping your 'client' identify and assess the gains and risks of acting in a situation where he or she feels blocked; and

3. helping him or her formulate an appropriate course of action based on a realistic assessment of gain and risk.
    Afterwards, reverse roles.
C   *In a training group*
    The trainer can facilitate a discussion of accurately anticipating gain and risk by presenting the concept, getting trainees to illustrate it from their personal and work experience, and himself or herself illustrating it with examples pertinent to the helping setting for which the group is being trained. The trainer may also break the group into pairs to practise along the lines of Part B. Furthermore, the trainer might set as homework the exercise in Part A.

PROBLEM MANAGEMENT TRAINING

In Chapter 5, I focused on helpers adopting a problem management approach to clients' difficulties. Taking this further, you may consciously choose to impart problem management skills to your clients. To a certain extent you will do this anyway if you use a problem management model. However, the skills of problem management may be systematically presented as a set of self-help skills. This does not necessarily mean that clients need take a calculated step-by-step approach every time they face a problem – life is too short! There are, though, circumstances where a more rigorous approach may be beneficial. These include: major decisions, role transitions, continuing negative feelings and behaviour, and potential and actual conflicts.

Interest in training in problem-solving was stimulated by an article by D'Zurilla and Goldfried that appeared in 1972.[20] In it they identified five stages of problem solving: (1) general orientation or 'set'; (2) problem definition and formulation; (3) generation of alternatives; (4) decision making; and (5) verification. Though having much in common with their work, the steps that I present below have differences as well. Furthermore, the term 'problem management' is favoured since, unlike 'problem solving', it has connotations more of *coping* than of *mastery*.

The steps below are also similar to the stages in the DOSIE problem management model in Chapter 5. However, it is one thing to present a model for helpers to use with clients and another to present one for clients to use on themselves. The latter has a rather different focus. Nonetheless, both models require simple expression for ease of memory and use.

CIDDA is a systematic self-help approach for managing problems. Its five steps are:

Step one: *Confront* the problem(s).
Step two: *Inform* yourself.
Step three: *Define* the problem(s).
Step four: *Decide* what to do.
Step five: *Act* and evaluate.

The five steps of this *confront–inform–define–decide–act* framework frequently overlap and interact.

Step one: confront the problem(s)

Confronting the problem(s) comprises a number of different elements.

● *Orientation.*   Orientation refers to a person's attitude towards problems. Relevant orientation considerations are the degree to which people believe that: problems are a normal part of life; the best approach to problems is to try to solve them; it is important to be skilled at identifying problems as they arise rather than when they are full-blown; and a 'stop-and-think' approach is better than impulsiveness.
● *Ownership.*   Ownership involves acknowledging problems when they exist rather than denying them or externalizing them on to other people.
● *Clearing a space.*   Confronting a problem is likely to involve clearing a space, so that the problem gets the time and psychological energy that it deserves.

Step two: inform yourself

Informing yourself about the relevant considerations and facts of the problem can take place both internally and externally. In both instances, clarity, specificity and comprehensiveness are desirable.

● *Inner information.*   Acquiring inner information involves self-examination. It can entail: inner empathy to discover what your deeper feelings are; trying to articulate your goals; analysing the way you conceptualize and otherwise think about the problem; and in many different ways exploring your skills deficits in relation to it.
● *Outer information.*   This includes information concerning other people and the environment. Information about others includes what they think about the problem and how supportive they may be. Information concerning the environment varies according to the problem.

Step three: define the problem(s)

In step two, a range of information is generated. In step three, you identify the relevant variables within your influence that hinder you from managing your problem effectively. This does not mean that sometimes people will not require professional help. However, there may be many instances in their lives where, by identifying their skills deficits more sharply, they are in a stronger position to act on their own. Also, helpers cannot always be around to support them.

You need to train your clients in operationally defining their problems in terms of the skills deficits that do or may diminish their ability to manage them. As mentioned in Chapter 5, the flip side of a statement of skills deficits is a statement of goals.

Step four: decide what to do

In step three, you identify one or more skills deficits and state these as goals. In step four, you decide what to do about them. Two components of step four are generation of alternatives and deciding.

● *Generation of alternatives.*   Here, you identify approaches to remedying your skills deficits. The principles of brainstorming may be useful here: for instance, deferment of judgement and 'quantity breeds quality'. At some stage, however, you need to narrow down your list to realistic alternatives that are clearly and specifically stated.
● *Deciding.*   Deciding entails evaluating alternatives and choosing one or more courses of action. Your choices are likely to be guided by considerations of utility and probability. D'Zurilla and Goldfried observe: 'The utility model which most closely parallels human behaviour in problematic situations involves a *subjective* estimate of the probability that each particular alternative will achieve any given outcome, as well as *subjective* determination of the value of the various outcomes.'[21] Your decisions may relate to regulating not only your overt behaviour but also your thoughts and feelings. In this step, you may focus more on strategies rather than tactics (the details of implementing strategies).

Step five: act and evaluate

Here, 'acting' encompasses any approaches you take to altering your thoughts, feelings and actions. This step includes four elements.

- *Planning.* You may need to fill in the tactics of how best to implement your decision(s).
- *Performance.* Carrying out your decision(s).
- *Monitoring.* Observing how to carry out your decision(s) and the emotional and behavioural consequences for yourself and for others.
- *Evaluating.* Assessing the adequacy of your performance and its emotional and behavioural consequences for yourself and others. Going back to earlier stages of CIDDA framework as necessary: for instance, gathering more information or redefining the problem. Alternatively, you may need to work on remedying specific skills deficits related to implementing your decision.[22]

Exercise 7.7 Problem management training within the CIDDA framework

This exercise may be done in a number of ways.

A *On your own*
1. Write out what you see as your skills resources and deficits within each of the five steps of the CIDDA problem management framework (confront–inform–define–decide–act). Use a two-column format, with resources in one column and deficits in the other.
2. Work within the CIDDA framework on a problem in your own life. Write down your thinking in each of the steps.

B *In pairs*
(a) Partner A counsels partner B, who assesses his or her skills resources and deficits in relation to each of the five steps of the CIDDA problem management framework.
Afterwards, reverse roles.
(b) Partner B attempts to train partner A in the skills of problem management within the CIDDA framework. This may be done in relation to a specific area of difficulty in partner A's life.
Afterwards, reverse roles.

C *In a training group*
The trainer introduces the CIDDA problem management framework. He or she then subdivides the group into fours to assess and discuss their skills resources and deficits within each of the five CIDDA steps. Afterwards, the trainer demonstrates training a group member in the self-help skills of problem management (in one session, this can only be an introduction). Then the group is divided into twos and threes to perform the training part of

the above pairs exercise. This is followed by a plenary sharing and discussion session. The trainer makes connections between problem management training and the work of the helping setting for which the group is being trained.

FACILITATING SELF-HELP

Thinking focused interventions are best viewed as ways of imparting self-help skills. Where possible, this emphasis on training in self-help should be built into the rationale helpers provide to clients for using these interventions. The concept of inner empathy requires expansion to include accurately listening not only to feelings and feeling fragments, but also to thoughts and thought fragments. The old adage 'Know thyself' can be further broken down into 'Know thy own feelings' and 'Know thy own thoughts.' Tuning in to what you think underlies each of the thinking focused self-help interventions mentioned here.

Some clients might be encouraged to engage in co-counselling and peer self-help groups. Co-counselling can be expanded so that partners work on not only their feelings but also their thinking. Especially, if some members already have some skills in the area of realistic thinking, peer self-help groups can have a focus that includes both thoughts and feelings. For example, a women's or a men's group can explore and try to alter the thoughts which contribute to women and men realizing only part of their potential. Self-help groups can have skilled helpers in the background. They can serve both as resource people for the whole group and also as a safety net for those requiring individual consultations.

8 Focusing on Action

Interviewer: How long have you been in psychoanalysis?
Woody Allen: Twenty-two years.
Interviewer: How is it going?
Woody Allen: Slowly.

Sometimes helping is viewed as stronger on talk than on action, with changes in clients' actions taking place slowly, if at all. The focus of this chapter is on helping clients change their observable behaviour. With apologies to John Lennon and Paul McCartney, I parody some lines of one of their most famous songs. This parody highlights the risks of allowing certain clients to wallow in self-pity rather than to encourage and assist them in assuming more responsibility for *acting* differently to meet their needs.

Yesterday, all your whinging seemed so far away.
Now it looks as though it's here to stay.
Oh, I believe in yesterday.

Feeling, thinking and acting, as I have already emphasized, are heavily interrelated. Consequently, the helper interventions of the preceding two chapters are relevant to altering clients' actions. However, here, I focus mainly on *direct* attempts to help clients change *specific actions*. Reverting to the notion of clients as choosers, this means helping clients make better *action* choices. Furthermore, clients should be assisted, if possible, to acquire the skills of making better action choices as self-help skills for their later lives.

SETTING GOALS

Though setting goals can focus on feelings, thoughts and actions, the last of these is the focus here.

Reasons For and Against Setting Goals

There are a number of reasons why it may be desirable to collaborate with your clients to set goals for acting differently. The *advantages of goal setting* include the following:

- *Clarity of focus.*   A well-stated goal clearly identifies the desired target actions.
- *Increased motivation.*   Goals can provide clients with something tangible to work for.
- *Increased persistence.*   Clients with clear and realistic goals are likely to work longer and harder on their problems than clients whose goals are more diffuse.
- *Increased action planning.*   Goals require implementation. This creates a pressure to plan for change carefully.

There are, of course, disadvantages too in setting goals. Such disadvantages may be more that the goals have been set either in the wrong way or at the wrong time than that they should not be set at all. Some *disadvantages of goal setting* include the following:

- *Creates dependence.*   The idea here is that basically clients' own goals will emerge given an adequate facilitative environment. They do not need to become dependent on others to help them set goals.
- *Too mechanistic.*   Goals may be set prematurely and in a simplistic way. This may both interfere with the development of a helping relationship and also curtail working on more fundamental concerns.
- *Too much pressure.*   Goals may lead to high expectations. These may cause unnecessary anxiety and resistance. Also, clients may experience failure rather than success.
- *Represent helpers' needs.*   Helpers may project onto their clients both their own ideas of what are appropriate goals and also their own anxieties about obtaining results.

Perhaps that is enough said to indicate that goal setting requires sensitivity and skill on the part of helpers. Furthermore, there may be occasions where overt goal setting is inappropriate.

Desirable Statements of Goals

There is an old adage: 'The road to hell is paved with good intentions.'
Let me provide a vignette and then discuss what might be desirable ways
of stating goals.

> Rex is a married man with two children. His wife increasingly complains
> that she and the children see little of him since he is so wrapped up in his
> work. On a number of occasions Rex has told his family that he intends
> spending more time with them. So far the only thing that has changed is an
> increase in resentment, because now Rex is also seen as not keeping his
> word.

Below are some considerations for cases when you and your clients
collaborate to set goals.

● *Goals stated in terms of actions.* Rex's wish to spend more time with
his family is an objective or intention rather than a statement of goals.
This intention requires clarifying to pinpoint the specific actions
required. Such actions might include: spending evenings at home;
having Sunday lunch with the family; and watching the children play
sport on Saturday mornings. Egan states that goals should be stated in
terms of accomplishments rather than behaviour.[1] For instance, if a
client says her goal is to get some training in communication skills,
'her goal is achieved only when those skills are *acquired, practised and
actually used* in interpersonal situations.' Another way of stating this
is that goals need to be stated in terms of desired outcomes rather than
just intervening processes.

● *Specific and measurable goals.* Behavioural psychologists collect
'baseline data' in order to be able to measure whether change has
actually taken place. For instance, spending evenings at home can be
quantified into which days of the week the evenings are; how many
evenings, both overall and on different days of the week; hours spent
at home, and so on. This does not deny that there is also a qualitative
element in what Rex does when he is at home. Some of this may also
be quantified: for instance, time spent with family as contrasted with
working in his study. The idea is that Rex's goals need to be stated so
specifically that they can be measured both to collect baseline data
and also to record changes, if any. For example, one of Rex's goals
might be to spend two evenings a week, one of which is either a
Saturday or Sunday, at home or otherwise with the family between
7 p.m. and midnight – work is not allowed during these family-focused
evenings.

● *Helpful and realistic goals.*   Goals are helpful if they are conducive to clients being better able to handle their problems. They require review if they do not contribute in some substantial way to this aim. Goals are realistic if they adequately acknowledge client, helper and environmental constraints. It is pointless and probably counterproductive to formulate specific goals that are beyond the emotional resources and personal skills of clients. The fact that their standards and hence their goals are unrealistic contributes to many clients' problems. The level and range of helper skills places constraints on what goals are attainable. Furthermore, helpers' values may limit whether they are prepared to offer their services, e.g. in condoning criminal behaviour. Environmental constraints include time, money and the degree to which the environment is supportive and/or alterable. For instance, the reason why Rex is only able to spend one weekend evening at home may be because his job requires him to be on duty the other evenings.

● *Goals tailored to and owned by the client.*   Goal setting should be a collaborative process between helpers and clients. This collaboration is important to maximize the chance of problems being clearly identified and operationalized. Goals are then being tailored in specific terms to remedying those skills deficits that sustain problems. Furthermore, clients' motivation to attain goals is likely to be much greater if they perceive that the goals are 'right' for them than if they do not. Lack of client motivation may be manifest in missing appointments and other resistances as well as in not completing homework assignments. To take Rex, he may have been prepared to own the goal of being at home for Sunday lunch, but not for Saturday lunch, since then he was accustomed to meeting with his friends prior to a round of golf.

Where there are several goals, you need to work with your clients to order priorities. Two important considerations are the degree to which specific actions contribute to a client's distress, and time constraints, such as the date of an impending exam. Goals are not immutable. They may require reformulation in light of either clients' progress or their changed circumstances.

It is possible to look at your helping contact with the client in terms of one or more 'contracts' of varying degrees of explicitness. Here the focus is not on the helping contract as such, but on the extent and way in which the client contracts to attain agreed goals. Contracts can be either implicit or verbally explicit. Additionally, sometimes it helps to write the goals down and let clients keep a copy as a reminder. On occasion such contracts are signed by both parties. They may contain rewards for compliance and penalty clauses for non-compliance.

Exercise 8.1 Setting goals for changing actions

This exercise may be done in a number of ways.

A   *On your own*
Analyse a problem in your own or in a client's life. Write down goals for changing the way you or your client acts in the problem area. Your goals for changed actions should be:
1.   stated in terms of actions;
2.   specific and measurable;
3.   helpful and realistic; and
4.   either tailored to and owned by you or tailored to and likely to be owned by your client.

B   *In pairs*
Either do the above exercise independently, then discuss;
or partner A counsels partner B in relation to a problem in his or her life, and facilitates him or her in setting goals for changed actions. The session ends with a discussion of the kind of helper–client contract that might be most appropriate to assist goal attainment. Afterwards, reverse roles.

C   *In a training group*
One option is for the trainer to give a demonstration interview on setting goals, using a group member as 'client'. Another option is for the trainer, after an introductory discussion, to set one of the exercises in Parts A and B above for either classwork or homework. The trainer then holds a plenary session in which group members present and receive feedback about the goals they have formulated.

USING MODELLING

Modelling involves demonstrating a sequence of behaviour and/or thinking to your client. Perry and Furukawa define modelling as: 'the process of observational learning in which the behaviour of an individual or group – the model – acts as a stimulus for similar thoughts, attitudes, or behaviors on the part of another individual who observes the model's performance'.[2] Here my primary focus is on demonstrating or providing demonstrations of observable behaviour to your clients. This may be used both for helping them acquire new responses and for either inhibiting or disinhibiting existing responses.[3] Another way of stating this is that modelling may be used for helping clients both acquire and develop action skills and also manage their anxieties. Additionally, modelling can be important when training your clients in thinking skills, either independently or in conjunction with action skills. Very often helpers use modelling as part of a package involving other interventions as well.

Characteristics of the Modelling Presentation

There are a number of options in how you provide a modelling presentation. This may focus on action skills, thinking skills or a mixture of the two. Table 8.1 illustrates some of your choices in presenting a model.

Table 8.1   *Some considerations for presenting a model*

	Model(s)			
	Live		Prerecorded	
	Self	*Other(s)*	*Self*	*Other(s)*
Action skills				
Thinking skills				
Thinking and action skills				

Some of the ways you may choose to use a model include the following:

- *Live modelling by helper.* Here, you yourself demonstrate the desired behaviours to your client or clients.
- *Live modelling by someone else.* For instance, you might use a recent graduate to demonstrate job interviewing skills.[4] Live modelling by someone else is more appropriate for group than for individual work. You may also encourage clients to observe skilled models in their everyday lives.
- *Prerecorded modelling by helper.* You may choose to make up videocassette or audiocassette recordings. These have the advantages of predictability, the opportunity to erase and correct poor performances, and reuseability. However, you may lose much flexibility and 'here-and-now' impact.
- *Prerecorded modelling by other people.* Here, even more than with live modelling by someone else, you may be able to control the

characteristics and performance of the model. Factors enhancing identification with the model include: similarity of sex, age, ethnic group and attitudes; and perceived competence which is not so outstanding that your client rejects the model's example. Other considerations which may enhance the model's attractiveness include prestige and warmth.

● *Covert modelling.* Covert modelling involves getting your client to use his or her imagination to observe someone else performing the desired actions. Your client might also be asked to imagine himself or herself as the model. This intervention requires you to check your client's capacity for imaging.

There are many other considerations in using modelling. Though the main emphasis should always be on modelling effective behaviour, your client may also learn from presentations of ineffective behaviours, so long as they are clearly labelled as such. Sometimes incompetence can be illustrated with much humour. You may choose to use graduated modelling procedures. Here either progressively more difficult skills or the use of the same skills in progressively more difficult situations may be demonstrated. Additionally, you may choose to use more than one model. You should pay attention to the instructions or commentary that accompanies the modelling so your clients know which desired actions to watch for. Indeed, either you or the model may summarize the skills that were used at the end of the presentation. A further consideration is whether your client observes the modelled actions to be rewarded. This is likely to increase significantly the willingness of your client to act similarly.[5]

Factors Enhancing Performance of Modelled Actions

In conjunction with or following the modelling presentation or presentations, there are a number of factors which may enhance both learning and also transfer of learning to outside situations. These include the following:

● *Rehearsal.* Rehearsal of modelled actions can be interspersed with observing the model. Rehearsal increases the probability of your clients owning, understanding, modifying where necessary and using the actions being modelled. As part of the rehearsal process, you may participate in role plays with your client.
● *Coaching.* You may need to instruct your clients in aspects of the

skill being modelled and then provide further feedback as they rehearse and practise it.

- *Teaching inner speech.* It is important that your clients have the correct inner speech to be able to direct their actions. They need to be able to instruct themselves rightly in the required sequence of behaviours.
- *Providing encouragement.* During rehearsals you can greatly assist your clients in skills acquisition by encouraging and rewarding their efforts and successes.
- *Practice.* Clients need to transfer performance of the modelled actions to their daily settings. This likelihood can be enhanced by repeated practice, homework, and, where possible, training in settings that approximate their daily surroundings.

Below is a vignette that draws together some of the points made in the previous two sections.

> Sharone, an attractive university graduate, went to see a Careers Adviser since, six months after graduation and despite many interviews, she was still unemployed. The Careers Adviser identified her as having deficits in interview skills. Amongst other interventions, Sharone watched a videocassette of the effective handling of a job interview. The model was someone of the same age and sex who had been in a similar predicament prior to improving her job interview skills. The videocassette contained a voice-over clearly identifying and labelling the desired skills. Afterwards, the Careers Adviser rehearsed and coached Sharone using role plays that approximated to her outside situation. Sharone was given much encouragement during this process. Rehearsal and practice were interspersed with reviewing excerpts from the video. Sharone was given the homework assignment of imagining herself using her improved job interviewing skills. She was then supported as she practised and monitored her use of the skills in real life.

Modelling Thinking Skills

I have already stressed the importance in modelling of clients' acquiring the required knowledge and inner speech to guide their actions. Additionally, all of the thinking skills covered in Chapter 7 lend themselves to being modelled. In fact, it is virtually impossible to train clients in thinking skills without using modelling. However, often in practice the use of modelling is not as systematic as is desirable. Thinking skills are easy to model by using audiocassettes, which may then be listened to by clients as part of their homework.

Exercise 8.2 Using modelling

This exercise may be done in a number of ways.

A *On your own*
Draw either on your personal experience or on your experience of a client and, in relation to acquiring or developing a skill, write out a programme using modelling as an intervention with:
1. a clear statement of goals;
2. a description of all important characteristics of your modelling presentation;
3. how you intend enhancing performance of modelled actions and, if relevant, thoughts; and
4. a statement of any other interventions you consider desirable in your treatment 'package'.

B *In pairs*
Counsel your partner, who draws either on his or her personal experience, or on his or her experience of a client. In relation to acquiring or developing a skill, design and implement, as far as possible, a programme using modelling as an intervention with:
1. a clear statement of goals;
2. modelling of the desired actions and, if relevant, thoughts (possibly by you);
3. ways of enhancing performance by your 'client'; and
4. use of any other interventions you consider desirable in your treatment 'package'.

C *In a training group*
In many of the exercises in this book, the trainer is encouraged to model the desired skills by giving demonstration interviews. In this exercise, the trainer might demonstrate the uses of modelling in counselling and helping. A further option is for the trainer, after a demonstration, to set either of the exercises in Parts A and B as either a class or a homework exercise. The trainer then holds a plenary session in which group members model and receive feedback about elements in their programmes.

USE OF REWARD

Helpers may choose to use reinforcement or reward to help develop specific actions. Such approaches are based on operant conditioning.[6,7] The term 'operant' emphasizes the fact that behaviour *operates* on the environment to produce consequences, as well as being controlled by or contingent upon the responses produced by that environment. Skinner observes that a response which has occurred cannot be predicted or controlled, but all that can be predicted is the probability of a similar response in the future. Where the client finds the responses rewarding, the probability of a given behaviour recurring increases, and vice versa.

Basic Concepts

Here, I use the everyday word 'reward' in preference to the more technical term 'reinforcement'. Below are some basic concepts about reward.

- *Positive reward.*   The provision of positive reward requires the presentation of a stimulus that increases the probability of a response: for example, money increases the probability of work responses.
- *Negative reward.*   Negative reward also increases the probability of a response through removing something from the situation: for example, removing a guard at a prison increases the probability of escape responses. Negative reward is not to be confused with punishment.
- *Contingencies of reward.*   To consider adequately the contingencies or circumstances involved in the provision of rewards, helpers need to take into account three elements: (1) the occasion upon which a response occurs; (2) the response itself; and (3) the rewarding consequences.
- *Schedules of reward.*   Basically there are three categories: reward each response; reward no response; and intermittently reward responses. Intermittent rewards can be very powerful, e.g. when gambling on either horses or dogs.
- *Self-reward.*   This controls actions through clients administering their own rewards.
- *Extinction.*   Extinction involves withholding or terminating rewarding consequences in relation to specific actions so that the probability of a response recurring declines, possibly to the point of extinction.
- *Prompting and fading.*   Prompts are verbal, physical or environmental cues that direct the client's attention to the desired actions. Often the prompts should be faded and then eliminated.
- *Shaping.*   Actions may be shaped by rewarding successive approximations to the targeted goals.
- *Covert conditioning.*   Using client's imagining to provide stimuli, responses and consequences of varying degrees of reward.

Identifying Rewards

When considering using reward in helping, it is important that you understand what individual clients find rewarding. Note that I say 'individual clients', because when it comes to rewards one person's meat may be another person's poison. There are numerous ways of finding out what clients find rewarding, including: asking them; asking others about them, though here you must be sensitive to issues of confidentiality; making your own observations; getting them to observe and monitor their own behaviour; and getting them to fill out self-report questionnaires in which they check off their reactions to lists of items that people might find rewarding.

MacPhillamy and Lewinsohn's Pleasant Events Schedule is an example of such a self-report questionnaire.[8,9] Those filling in the questionnaire rate each of its 320 items, which consist of events and activities generated after an extensive search of possible 'pleasing events', on a five-point scale of pleasantness. The idea behind the questionnaire is basically expressed in the old adage 'a little of what you fancy does you good'. Put another way, the authors of the questionnaire believe that one of the ways to control clients' depressive tendencies is to get them to identify and participate in more pleasant events and activities. Illustrative pleasant events include: being with happy people; thinking about friends; breathing clean air; listening to music; reading a good book; petting and necking; eating good meals; being seen as sexually attractive; seeing beautiful scenery; and visiting friends.

When working with children, pictures may be used instead of words to portray rewards. An example of this is the 'reinforcement menu' devised by Daley for finding effective rewards for eight-year-old to eleven-year-old mentally retarded children.[10] Twenty-two high-probability activities, such as talking, writing and colouring, were drawn in colour by an artist and enclosed in a single book or 'menu' with one activity per page. Children were encouraged to identify the activities in which they wanted to engage.

So far I have mainly been describing how to identify what people find rewarding outside helping. However, a possible view of the helping process is to see the role of the helper as a dispenser of intentional and sometimes unintentional rewards: for instance, praise, attention, eye contact, smiling, empathic responding, warmth and genuineness. In a well-known study, based on recordings of his interviewing, even Carl Rogers was found to be differentially rewarding certain categories of client utterances.[11]

Exercise 8.3 Identifying rewards

This exercise may be done in a number of ways.

A *On your own*
    1. List as many things, events and activities as you can think of that you
    find rewarding. Then note each item on your list using the following scale:

        Engaging in ———— is ———— for me.

extremely rewarding	4
very rewarding	3
moderately rewarding	2
slightly rewarding	1

    2. Write out a list of rewards which helpers may intentionally or uninten-
    tionally administer to their clients. Then make a list of possible ways in
    which clients reward the behaviours of their helpers.

B *In pairs*
    1. Working with a partner, together spend the next fifteen minutes writing
    down as many things as possible that people might find rewarding in
    their lives. Then independently rate each item for how rewarding
    engaging in it is to you, on the scale used in Part A above. Rate as 0 any
    item which you would not find rewarding.
    2. Again working with a partner, together use the next ten minutes to write
    down as many ways as you can think of that helpers and clients may be
    intentionally or unintentionally adminstering rewards to each other. At
    the end of the ten minutes, discuss and give your opinions of which are
    the most important ways.

C *In a training group*
    One option is for the trainer to do the exercise in Part B above as a
    whole-group exercise from the start. Another option is for the trainer, after
    an initial discussion of what is required, first to let the group members do the
    exercise in Part B above in pairs, and then to conduct a whole-group
    sharing and discussion session in which lists of 'rewards in life' and
    'rewards in helping' are compiled for the group as a whole.

Graded Task Assignment

Apart from subtle inflections of voice and body language, there are many
obvious ways in which helpers reward clients. In writing about modelling,
I mentioned encouragement as one of the factors enhancing performance, and used an example from careers work. Even without using

modelling, a careers adviser may reward all attempts by a client to gather information relevant to a career decision. The rewards may include comments like 'good', 'well done', or 'that's helpful'.

Another example of the use of reward is with clients who need to engage more in activities that are rewarding for them. Here, after working with them to identify such activities, you may have to encourage and reward them as they formulate goals and then take steps to attain them.

Graded task assignment is a way that helpers can use reward with their clients as they either acquire or strengthen and develop desired actions.[12] Sometimes clients fail either to carry out a task or to manage an anxiety because they have tried to do too much too soon. Graded task assignment allows them gradually to build up their skills and coping capacities. It uses reward in at least two ways. First, as clients take the first small steps they experience the internal reward of success. Subsequently they experience more reward as they cope with increasingly difficult tasks. Second, helpers can externally reward clients both for their efforts to take risks and change, and also as they attain specific tasks.

Graded task assignment involves shaping behaviour by rewarding successive approximations or component parts of the eventual target actions. It includes the following elements.

- Assessing whether or not the client is ready for graded task assignment.
- Formulation of ultimate goals.
- Formulation of intermediate tasks, starting with first small steps and then moving on to more difficult tasks.
- Ownership by client of success experiences. Clients are encouraged to acknowledge both when they attain tasks and also that they have attained them through their own effort and skill.
- Encouragement of realistic evaluation of performance. This includes helping clients assess their skills resources and deficits in relation to completing past, present and future tasks.
- Helping clients ventilate their doubts, anxieties and difficulties.
- Rewarding clients for effort and successful performance of tasks.
- Revising and devising different and either more easy or more difficult tasks as necessary.
- Encouraging practice and homework.
- Working with client's thinking deficits as necessary.

Below is a vignette that briefly illustrates graded task assignment.

Sid is a shy seventeen-year-old working-class young man whose goal is to develop a close relationship with a girl. Sid and his counsellor discuss possible intermediate tasks to attaining this goal and how they might be ranked in terms of small steps first, with bigger steps coming later. Some of the items on Sid's list in ascending order of difficulty are: being more open about himself with his mother and sister at home; holding conversations with girls when he is with a group of friends; asking a girl out for a drink; asking a girl to go to a disco; holding hands with a girl; kissing a girl and so on. Sid discusses with his counsellor how best to go about each task. As he reports back his progress he receives rewarding comments like 'good' and 'well done'. Tasks are revised as necessary.

In this particular example Sid had access to suitable female companions. Otherwise, getting access to them would have been a priority task.

Exercise 8.4   Graded task assignment

This exercise may be done in a number of ways.

A   *On your own*
Design and write down a graded task assignment programme either for yourself or for a client. Clearly indicate how you intend reward to be part of your programme.

B   *In pairs*
Either independently do the above exercise, then discuss;
or together with your partner design a graded task assignment programme, either for one of yourselves or for a client, clearly indicating the ways in which reward is to be used.

C   *In a training group*
The trainer introduces the topic of graded task assignment. He or she models it by working with a group member to design a programme to attain that person's goals. The group is then broken up into pairs or threes (helper, client and observer) who practise designing graded task assignment programmes. Afterwards there is a plenary sharing and discussion session.

Training Clients to Use Self-reward

Kanfer and Gaelick make a distinction between an *administrative* and a *participant* model of treatment.[13] In the administrative model, the helper administers a treatment or intervention to which the client submits. In the *participant* model, there is an emphasis on client responsibility or self-help, and the helper is viewed as 'a transitory social support system'. Throughout this book, there has been an emphasis on the participant rather than on the administrative model. Training clients to use self-reward further reflects this emphasis.

Training clients to use self-reward is often termed a self-control or self-management strategy. It can involve all the focusing on action concepts covered so far: goal setting, modelling, identifying rewards and graded task assignment. In helping clients to design self-reward programmes it can be important that they perceive both that *they* have chosen their goals or target behaviours and also that they have the confidence to complete tasks that will bring desired outcomes. Consequently, graded task assignment is often used to ensure that clients build up their confidence with success experiences. This enhances motivation both initially and later. Some clients may require preliminary work to overcome dependency patterns and the need for secondary gain. Others, who may be genuinely prepared to change, may have to build up component skills prior to initiating a self-management programme.

Self-observation

Self-observation or self-monitoring can provide an important way of enhancing motivation and clarifying goals. However, as a treatment intervention, the effects of self-observation alone are often short-lived. Though self-observation can focus on thinking, here our focus is on recording externally observable behaviours.

Self-observation is important at the start of, during and after a self-reward programme. Initially, it establishes a baseline and increases awareness. During a programme, it acts both as a reminder and also as a check on progress. Afterwards, it is relevant to maintaining gains, though at this stage self-observations are unlikely to be collected so systematically.

Basically self-observation involves collecting quantitative data. Self-recording devices include:

● Charts and tally sheets: for example, a daily weight chart or a daily tally of number of cigarettes smoked.
● Wrist counters and pocket counters: for instance, a shy adolescent may record the number of times she engages in conversations with peers.[14]

However, self-observation can be expanded to include noting both the internal and external cues that come before actions and also the consequences of actions. Clients may require relevant training in self-observation.

Environmental modification

There are two main strategies of reward that clients can use in order to influence their actions. First, they can try modifying their environment to control target actions *prior* to their execution. Second, they can self-administer a reward *following* or *contingent upon* an action or series of actions that achieves either a goal or a subgoal.

Stimulus *control* is one form of environmental modification. This entails choosing to modify the stimuli or cues associated with undesirable action responses. For instance, Terry has a goal of losing 12 kg over the next three months. Ways in which she can modify her environment to control her food intake include: ensuring that food is put out of sight and easy reach; equipping her refrigerator with a time lock; and only keeping as much food in the house as can be consumed in a short period of time. Additionally, Terry may try to control her environment by associating with people who are counting calories and interested in exercise.

Terry might also be encouraged to engage in stimulus *narrowing*. This involves reducing the number of stimuli associated with her undesirable actions: for instance, she might choose to eat only in the dining room or in the presence of certain family members.

Positive self-reward

The second main strategy of reward that Terry might use is the administration of positive self-reward. Such self-administered reward would be contingent upon her attaining a subgoal, say losing 2 kg. There are two main categories of positive reward that clients can administer to themselves:

- *External reward.*   External reward includes: (1) self-administration of new rewards that are outside the client's everyday life, such as a new item of clothing or a special event; and (2) initial denial of some pleasant everyday experience and later administration of it contingent upon a desired action.
- *Internal reward.*   This includes inner speech statements like 'That's great', or 'Well done', or 'I'm glad I made it' that clearly indicate the client's satisfaction with the achievement of a target action.

In setting up positive self-reward programmes, there are a number of considerations pertinent to attaining goals. You and your client need to identify suitable rewards. As mentioned earlier, you may need to break tasks down so that clients reward themselves for attaining graded steps. Additionally, the connections between achievement and reward must be clear. Furthermore, the client may be encouraged to draw up a unilateral contract which specifies the relationship between positive self-rewards and desired actions. Alternatively, a contract may be bilateral between helper and client. This, however, should only be a transitional phase in a programme aimed at developing self-help skills. Kanfer and Gaelick observe that wherever possible a positive self-reward should be relevant to the target behaviour. They write: 'the ex-smoker might select the purchase of new perfume or having teeth cleaned and polished, because such rewards emphasise the positive aspects of not smoking in terms of whiter teeth and increased sensitivity to smell.'[15]

Above, I have emphasized environmental modification and positive self-reward. However, though less frequently used, aversive consequences can also be self-administered: for example giving to charity a specified sum of money for every 100 calories in excess of a daily limit; and presenting yourself with a noxious odour after each extra snack.[16] Furthermore, clients can also imagine themselves undergoing aversive consequences if they perform undesirable actions. This process is known as covert sensitization.[17]

   When collaborating with a client to design a self-reward programme, you should be mindful of external resources that the client can use. For example, participation in activities of a social, educational, recreational or religious nature may provide opportunities for gaining confidence and skills. Additionally, reading appropriate self-help books and manuals can be incorporated into a programme. Such material should be easily comprehensible to the client, but this is often not the case.[18]

Exercise 8.5   Designing a programme using self-reward

This exercise may be done in a number of ways.

A   *On your own*
   Design a programme using self-reward to acquire or alter a specific action. Write down:
   1.   how you intend to observe and monitor your actions;
   2.   a clear statement of your goal;
   3.   the steps in your programme to achieve your goal, including whether you will use graded tasks and also how you will incorporate environ-

    mental modification and positive self-reward; and

4. how you intend to ensure that your actions last once your goal has been achieved.

B   *In pairs*

Counsel your partner and collaboratively design a programme using self-reward, based on the outline in Part A above, for helping him or her to acquire or alter a specific action. Afterwards, reverse roles.

C   *In a training group*

One option is for the trainer to present case material, drawn from a helping setting relevant to the group. This focuses on ways of helping clients attain action goals through environmental modification and positive self-reward. Another option is for the trainer to give a demonstration interview with a group member as 'client', in which they collaborate to design a programme using self-reward to help that 'client' acquire or alter a specific action. A further option is for the group, after an introductory discussion and/or demonstration, to break up and do the exercise in either Part A or Part B above. The trainer then holds a plenary session in which members' programmes using self-reward are presented and discussed. Members are encouraged to implement their self-reward programmes in their everyday lives.

ROLE-PLAYING, REHEARSING AND COACHING

Imagine you are Steven Spielberg about to start directing a new film. You have picked your actors and actresses and now you want them to become proficient in their roles. Much of your work involves building their skills through coaching them at rehearsals in which they try out or 'role-play' their parts. As helpers you may find yourselves in the position of a director who helps clients acquire and/or develop skills for playing their parts. In Chapter 6, I mentioned the use of role-playing for helping clients release and explore their feelings. Here the focus is on using role play, rehearsal and coaching as ways of helping clients act more effectively. Role-playing is likely to be used as part of an intervention package. Other interventions beside rehearsal and coaching may include: modelling, graded task assignment, use of reward, use of self-reward and appropriate inner speech.

Role Play as Part of Assessment

Role-playing can be used to identify where a client's skills deficits lie.

Though there may be differences between how your client behaves in a simulated and in a real setting, valuable observations and self-observations may be gained from role-playing.[19] A reason for this is that, unlike self-report, role-playing may highlight vocal and body as well as verbal messages.

> Janis was a client who was having difficulty terminating a relationship with Hank, her boyfriend of the previous six months. Hank would keep coming round to her flat asking to have a talk. Janis found it difficult to handle this situation. Janis's counsellor asked her to role-play how she acted when Hank came round. As a result of their role play it became apparent that, amongst other things: (1) Janis had no strength in her voice when she told him she wished he would stop coming around; and (2) he only had to push very lightly on the door and Janis would offer no resistance. In short, the role play highlighted both vocal and body messages that interfered with Janis's attaining her goal of terminating the relationship.

Clients may feel uneasy when asked to role-play a scene in their lives. Part of your skill lies in helping them acknowledge that this may help identify ineffective patterns of acting on which they can then work. Furthermore, you can help disinhibit them by yourself being prepared to participate without self-consciousness in their role plays.

Preparatory Considerations

Goal setting and presenting a rationale are two important preconditions for successful use of role play.

- *Goal setting.* All the criteria for stating goals I mentioned earlier in this chapter are relevant. As far as possible, goals should be: stated in terms of actions: specific and measurable; helpful and realistic; and tailored to and owned by the client. Graded task assignment involving intervening goals may be used if the ultimate goal is too difficult.
- *Presenting a rationale.* In presenting your rationale, you could use the analogy of a well-known stage or film director (as I used the illustration of Steven Spielberg), who wants to help the client develop a new role or new skills. You can emphasize that, in addition to assessment, role-playing provides a safe situation in which new ways of acting can be tried out and developed. Goldfried and Davison give the example of a therapist preparing a client for role-playing, saying: 'In a sense, (it's) going through a dry run. It's safer to run through some of these situations here, in that it really doesn't "count" if you don't handle them exactly as you would like to. Also, it can provide

you an excellent opportunity to practice different ways of reacting to these situations, until you finally hit on one which you think would be best.'[20] You may mention in your rationale that some people may have feelings of unease and artificiality as they get used to role-playing.

The Rehearsal Phase

During the rehearsal phase, you discuss and try out different ways of acting. In all probability Steven Spielberg does not just tell his cast what to do. Rather he collaborates with them to identify different behaviours that are both within the resources of any particular cast member and also appropriate for that scene. This is likely to include a considerable degree of improvisation on a 'trial-and-error' basis.

There are a number of different interventions involved in the rehearsal phase.

- *Choosing appropriate 'scripts' and actions.*   You and your client generate and review alternative scripts. This involves looking at verbal, vocal and body messages. Furthermore, you explore coping with different responses on the part of others.
- *Role-playing.*   This involves enacting one or more of the 'scripts'. The helper may model desired actions. The helper may also play a part in the enactment: for instance, the part of a friend, partner, parent, child, workmate or boss. The role plays are repeated as many times as is necessary and feasible. A variation of role-playing is the empty chair technique. Here the client role-plays talking to an imagined other who occupies the empty chair.
- *Coaching.*   Before, during and after role plays, helpers can coach their clients in how to behave. Their coaching can have two main components. First, helping clients with their observable behaviour. Second, helping clients acquire the appropriate inner speech so that they can instruct themselves in how to act independent of their helpers.
- *Feedback.*   Feedback can come from either clients, helpers or observers. It is important that clients learn both during and between sessions to monitor and realistically evaluate the adequacy of their own performance. This process may be accelerated by replays of audiocassettes or, preferably, videocassettes. These may be played back during sessions as well as loaned to clients for homework. Feedback is a form of coaching during and after an enactment. Role

reversal, involving client and helper exchanging roles, provides an additional means of clients obtaining feedback, both regarding what it feels like to be the other person in an interaction and also from their helper's performance of how they behave. Another variation is to have the helper directly mirror the client's verbal, vocal and body messages. Feedback includes the use of positive reward by helpers as clients perform desired actions. Additionally, clients may receive reward both from developing and using their skills and also from using positive self-statements.

- *Rehearsing thinking skills.* Helpers may train their clients in appropriate thinking skills.[21] These may be self-instructions to guide new ways of acting. Alternatively, the focus of a rehearsal could be more on acquiring thinking skills in their own right (for instance, problem solving), without having any particular social situation in mind.
- *Homework.* As clients satisfactorily role-play desired actions, they should be encouraged to try out their new skills in real life. Helpers can help clients anticipate problems and develop coping strategies for them. Furthermore, you can: support your clients as they try out their skills outside; debrief them and monitor their progress; and help them to own any positive consequences of their changed behaviour. Also, you can do further role-playing, rehearsing and coaching as needed. A final point is that rehearsing thinking skills also lends itself to being done as homework.

Exercise 8.6 Using role-playing, rehearsing and coaching

This exercise may be done in a number of ways.

A *On your own*
Design and write out a programme, using role play as a central intervention, so that either you or a client can act more effectively when performing a specific task. Your programme should contain the following elements:
1. use of role play for assessment purposes;
2. presentation of a rationale;
3. a statement of goals;
4. choosing appropriate 'scripts' and actions;
5. role-playing;
6. coaching;
7. feedback;

8.   rehearsing related thinking skills; and

9.   homework.

B   *In pairs*
Partner A counsels partner B and, along the lines of Part A above, uses role play as a central intervention in helping him or her act more effectively when performing a specific task.
Afterwards, discuss, then reverse roles.

C   *In a training group*
The trainer discusses the use of role-playing, rehearsing and coaching in helping. He or she gives a demonstration of how to use role play to help a group member 'client' act more effectively when performing a specific task. Then the group does the pairs exercise, prior to coming together for a plenary sharing and discussion session. Group members are encouraged to use in real life the skills on which they worked.

IMAGINAL GOAL REHEARSAL

Imaginal goal rehearsal is another intervention focused on helping clients act effectively. I have already mentioned the use of imaging in systematic desensitization. In this section, imaging is used as a coping skill not only for containing anxiety but also for imaging and rehearsing successful execution of tasks.[22] Lazarus writes 'If you repeatedly and conscientiously picture yourself achieving a goal, your chances of actual success will be greatly enhanced.'[23]

> Jake was a middle-aged man with a fear of driving over high bridges on his own. Consequently, he avoided them. As he was driving back one day to the city where he lived, he had to choose to take either the long route with no threat or a short route involving going over a raised high bridge. In the hour or so before he came near the city, Jake repeatedly visualized successfully driving over the bridge. This gave him the confidence to commit himself to staying on the road that led to the bridge. He kept using his goal-directed imaging until getting on the bridge. Additionally, he used coping self-instructions to help him manage his anxiety before and whilst on the bridge, which he drove over successfully. Then he used positive self-reward to acknowledge his achievement.

All of us can use imaginal goal rehearsal before situations, such as job interviews, that are important to us. Beck and his colleagues use the term 'cognitive rehearsal' to refer to asking patients to imagine each successive step in the sequence leading to completion of a task.[24] Assuming that people possess the requisite skills other than confidence to perform tasks successfully, there are at least three reasons why imaginal goal rehearsal may assist them. First, it influences them to identify the component parts of the task they face. Second, it helps their mind stay focused on the task. Third, repeated imagings of acting competently and successfully both enhances their task-relevant skills and inhibits interfering anxiety.

Imaginal goal rehearsal can be used either on its own or as part of a package involving other interventions such as live role-playing, rehearsing and coping inner speech. It involves training clients in the use of imaging and then getting them to engage in repeated mental rehearsals. As with any intervention using imaging, helpers should check the extent to which their clients can visualize scenes.

Exercise 8.7   Using imaginal goal rehearsal

This exercise can be done in a number of ways.

A   *On your own*
Think of a task in your life that currently you do not handle as well as you would like. Identify the component parts of successful performance, then repeatedly rehearse imagining yourself performing this task competently and successfully. Then, if possible, try out the task again in real life after you have prepared yourself by means of imaginal goal rehearsal.

B   *In pairs*
Partner A trains partner B in imaginal goal rehearsal in relation to either the task he or she worked on in Exercise 8.6, or another task.
Afterwards, discuss, and reverse roles.

C   *In a training group*
The trainer introduces the topic of using imaginal goal rehearsal to facilitate performing specific tasks successfully. He or she trains a group member 'client' to use imaginal goal rehearsal. Afterwards, the group breaks into twos or threes (helper, client and observer) to perform the pairs exercise. This is followed by a plenary sharing and discussion session.

FACILITATING SELF-HELP

Interventions focused on action, like those focused on feeling and thinking, should be presented where possible as imparting self-help skills. Training clients in the use of self-reward clearly falls into this category. Goal setting, identifying rewards, graded task assignment and imaginal goal rehearsal also fit easily into a self-help framework. Additionally, clients can be helped to use role-playing and rehearsal as self-help skills. However, they may have to be their own coaches is they cannot find someone to help them. Even modelling can be transformed into a self-help skill. This is done by encouraging clients to observe closely the actions and thoughts of appropriate models.

I started these three chapters on interventions focused on feeling, thinking and action by stressing that changes in each area were capable of influencing the other two. As helpers, you have to choose and negotiate where and how best to intervene. Unfortunately, there are distinct limits to which these skills of appropriate judgement can be conveyed in a book such as this. Having your practical work supervised by someone skilled at both helping and supervising can be an excellent way of learning these skills of judgement.

9 Facilitating Groups

Question: How many counselling group members does it take to change a light bulb?

Answer: Eight. One to change it and the remainder to discuss doing it before and to offer support afterwards.

There are two main forms of helping in groups: group counselling and life skills training. A word about my use of terms. I use *group counselling* to signify interactional or encounter groups that meet regularly over a period of months. I use *life skills training* for structured groups that last for a stipulated number of sessions with the object of teaching trainees one or more specific skills. I use the words *facilitator* and *trainer* for the helper roles in group counselling and life skills training, respectively. Many of the helping in groups skills that are discussed in the next two chapters can be used in informal settings.

Two different but interrelated ways that you can operate underlie group counselling and life skills training. The assumption in group counselling is that you are a *facilitator*. You influence and utilize the resources within the group to assist individual members in confronting and working on their problems in relating and living. Another way of viewing group counselling is that clients participate in relatively unstructured groups that emphasize experiencing of feelings, 'here-and-now' interaction, and skills acquisition for outside life. Group counselling is sometimes distinguished from group therapy because it focuses on the problems of 'ordinary' or 'normal' clients rather than on those of the 'deviant', 'abnormal' or 'severely disturbed'.[1] There can be much overlap between these two groups of clients.

The assumption in life skills training is that you are an *educator* or *trainer*. You run structured groups that train clients in specific life skills. In reality, there are many intermediate positions. Group facilitation can include providing members with feedback about their thinking and relationship skills. Life skills training can be performed in ways that allow participants to explore and experience their feelings. Though the major emphasis in this chapter is on group counselling, much of it is also relevant to the following chapter on life skills training. For instance, you require good group facilitation skills to be an effective life skills trainer.

DECIDING TO RECOMMEND GROUP COUNSELLING

You and your client may decide that joining either a counselling group or a life skills training programme is a preferred intervention. Below are some of the reasons why you might choose group counselling. The potential *advantages* of group counselling include the following:

- *Economizing on time.*   It is arguably 'cheaper' in terms of time to see eight clients together once a week for one and a half hours than each separately for forty-five minutes, a total of six hours, that is, four times as long.
- *Giving clients practice at relating.*   Clients are usually deficient in relationship skills. A group allows them a protected arena within which to develop and practise their skills.
- *Healing potential of other group members.*   A concept known as 'cohesiveness' is said to define the more successful counselling groups. Yalom writes: 'By definition, cohesiveness refers to the attraction that members have for their group and for the other members. Members of cohesive groups are more accepting of each other, more supportive, more inclined to form meaningful relationships in the group.'[2]
- *Participant-observer role of the group facilitator.*   The facilitator has an excellent opportunity to observe in the here-and-now the members' skills resources and deficits.
- *Improved client motivation.*   There are at least two ways in which group counselling may improve client motivation. First, some clients enjoy the companionship and opportunity for intimacy that groups provide. Second, they may be motivated by other group members to act more effectively. This may come about either through observing their behaviour or through their suggestions and encouragement.

Despite the fact that group counselling has many advantages, it also has its share of problems and disadvantages. However, these can be lessened

by good group leader skills. The potential *disadvantages* of group counselling include the following:

- *High dropout rate.* Groups which do not attain a state of at least
  moderate cohesiveness are likely to start losing many of their members. The risk of losing clients in group work, where clients are forced
  to relate to other group members who often are there precisely
  because they have communication difficulties, is probably far greater
  than that of losing them in individual work, where the client is likely to
  have a relatively safe relationship with the helper.
- *Pressure for conformity.* All groups are likely to develop norms, or
  spoken and unspoken rules about how members should behave in the
  group. There is a risk that some of these norms may help members to
  avoid rather than deal with their problems.
- *Unethical facilitation.* Unethical facilitation may take many forms.
  Some group facilitators may be untrained for the task they are
  undertaking. Facilitators can also exploit clients emotionally and
  sexually. Furthermore, there is the opportunity for facilitators to
  make a lot of money by charging excessive fees. Additionally, group
  members may be inadequately protected by unethical facilitators
  from being emotionally damaged within the group.

As helpers you may decide that group counselling is desirable for
clients either *instead of*, *concurrently with* or *after* individual work.
However, you may either not currently run a group or, if you do, not have
a vacancy in your existing group or groups. In such circumstances, you
may wish to recommend another group to a client. Table 9.1 is a brief
checklist of questions for assessing counselling groups. Some of this
information may not be readily available, but all of it is relevant to an
informed decision about whether or not to recommend a particular
group.

It is possible that, increasingly, those conducting counselling groups
will be required to become more overtly accountable and to provide the
kinds of information that Table 9.1 checks. In the meantime, helpers are
advised to make as much personal contact with potentially suitable group
referral sources as they can.

Table 9.1 *Checklist for assessing counselling groups*

---

1. What is the theoretical orientation and/or purpose of the group?
2. What are the methods that may be employed during its life?
3. What is the pertinent training and experience of the facilitator or facilitators?
4. What are the size and criteria for membership of the group and is there a screening or
   selection process prior to entry?

Table 9.1 *(contd.)*

---

5. When is the group likely to start? How long is each session? Over what period will the group sessions continue? Where will the group be held?
6. What, if any, is the fee for the group and are there any additional expenses that may be incurred?
7. To what extent is there a clear understanding or contract concerning the amounts and kinds of responsibility that are to be assumed by the facilitator and by the group members?

STAGES IN GROUP COUNSELLING

Many writers on group counselling observe that groups go through stages. For instance, Mahler cites four stages: involvement, transition, working and ending.[3] The Coreys have six stages: pregroup, initial, transition, working, fixed, and postgroup.[4] Rogers lists fifteen 'process patterns' in 'roughly sequential order'.[5] Illustrative patterns from this list are: one, milling around; seven, development of a heading capacity in the group; and fourteen, the expression of positive feeling and closeness. In short, there are two main strands in the development of cohesive groups. First, the movement from *social distance* to *intimacy*. Second, the movement from *talking about problems* to *actively working on them*.

Though there are differing goals and emphasis among counselling groups, I propose four main stages in the life of a counselling group:
1. Preparatory stage.
2. Initial stage.
3. Working stage.
4. Ending stage.

Stage One: Preparatory Stage Skills

Thorough preparation for any group you facilitate is likely to increase its chances of success and decrease its chances of failure. Below are some of your choices in preparing a group.

- *Objectives.* 'What outcomes do I wish to achieve by facilitating a group?' You need to think through as rigorously as possible what outcomes you want from the group both for your clients and for yourself. For instance, group facilitators differ in the extent to which they emphasize changing feelings, thoughts or actions. Even within these areas, greater specificity is necessary to stipulate what aspects of feeling, thinking or action the group aims to change. For instance, a group focused on feelings might help members to tune into and experience feelings, own and express feelings, regulate feelings, become better at understanding and responding to others' feelings, and so on. Clearly your objectives will be tempered by your theoretical orientation, level of skill, confidence and by the expectations and constraints of any setting in which you work. Furthermore, an important choice can be how much leniency and responsibility you allow for clients to negotiate or decide upon the objectives of the group. In short, the answer you seek to provide to a direct question regarding your objectives is: 'If this group is to be regarded by me as successful, it will have the following outcomes: ————.'

● *Interventions.* 'What are the main interventions I am likely to use to achieve my objectives?' At its simplest this may be a decision to run either an experiential counselling group or a life skills training group. However, you need to go beyond this and think of the specific skills you are likely to use. Some of these skills are mentioned in this and the next chapter.

● *Evaluation.* 'How do I evaluate the processes and outcomes of the group?' It can be helpful to think through in advance how best to evaluate the progress of members at the start, during, at the end of, and as a follow-up to the group.

● *Number of facilitators.* 'Do I want to facilitate the group on my own or together with another person?' Co-facilitating with a more skilled and experienced person is an excellent way of learning group facilitation skills. Not only do you have a model to observe, but your anxieties about the task may also become less. Other reasons for having two facilitators include: it is more likely that each group member will relate well to at least one facilitator; two facilitators are likely to observe more and consequently give better feedback to members; the facilitators can review the progress of the group and provide feedback to each other; it allows for differences in helper characteristics, for example, gender; and it allows for differences in helper roles, for instance, one might be more nurturing while the other might be more task-oriented and confronting. Reasons for not having two facilitators include extra expenditure of resources and the possibility of conflict between them. However, conflict can be for good and ill. Rogers observes: 'I think it does an enormous amount of good for a group to find that the co-leaders are human and can differ openly and work out their differences right in front of the group.'[6]

● *Clientele.* 'What kinds of member do I wish to have in the group?'

Sometimes group facilitators run groups for a *homogeneous* clientele, for example, single people, women, married couples, people with public-speaking difficulties, alcoholics, gay people, etc. Other group facilitators aspire to form *heterogeneous* groups composed of a range of different personalities and presenting concerns and members of both sexes. The homogeneous versus heterogeneous distinction is imprecise since, for instance, even in a single-sex group there can be a range of different personal styles. Given the importance of cohesiveness, this is something that, up to a point, can be planned for in group selection. Some considerations here are: each group might have a few members who are reasonably outgoing and who can act as catalysts; probably there should not be too wide discrepancies in the members' level of psychological wellbeing; and compulsive monopolisers, extremely aggressive people and those likely to terminate early should be excluded.

- *Advertising.* 'How am I going to obtain members for the group and make its availability known?' Sometimes facilitators run groups made up entirely of people who either have been or are still undergoing individual helping with them. Letting colleagues know about your intention to form a group is another method of obtaining members. Once someone is established as a group facilitator, a number of clients may come either self-referred or referred by others. Sometimes facilitators advertise their groups by such means as posters, hand-outs and insertions in appropriate newspapers, newsletters and journals. There are ethical issues where such advertising is concerned, for example, not overselling.
- *Closed or open group.* 'Do I want the group, once under way, to be closed or am I prepared to admit new members during the life of the group?' *Closed* groups meet for a fixed time span, say six months or a year, and once started admit no new members. One of the stated reasons for this is that it allows members to develop a deep level of intimacy without the possible disrupting effect of new members. *Open* groups may meet for either a fixed or an unspecified length of time. Members may leave when they feel ready to and others may join if this is deemed appropriate by the facilitator, possibly in consultation with existing group members.
- *Group size.* 'How big do I want the group to be?' There is a conventional wisdom in group counselling that seven is an ideal size for an interactional group, with from five to ten members being an acceptable size. Reasons for not going below five members include the large gap caused by anyone leaving and the fact that a very small group may not provide the desired range of personalities and oppor-

tunities for different kinds of interaction. Large groups may get impersonal. Furthermore, they may inhibit shy members from participating at all. Also, large groups may split into subgroups. In some closed groups, the facilitator may start with ten members to allow a few people to drop out without causing serious disruption.

- *Duration of group and frequency and length of sessions.* 'Over what period of time do I want the group to meet, how often, and how long should each session be?' Counselling groups with a developmental emphasis tend to meet for a minimum of three months and often last for a year or longer. Many groups meet once a week. However, some facilitators prefer to run counselling groups on a twice-weekly basis so that the group does not lose momentum between sessions. Where the group has difficulty coming together, a facilitator might be prepared to hold the sessions bi-weekly or even monthly. For many counselling groups the length of each session is ninety minutes to two hours. Sessions of less than ninety minutes may not give enough time for all members to participate and for different themes to be developed. Sessions longer than two hours may be tiring for some participants and also difficult to spare time for on a regular basis. However, longer sessions (for example, of three hours' duration) might be held, especially if the group meets less frequently than once a week. Sometimes, either as part of a continuing group or as an event on its own, a 'marathon' group session will be held. This might entail six three-hour sessions spread over a couple of days, with breaks for eating and sleeping.
- *Location, physical setting and facilities.* 'Where is the group going to be held and is it a suitable location for attaining the group's objectives?' Facilitators who run interactional groups need to have access to suitable premises for those purposes, though in the real world compromises may have to be made. Ideally the room in which the group is held should have the following characteristics: quiet; privacy; pleasant decoration; reasonable size, neither too large nor too small; adequate heating (or cooling), lighting and ventilation; enough comfortable chairs so that the group may be seated in a circle; and guaranteed availability. Sometimes group members are formally seated round a table rather than in easy chairs and, on other occasions, they may be seated informally on cushions on the floor.
- *Contract.* 'What is the contract between the group members and me and how explicit do I intend to make it?' All groups operate within 'contracts' of varying degrees of explicitness. These contracts represent agreements about the behaviours that the group facilitator and group members may expect from each other. Some facilitators prefer

to make details of the contract explicit either beforehand or at the start of the group. Others are prepared to regard the development of a contract as the group proceeds as a valuable part of the group experience. Contracts can take many forms, from being largely unstated, to being verbal, to being written and unsigned, to being written and signed by all parties concerned. Some issues that might be covered in a contract include: size of group; admission of new members; minimum attendance; contact with the leader between group sessions; any limitations on extra-group socializing and confidentiality. Furthermore, certain contracts offer guidelines on desirable behaviours within a group, for example, honesty about oneself and not interrupting others.

Exercise 9.1   Planning a counselling group

This exercise may be done in a number of ways.

A   *On your own*
Write out a plan for a counselling group to be run in an agency or setting of relevance to you. Make sure that you have thought through each of the following points:
  1.   the objectives of the group;
  2.   the main interventions you are likely to use;
  3.   how you intend evaluating the processes and outcomes of the group;
  4.   the number of facilitators involved;
  5.   the clientele;
  6.   advertising the group; whether the group is closed or open;
  7.   the size of the group;
  8.   the duration of the group and the frequency and length of its sessions;
  9.   the location, physical setting and the facilities required; and
  10.   the nature of the contract.
B   *In pairs*
Either each partner writes out a plan for a counselling group covering the points in Part A, then partners come together for a sharing and discussion of their plans;
or together with a partner you write out a plan for a counselling group covering the points in Part A.
C   *In a training group*
The trainer may illustrate the planning of a group with case material drawn from the setting for which the group is being trained. Alternatively, the trainer and the group can together plan a counselling group. Another option is for the trainer to set either the individual or the pairs part of this exercise

and afterwards hold a plenary sharing and discussion session on planning counselling groups.

Intake interviewing

Intake interviews are individual interviews with prospective members prior to starting a group. Obviously, groups composed from a facilitator's own clients do not need such interviews, but intake interviews are desirable for most counselling groups. First, they allow both facilitator and client to get to know each other. This may reduce the likelihood of the client's leaving the group early. Joining a group can be a very threatening experience, especially for shy and socially awkward people. The importance of members feeling that they have a relationship with the facilitator should not be underestimated. Second, intake interviews enable facilitators to implement their criteria for group selection both by enrolling suitable members and by excluding the unsuitable. Third, intake interviews enable the facilitator to explain the objectives and methods of the group and to answer questions. Some facilitators go beyond this to suggest ways in which clients can prepare themselves for the group either by reading (for example, about the basic principles of the helping approach being used), or by listening to audiocassettes or watching videocassettes (for example, those illustrating desirable group-member behaviours in sending and receiving communications).

Exercise 9.2   Intake interviewing

This exercise can be done in pairs or in a training group.

A   *In pairs*
In Exercise 9.1, you planned a counselling group. Imagine that you advertised for members for the group and that your 'client' has come to you to ask about the feasibility of joining your group. Conduct an intake interview with your partner in which you:
1.   help your 'client' to express and explore his or her reasons for wanting to join your group;
2.   assess whether your client meets the criteria for inclusion;
3.   if so, explain to your client the objectives and methods of the group you

intend to run, as well as allowing ample time for answering any questions your 'client' may have; and

4. check with your 'client' whether he or she still wishes to join your group and is clear about its objectives and administrative arrangements. Afterwards, reverse roles.

B   *In a training group*
The trainer may illustrate points about intake interviewing for counselling groups with case material drawn from the setting for which the group is being trained. The trainer may also conduct a demonstration intake interview using a group member as a 'client'. Another option is for the trainer to demonstrate, by means of an audiocassette or videocassette, an intake interview with a real client. Yet another option is for the trainer to set the pairs parts of this exercise and afterwards hold a plenary sharing and discussion session on intake interviewing for counselling groups.

Stage Two: Initial Stage Skills

The initial stage lasts for the first session or early sessions. The seating for your group should be circular so that participants may easily see each other. Also, a circular seating pattern helps participants to talk to each other and not just to you. This communication pattern highlights a basic difference between individual and group work. In individual work, the helping interventions come from you. In group work, the helping interventions come not only from you but also from the other group members. Consequently, you facilitate the helping processes of the group.

Counselling groups differ in the extent to which they focus on specific member skills. Here my assumption is that the skills you as facilitator require in the initial stage are more person-oriented then directly task-oriented. They are the skills of creating an emotional climate conducive to the movement of members towards both working on problems and also engaging in direct and open communication. Let us look at some of the group facilitation skills you require.

Structuring

If you conducted intake interviews, you started then the process of structuring members' expectations about the group. However, when members get together for the first time you may want to make some opening remarks. You need to tailor your initial structuring to the goals of your group. Furthermore, since members are often very anxious at the first session, they may not listen to the detail of your opening remarks, but rather be sensitive to your emotional impact. Further structuring may take place throughout the life of a group both by specific statements intended for that purpose and also by your vocal and body language and by your responses to specific member statements.

The kinds of topic that may be covered in an initial structuring include the following:

- Calling the session to order.
- Introducing yourself.
- Welcoming the members.
- Communicating the time limits both of individual sessions and of the life of the group.
- Stating your purposes for the group.
- Clarifying your own role.
- Indicating members' roles.
- Encouraging members to participate.
- Giving an opening 'permission to talk'.

As in individual helping, it is not only what you say but how you say it that counts. A few guidelines here include: making eye contact with each member; talking direct to the members in 'you–me' language; showing commitment to the task and not being diffident; having your verbal and vocal communication clear; having relaxed and interested body language; and brevity. Below is an example of a possible initial structuring.

> Hello. I would like it if we could start now. As you know, I'm [state name]. Welcome to this first session of our group. Each session will last for two hours and we plan to meet weekly for four months. The group's stated purpose is to enable you to share and work on your concerns, especially with regard to how you relate. While I will help you do this, I believe as time goes by you will help each other both by taking risks and revealing more of yourselves and also by giving open and honest feedback. I wish to share with you responsibility for what goes on in our sessions. Also, I want you to talk with each other and not just to me. When somebody is ready, please start.

Encouraging participation and responsibility

When running groups, it is vital that you do not dominate the group, but facilitate interaction *among* group members and responsibility *by* group members. Knowing that you do not have to assume responsibility for everything, which is impossible anyway, may help you to feel more relaxed. This in turn will contribute to lowering the anxiety level in the group.

The following are skills you can use to encourage group member *participation*.

● *Initial structuring.*   You can include remarks that encourage members to talk to each other.
● *Encouraging cross-talk.*   You may encourage talk between members by asking a member who talks to you to talk to the group as a whole. The same message may be conveyed by an arm gesture.
● *Linking statements.*   You can find ways of relating what one member says to what others say.
● *Invitations to participate.*   You can give invitations to contribute either to the whole group: for example, 'Does anyone else have anything they would like to share about what Pete has been saying?'; or to specific members who may have trouble breaking the ice without encouragement: for example, 'Gail, I've been watching your expression as Pete has been talking, and wondering whether you would like to say anything.'
● *Supporting.*   You support members' participation where you consider it productive. Also, if necessary, you help them to cope with negative reactions from others.
● *Using rewards.*   There are many ways you may use rewards. You may verbally empathically respond to a group member. However, you have to weigh the pros and cons of responding verbally yourself or allowing other group members to speak. In virtually all instances, you can encourage members' participation by use of body language, such as eye contact and head nods, that shows that you are interested and care.
● *Fostering constructive group norms.*   Any group develops implicit and explicit rules or agreements about the behaviour appropriate for its members. As a facilitator, you can influence the development of helpful rather than harmful norms. For instance, you can encourage punctuality. Also, you can show sensitivity to those who are taking the risk of being open and honest, and acknowledge this to the group: for example, 'Kathy, I admire your courage in talking about that.' Furthermore, you can help the group air and deal with its concerns about confidentiality. In short, you help establish norms that are conducive to developing trust.

The following are skills that you can use to develop group member *responsibility* both for the group and for themselves.

● *Initial structuring.*   You can include remarks that encourage members to assume responsibility for the processes and outcomes of the group.

- *Establishing agendas.* You can share with members the responsibility for deciding what goes on in a session.
- *Encouraging self-referent talk.* You encourage members to own and talk about their thoughts, feelings and actions by means of 'I' statements. Also, you discourage intellectualization and generalization, if they go on at all long.
- *Encouraging direct 'here-and-now' communication.* You assist members in talking directly to each other openly and honestly.
- *Facilitating ownership of problems.* Even early on, but using judgement, you may encourage individual members to own rather than distance themselves from their problems and skills deficits.
- *Modelling personally responsible communication.* You use 'I' statements yourself and are direct and open with the group.

Empathic responding

Though you may choose to respond empathically to individual members, there are at least five ways in which empathic responding may be different in group and in individual work. First, you may wish to respond empathically to an interaction between two or more members. One way to do this is to clarify what each has said. Another way is to summarize themes in the interaction. Second, you may respond to the group as a whole. For example, you may reflect pleasure at having had a good session, frustration at lack of progress, and resistance to dealing directly with a theme that may be just below the surface. Third, you may respond to the unspoken needs of members who are not overtly participating and/or who may feel particularly vulnerable. Fourth, you may try, implicitly or explicitly, to release the healing capacity of the group and encourage members to respond empathically to each other. Fifth, you may identify empathic responding as a useful self-help skill and encourage members to use it not only inside but outside the group.

Further facilitation skills

All of the further facilitation skills you use in individual work are helpful in facilitating groups. I have already mentioned the importance of encouraging self-talk. Other further facilitation skills you can use in group work, often with modification, include the following. However, always remember that you need to weigh carefully whether to speak yourself or allow others to do so.

- *Helpful questioning.* As well as questions addressed to individuals, some of your questions may be addressed to the group. These include: 'Vickie has raised the issue of confidentiality. What does the group think?'; 'Does anyone have any further thoughts and feelings about what Joanne has just said?'; and 'It seems to me that Dino would like some feedback or help from the group. Is anyone willing to provide this?'.
- *Facilitative confronting.* When confronting individuals you need to be sensitive to the effect, for good or ill, that this may have on other group members. There may be times when you choose to confront the whole group: for instance, if you think they are focusing excessively on one member's concerns as a way of avoiding dealing with their own.
- *Self-disclosing.* An issue in group counselling is that of how much of a participant the facilitator chooses to be. You may both show involvement and also disclose experiences in ways that help or harm. The level of psychological wellbeing of group members is an important consideration in the degree to which and manner in which you disclose. Showing involvement seems desirable in most groups. However, disclosing experiences and working on personal issues can be more risky. Consequently, this requires more careful consideration of the advantages and disadvantages in each situation.
- *Summarizing.* In general when facilitating groups it is undesirable to provide lengthy summaries of what individuals have said. This smacks of doing individual work in a group setting and may block the group process. However, summaries can be very useful in picking up the main feelings, themes and emerging directions of the group. They may be made both during and also at the end of a group. Also, some group leaders summarize the previous session at the start of a subsequent one. At the end of a session it can be useful to obtain feedback on how members consider the session has gone.

There are special problems in training people in group work. It requires access to many clients. Trainees tend to get more nervous about group than individual work. Also, there is the difficulty that group counselling tends to be medium- to long-term rather than short-term, and so on. Because of these and other problems, often all the trainer can do is to offer a laboratory experience in group counselling. This is unsatisfactory, but much better than nothing.

Exercise 9.3 is designed to give you practice at facilitating the initial stage of a counselling group. A suggestion for trainers with large classes is that they break them into groups of six to eight trainees. These groups stay together for Exercises 9.3 to 9.7 so that trainees get the experience of the initial, working and ending stages of a counselling group. Some class time can still be devoted to presentations and discussion as a whole group. I have received positive feedback from trainees when teaching group facilitation skills this way.

Exercise 9.3 Facilitating the initial stage of a group

This exercise is best done in groups of six to eight.

The idea is that each trainee acts as facilitator for a session, with the others being group members. However, first the trainer models facilitating a group lasting thirty, forty-five or sixty minutes, depending on the time available. The skills to be used include the following:

1. structuring;
2. encouraging participation;
3. encouraging responsibility;
4. empathic responding; and
5. further facilitation skills (for example, where appropriate, questioning, confronting, disclosing and summarizing).

Each session is to consist of three distinct parts: (1) initial structuring; (2) the bulk of the time spent on facilitating discussion; and (3) time at the end for a summary by the facilitator and feedback from group members. After the demonstration session, each trainee facilitates the group for a session. At the end of each session there is a brief feedback period. The sessions may need to be spread over a number of weeks.

There are many variations of this exercise. They include: using smaller groups, say one facilitator and three members; using co-facilitators; and using the 'fishbowl' format, in which the inner ring are trainees seated in a circle who hold a group counselling session, and the outer group are observers who may be invited to provide feedback at the end of the session and who, on another occasion, act as the inner group.

Handling aggression

I mention the skill of handling aggression here because many beginning facilitators find this a potentially disturbing aspect of group work.

Counselling groups have the potential to be, and sometimes are, destructive. Aggression in groups tends to manifest itself in two main ways: aggression between members, and aggression directed towards the facilitator. Aggression between group members may be handled in a number of ways. First, it may be allowed to run its course without any intervention from you. Second, you may encourage group members to own their hostile feelings and to express them as 'I' messages, along the lines of 'I feel . . .', rather than as 'You' messages, along the lines of 'You are . . . (followed by a derogatory statement).' Third, you can endeavour to help group members to explore the feelings, thoughts and standards that underlie their anger. Fourth, you may support vulnerable group members until they are able to handle other people's aggression by themselves. This may include setting limits on another member's expression of anger. Protection of vulnerable individuals can demand a great deal of vigilance. I have already suggested that extremely hostile people might be excluded when forming a group. Fifth, in some instances, it may be appropriate to help members to identify the behaviours by which they may be setting themselves up as targets for attack.

Expressions of anger, especially when directed at you, can also be very threatening. It may help to co-facilitate a counselling group until you feel confident enough to facilitate one on your own. A number of the points about coping with inter-member aggression are pertinent to the ways you might choose to handle aggression directed at you: namely, not over-reacting to it, encouraging it to be expressed and responding to it by means of 'I' messages, and exploring the thoughts and feelings that underlie it. There is a need for you to be more assertive in group than in individual work. Eric Berne, the originator of Transactional Analysis, used to joke that a friend of his, Dr Horsley, could tell from the way psychiatrists answered the phone whether they did individual or group work! Aggression is one of the first *current* or here-and-now feelings that may be expressed in a group.

Stage Three: Working Stage Skills

The skills required in the working stage depend upon the objectives of the counselling group. I suggest that the working stage of most counselling groups centres on two main modes of interactive work:

- *Working in the 'here and now'* – developing the skills of intimacy.
- *Working in the 'there and now'* – developing the skills of managing problems.

I acknowledge that there is overlap between these two modes of work, and also, that some groups emphasize both modes rather than one or the other.

Comparisons with life skills training

The working stage of counselling groups overlaps with, but should not be confused with that of life skills training groups. The following are some of the differences. First, the greater length and more unstructured nature of counselling groups allows for more emphasis on accessing and working with feelings, anxieties and defensive processes. Second, a wider range of behaviour can be worked with than in a life skills training group. Third, in cohesive counselling groups the members participate more than in life skills training groups in showing involvement with, providing feedback for and helping each other. There is greater opportunity for intimacy to develop in counselling groups. Fourth, the role of the helper remains more facilitative in counselling than in life skills training groups. In life skills training groups, the helper tends to lead from the front and use *initiating* skills. In counselling groups, much of the work of the helper involves using the *responsive* skills of working with and helping members to work with the material generated in the group.

The transitional phase

Some groups fail to reach the working stage. Those that reach the working stage tend to have a transitional phase which straddles the ending of the initial stage and the beginning of the working stage. Even the most cohesive of groups is likely to move in fits and starts from one stage to the other. Coping with resistances and defences and fostering working norms are two important and highly interrelated skills relevant to both the transitional phase and the rest of the working stage.

● *Coping with resistances.* There are many manifestations of resistances and defences. One set revolves around fears and anxieties about a deeper involvement in the group experience. Some of these anxieties may be well established. Clients may need the healing process of the group over a period of time before they may be ready to acknowledge and work in sensitive areas. Other clients' resistances and defences may be much more accessible. They may reflect fears that include: being exposed, feeling rejected, being the subject of ridicule and aggression, being in conflict, showing vulnerabilities and strengths, receiving affection and approval, acknowledging needs for other people, being dependent, assuming independence, acknowledging past mistakes and damage to others, and owning responsibility for sustaining problems. Resistances and defences may be both individual and collective. The latter point can be illustrated in the joke about the family who went for family therapy.

Family:	Father thinks he is a chicken.
Family therapist:	Oh . . . I can easily cure that.
Family:	We don't want you to cure him. We need the eggs.

Where appropriate, the facilitator can work with resistances and defences by using skills such as empathy, facilitative confrontation, helpful questioning and encouraging disclosure and feedback from others.

● *Fostering working norms.*   In the initial stage you focus on developing norms appropriate to developing trust. In the transitional phase you build on this by fostering norms conducive to even more honest and open communication. This includes both rewarding and also helping members to value: deeper levels of disclosure, the dropping of defensive facades and manipulative tendencies, and the ownership of skills deficits in relation to problems. In short, fostering working norms entails encouraging group members to accept, work on and help each other to accept and work on the reality of themselves, each other, and the skills deficits sustaining their individual and collective problems.

Working in the 'here and now' – developing the skills of intimacy

Many join counselling groups because of difficulties in relating. For instance, some may be lonely and isolated and lack the confidence and skills to start and develop relationships. Others may lack the skills of sustaining and deepening relationships. Instead, they may act towards others in destructive ways that leave them feeling violated. Life skills training provides one approach to people wanting to acquire and improve their relationship skills. However, group counselling also has much to offer. Unlike life skills training, group counselling gives members the psychological space and time to start developing intimate relationships with each other. Facilitating open mutual feedback and providing knowledge and feedback regarding members' relationship and thinking skills are two important skills of the counselling group facilitator.

Facilitating open mutual feedback   Carkhuff developed the concept of the helper-offered skill that he labelled *immediacy*.[7] It involves the helper in responding immediately to his or her experience with the client. This is a form of self-involving disclosure that requires the helper to be aware of and share thoughts and feelings about what is going on in the here and now of the helping relationship. Ivey and his colleagues call this skill *direct mutual communication*.[8,9] They describe the skill as 'one in which two individuals attempt to focus on their interaction as they perceive and feel it, and attempt to share with each other their experience of the other'. Egan has translated this skill to everyday relationships and called it *you–me talk*.[10] He distinguishes between *relationship immediacy* – your ability to discuss where you stand in your overall relationship – and *here and now immediacy* – your ability to discuss what is happening in the here and now of any given transaction.[11] I prefer to use the term *open mutual feedback*. This can refer to feedback about either the overall relationship or any interaction in it, especially in the immediate present.

Open mutual feedback between group members is a complex skill containing a number of different components. These include empathy to your own thoughts and feelings, to the other person's thoughts and feelings, and to what may be important or left unsaid in either an interaction or a relationship. Additionally, members require sufficient involvement to share and discuss openly their thoughts and feelings about the interaction or relationship. This feedback is more likely to be effective if it: uses 'I' statements; is not dogmatic, but invites discussion; is as clear and specific as possible; and, though confronting, also signals a cooperative intention not only to receive feedback in turn but also to work on problems together.

As a group facilitator, you can encourage the skill of open mutual feedback in a number of ways.

- Clearly identifying it as a relationship skill important in the development of the group.
- Acknowledging and rewarding members who do 'level' with each other.
- Modelling the ability to give and receive open mutual feedback.
- Providing feedback to members on how they may block open mutual feedback. Below is an example.

> Geoff, Diana seems to be saying that every time she wishes to discuss your relationship, you change the subject and that this makes her feel shut out and resentful. I also think that you have a tendency to block discussing difficult topics, not only by changing the subject but also sometimes through the use of humour as a distancing device. You did that a moment ago.

Exercise 9.4   Facilitating open mutual feedback

This exercise may be done in triads or in training groups of six to eight.

A   *In triads*

Person A acts as group facilitator.

1.   Person A explains the concept of open mutual feedback to persons B and C.
2.   Person A encourages person B to use 'I' statements and tell person C his or her current thoughts and feelings about him or her and their relationship. Then person C has the opportunity to comment on this feedback. When this is finished, person A shares his or her thoughts and feelings about what has been left unsaid in the feedback. This sequence is repeated for person C's feedback to person B.
3.   Person A then facilitates person B and C in: (a) discussing their relationship using open mutual feedback; and (b) reviewing their skills, resources and deficits at giving and receiving open mutual feedback, both concerning specific interactions and also concerning overall relationships.

Afterwards persons B and C get turns acting as group facilitator.

B   *In a training group*

The trainer discusses the importance of open mutual feedback in the development of group cohesiveness. This includes not only feedback within pairs but within the group as a whole. He or she models the skill with a group member. The trainer then may get the group to do the triad exercise one or more times as a stepping stone to coming together as a whole group. In the whole group, the trainer facilitates open mutual feedback among group members. One variation of this is for members to take turns in the hot seat, getting feedback from the group and then being given the chance to react to it. Inasmuch as possible the trainer encourages here-and-now feedback, including expression of feelings as well as thoughts. The trainer also encourages the group members to give open mutual feedback as they explore their blocks and defences regarding giving and receiving feedback. After the trainer's modelling, members may get the opportunity to facilitate the group as it focuses on open mutual feedback.

Providing knowledge and feedback   As implied earlier, there is a tension both in life skills training and in group counselling between being a facilitator and a trainer. Some training input is appropriate in group counselling and some facilitation is desirable in life skills training. A major difference is that much of the training in group counselling is done *in response* to material manifested in the interactions in the group. Furthermore, training interventions in group counselling tend to be relatively brief. They frequently involve raising members' awareness concerning their behaviour, its impact on others, and its consequences for themselves. If necessary, the facilitator's interventions may provide basic knowledge by articulating specific relationship skills that group members need to become more aware of and use, either individually or collectively. Furthermore, some group members may require help in understanding that there is a repertoire of skills to be acquired and developed for use in their relationships.[12] It is not just a matter of 'doing what comes naturally'. Additionally, the assumption that group members are personally responsible for their feeling, thinking and action choices in their relationships should be implicit, and sometimes explicit, in all group leader interventions.

In my book, *Human Relationship Skills*, I propose some of the characteristics of close personal relationship.[13] Below I have listed those characteristics or skills areas that lend themselves to the provision of knowledge and feedback in group work.

- Assuming responsibility.
- Showing respect.
- Showing affection.
- Showing commitment.
- Showing caring.
- Being open and revealing.
- Giving and receiving feedback.
- Lack of defensiveness.
- Showing understanding.
- Constructive use of anger.
- Collaborative management of conflicts.

Often, other group members provide valuable feedback on the way a member 'comes across' to them. Sometimes facilitators may choose to reflect such feedback as a way of emphasizing its importance. On other occasions, facilitators may themselves provide feedback concerning relationship skills, though they must be careful not to dominate the group. Some illustrative facilitator statements include the following:

> Jane, at first when you started crying in these sessions you seemed to gain sympathy from the group. Now I detect a fair amount of impatience when you cry, as though you may often seek sympathy rather than deal directly with your problems in relating.

> Betty, I think that you have the habit of disguising your own thoughts and feelings by asking questions of other people. You've just done this with

Bill. Do you consider that's a valid point? If so, please remember our guidelines about making 'I' statements.

Keith, I felt that you were recounting a very painful experience and yet every so often you smiled. The effect that this seemed to have was to make it very difficult for the group to experience how vulnerable you felt.

Facilitators can also provide knowledge and feedback in the area of thinking skills. Some of these thinking skills were reviewed in Chapter 7. They include: attributing responsibility accurately; using coping rather than task-irrelevant and anxiety-engendering inner speech; anticipating the future accurately; discarding unrealistic inner rules; and developing different perceptions. An illustrative group leader statement in the area of thinking skills is as follows:

Nick, I sense that you are thinking: 'If the group really gets to know me they will think I am a pretty rotten person.' If that is correct, let's look at the evidence for assuming the group might think that.

Much of the value of group counselling is derived from the opportunity it provides for members to test and discard distorted perceptions about themselves, others and the environment. In all sorts of ways group members' negative and positive self-conceptions are likely to be challenged and often changed. On the surface, group counselling may seem to emphasize relationship rather than thinking skills. However, underneath it is frequently changes in thinking skills that allow for the development of intimacy.

Exercise 9.5   Focusing on members' relationship and thinking skills

This exercise can be done in triads or in larger groups of six to eight.

A   *Without a trainer*
This part of the exercise requires three people, though it may be done with up to eight. You act as facilitator while your 'group members' interact with each other about either their helping skills or the way they relate. Do *not* intervene after each statement. However, at appropriate moments:
1.   reflect comments, if any, from other group members about another member's manner of relating and/or thinking;
2.   give constructive feedback, using 'I' statements, to one or more members concerning their relationship and/or thinking skills; and
3.   give the recipients of your feedback the opportunity to react to it and explore its implications, possibly with the help of the other 'group members'.

Afterwards, if feasible, each of your 'group members' should have the opportunity to be the facilitator for this exercise. If the training group consists of more than six, using two facilitators at a time might be considered.

B *In a training group*
The trainer may discuss interventions for providing knowledge and feedback concerning group members' relationship and thinking skills. The trainer may provide some audio-recorded or video-recorded illustrations of such interventions, preferably drawn from the setting for which the group is being trained. Where possible the trainer should discuss the choices involved in formulating and sending knowledge and feedback messages. Then the trainer may ask the group to do the exercise in Part A above, prior to coming together for a plenary sharing and discussion session.

Working in the 'there and now' -- developing the skills of managing problems

In a life skills training programme focused on the skills of managing problems, such skills are specifically taught. In group counselling, members bring into the group problems from their outside lives. There is no easy dividing line between emphasizing here-and-now interaction and allowing members to discuss their outside problems. Problems members bring into the group from outside *may* be a stimulus for here-and-now interaction which in turn may trigger off exploration of problems outside. However, both the facilitator and the group may either have or develop an idea of what they want the balance to be between focusing on inter-member relating and managing outside problems.

When members bring in their outside problems for discussion in the group, this is a form of sharing with the whole group and not just with the facilitator. The topic of managing problems has already been discussed in Chapters 5 and 7. Here I focus on skills of facilitating this kind of group work. Again, I stress that the helper's role, unlike that in life skills training, is more *responsive* to material generated by the group than initiating. Furthermore, much of the time the facilitator does not help individual members manage their problems, doing individual work in front of the group. Instead, the facilitator helps group members develop the skills of helping each other. Below are a few of the skills a facilitator might use.

●   *Facilitating group member empathy.* Intervening in ways that encourage members to be sensitive to and accurately listen to wha another member thinks and feels as they bring a problem into the group. Identifying and encouraging the skill of not just understanding but *showing* understanding and caring.

● *Facilitating group members in operationalizing each other's and their own problems.* Helping members acknowledge and help each other acknowledge the importance of assuming responsibility for their role in sustaining problems. Helping members break down and help each other break down problems in such a way that any skills deficits sustaining the problems are clearly identified.

● *Facilitating members to set goals and help each other to set goals and to develop action plans.* Helping members understand the importance of translating insight into action. While keeping personal responsibility for outside actions clearly with individuals, encouraging members to discuss in the group their goals and plans to achieve them. Helping members assess the impact of their actions on others and the likely consequences of this for them.

● *Encouraging the formation of productive norms and behaviours.* Facilitators need to influence the development of norms that help members manage problems. Pressures for conformity, dependency on group decisions, and intellectualizing about rather than working on problems are all norms to be discouraged. Avoiding destructive norms can mainly be achieved by encouraging the formation of constructive ones.

● *Linking.* Finding ways of helping members see relevant connections between others' problems and their own. Helping members more fully acknowledge that having problems is part of living. Also, that they can develop the skills of managing problems not only by working on their own but also by observing and helping each other work on their problems.

The purpose of Exercise 9.6 is to raise your awareness that much of the work of the group leader is that of facilitating members in doing work for each other. These member skills develop over time in a cohesive group.

Exercise 9.6   Facilitating group members to help each other manage their problems

This exercise is best done in groups of six to eight. The trainer leads a demonstration group of about an hour's length. Members are asked to share problems that they and the group might work on. The trainer and the group negotiate which person starts with his or her problem as the group's focus. The trainer then facilitates both this member and the group collaborating to work together on managing the problem. The trainer, where appropriate, facilitates the group's empathy, operationalizing of problems, goal setting and action planning skills. Furthermore, the trainer encourages constructive norms and uses linking skills. The group may move on to working with another member's problems.

Though it means holding further groups, ideally each trainee should have a turn both as facilitator and also as the member whose problem is subject to a collaborative problem management approach. The trainer may engage in identifying skills, coaching and feedback, and inviting further discussion as deemed appropriate.

Stage Four: Ending Stage Skills

The group facilitator uses ending skills in the following ways: with individual members who terminate during the life of a group; in the lead up to the group's final session; in the group's final session; and in follow-up contact with individuals and possibly the group as a whole. Though this section is not about individuals who terminate *during* a group, where possible these decisions should be discussed and prepared for over a series of sessions rather than be implemented abruptly.

There is no easy dividing line between the working and ending stages. The ending stage may be viewed as providing a form of closure to the working stage. For instance, the working stage has probably focused on the development of here-and-now intimacy between members. The fact that some of these relationships are about to end needs to be prepared for and dealt with. Also, members may have been working with the help of the group on managing their problems. They now need to prepare to manage their problems without the help of the group.

Tasks and skills of the group facilitator during the ending stage include helping members to do the following:

- Experience and express their feelings and thoughts concerning parting.
- Articulate and consolidate self-help skills for dealing with their relationships and problems after the group. Changes perceived as deriving from members' *choices* are more likely to persist.[14]
- Plan for any actions that need to be taken after the group for members either to make changes in their own lives or to seek further help.

- Review the progress of the group and understand the learnings to be derived from this.
- Provide feedback to the facilitator on the strengths and weaknesses of the way the group has been led. Members can be asked to write their comments on index cards so that they may be reviewed later.
- Understand the thoughts and feelings of the leader, where appropriate, about the group, its members and any follow-up evaluation and contact.

For facilitators, and sometimes group members, the ending stage of the group often extends beyond the final session. Facilitators may perform the following tasks *after* the final session.

- *Exit interviewing.*   Exit interviews are for individual group members who think they require them or whom you think require them. Such interviews can focus on matters like consolidating self-help skills, further developing action plans, supporting still vulnerable members and identifying resources for further individual and group work.
- *Holding follow-up sessions.*   In conjunction with group members, the facilitator may arrange one or more follow-up sessions, say three and/or six months after the end of the group. Follow-up sessions may motivate members to work harder on maintaining and developing their skills in the period intervening, after the final session.
- *Evaluating the group's effectiveness.*   Systematic evaluation of the group's effectiveness ideally requires planning in advance of the group. Even if baseline data have not been collected, there is still merit in collecting and analysing final session and follow-up data regarding both the processes and outcomes of the group.

Exercise 9.7   Ending a group

This exercise may be done in pairs or in a training group.

A   *In pairs*
Partner A and partner B discuss what are the important issues for facilitators to bear in mind during the ending stage of a group. Then partner A, acting as facilitator, role-plays an exit interview after a counselling group with partner B, acting as a member of the recently finished group. The following are topics that may be covered in such an exit interview:
1.   feedback about the group;
2.   consolidation of self-help skills;

3. development of further action plans;
4. identification of resources for further individual and group work; and
5. dealing with residual feelings, such as vulnerability or sadness.
   Afterwards, reverse roles.

B   *In a training group*
   *Either*the trainer leads a discussion concerning the tasks and skills required in the ending stage of a group. The group then breaks up into pairs or triads to do the Part A exercise above. This is followed by a plenary sharing and discussion session;
   or, if the group has done Exercises 9.3 to 9.6 together, the trainer facilitates the ending session or sessions of the group, dealing with ending stage issues as appropriate. This session or sessions could be video-recorded and played back to the group for discussion of facilitator ending stage skills. Even without the video-recording, a final discussion is desirable.

FACILITATING SELF-HELP

Throughout this chapter I have tried to emphasize that counselling groups are not just ends in themselves. Instead their aim is, like that of individual helping and life skills training, to provide clients with the knowledge and skills to be able to help themselves.

At the end of Chapter 6, I mentioned co-counselling, the development of support networks and peer self-help groups as ways in which individuals can work in the area of feelings. Co-counselling, developing support networks and peer self-help groups are all group approaches with a wide range of applications. Where appropriate, group facilitators can bring these ways of working to the attention of group members, either collectively and/or individually.

Support networks   Without wishing to denigrate the value of co-counselling and peer self-help groups, there is an even more widespread need for people to be effective in developing their own support networks.[15,16] Murgatroyd rightly observes: 'When a person seeks help from a stranger it is often a sign that their own helping networks are inadequate. It may be that the person is disconnected from their own networks – family, friends or relatives – or that they have never been connected to such a network. It may be that they are connected to this network, but its resources are inadequate given the problem the person is experiencing.'[17] In reality, an individual's network comprises participation in many different networks: family, friends, work colleagues, clubs, church, etc., as well as access to voluntary or professional helpers.

Either in a counselling group or in individual helping, you can explore with clients: whether they understand what a support network is and why it is important; the realistic characteristics of their existing support network; whether and in what ways they can use their existing network to better effect than they have up until now; and, if appropriate, ways of expanding and developing their support network for the future. Furthermore, if necessary, clients should be helped to understand the notion of reciprocity in support networks: namely, that they involve *giving* as well as *receiving* support.

10 Life Skills Training

Peter Ustinov tells the story of how, towards the end of a White House reception for Prince Charles, he went up to President Reagan and tried to make small talk.

Peter Ustinov: You may remember, sir, that forty years ago we had dinner together in a French restaurant in London called Les Ambassadeurs.

President Reagan: (after a pause) What ambassador?

Training politicians in the life skill of accurate listening — that's a thought, if not an uphill struggle.

Life skills training is a growing area. You may train clients in life skills as part of either individual helping or group counselling. However, life skills training most often implies running structured groups of limited duration to train participants in one or more specific skills. Sometimes terms like 'personal and social education', psychological education' and 'social skills training' are used instead of 'life skills training'.

The reasons for the growth of life skills training include the following.

- *It has a developmental emphasis.* The target of life skills training in an ideal world would be to train everyone in the skills required to meet each task at every stage of their life span. Such training has a developmental rather than a remedial or rehabilitation emphasis.
- *It has a preventive emphasis.* Developmental life skills training also has a preventive emphasis. For instance, Daws, writing of the need for preventive work in British schools, argues that the strongest expression of the preventive principle is work devoted to the personal

and social education of *all* pupils in such a way that it anticipates their developmental needs.[1]

- *Problems of living are widespread.* The world is full of the walking wounded. The statistics on marital breakdown provide one indication of this. In Britain, approximately one in three marriages ends in divorce with the vast majority of children involved being under sixteen.[2] In Australia, the overall divorce rate is probably 30–35 per cent.[3] In the US, nearly half of all marriages end in divorce and, by the time they are eighteen years old, one out of every two children experience an upbringing in a single-parent household.[4] Also, throughout the world many people are underfunctioning in most of the other developmental tasks.

- *Pressures are increasing for helper accountability.* Some helpers argue that their cost-effectiveness is much greater if they actively engage in developmental and preventive interventions, like life skills training, rather than passively wait in their offices for clients needing remedial help. They seek ways to make an impact on as many people as possible.

- *The influence of cognitive-behaviourism has increased.* The theoretical foundation for much of life skills training rests on the behavioural (actions-focused) revolution in helping of the 1960s and the subsequent cognitive (thinking-focused) revolution of the 1970s. Behavioural and cognitive approaches have come together in a hybrid called cognitive-behaviourism. Now most life skills training programmes focus on both thinking and action skills.

WHAT ARE LIFE SKILLS?

In Chapter 1, I mentioned that the essential element of a skill is the ability to make and implement an effective sequence of choices so as to achieve a desired objective. Furthermore, the concept of skill is best viewed not as an either/or matter. Rather, it is preferable to think of people possessing skills *resources* and *deficits* or a mixture of the two in each skills area. The object of this book is to help you shift the balance of your helping skills resources and deficits more in the direction of resources. Likewise, the object of life skills training is to help people increase the probability of making good rather than poor choices in the targeted skills.

As indicated, one way of viewing life skills is to relate them to developmental tasks throughout the life span. Lists of developmental tasks (focused on North American culture) have been provided by writers such as Havighurst, Blocher, and Egan and Cowan.[5,6,7] Havighurst considers that tasks based mostly on biological maturation, such as learning to walk, show least cultural variation, whereas those growing out of social demands show most variation.

Another way of viewing life skills, albeit interrelated with developmental tasks, is as the skills of effective living, psychological health or high-level human functioning. Put another way, if you are to assume effective responsibility for your life choices, what are the areas in which you require skills? Elsewhere, I have suggested that you require life skills in four broad areas, the four Rs: *responsiveness*, in experiencing feelings; *realism*, in thinking, language and inner speech; *relatedness*, in self-definition and communication; and *rewarding activity*, in finding meaning in occupation.[8]

In Exercise 10.1, I list life skills in seven broad areas: feeling, thinking, relationships, study, work/handling unemployment, leisure and health. Rather than just list the skills, Exercise 10.1 asks you to rate yourself on them. The idea is to make it more interesting for you by encouraging you both to look at your own life skills and also to identify skills in which you might train others. The listing of life skills in Exercise 10.1 is far from exhaustive.

Exercise 10.1 Assessing your life skills

This exercise may be done in a number of ways.

A   *On your own*
   The questionnaire that follows lists a number of life skills in seven broad areas. Rate how satisfied you are with your skills in those of the seven areas that are relevant to you by using the rating scale below:
   3   *much* need for improvement
   2   *moderate* need for improvement
   1   *slight* need for improvement
   0   *no* need for improvement
   Put a question mark (?) rather than a rating by any skill whose meaning is not clear to you. If a skills area is not relevant to you, (for example, study) you may choose not to respond in that area.

   Your rating   *Skills*

   _____   *1. Feeling*
   _____   Acknowledging the importance of your feelings
   _____   Awareness of and openness to your feelings
   _____   Awareness of your wants and wishes
   _____   Inner empathy/ability to 'tune in to' and explore feelings

_____ Awareness of your body sensations
_____ Capacity to experience your sensuality
_____ Capacity for spontaneity
_____ Ability to express feelings appropriately
_____ Ability to understand and regulate negative feelings
_____ Full awareness of the parameters of existence: for example, death, suffering, fate

2. Thinking

_____ Having a realistic conceptual framework
_____ Assuming personal responsibility for the choices that 'make' your life
_____ Attributing responsibility accurately
_____ Using coping inner speech
_____ Ability to develop different perceptions
_____ Accurately anticipating risk and gain
_____ Possessing realistic inner rules
_____ Absence of defensive thinking
_____ Accurate evaluation of personal characteristics
_____ Decision-making skills
_____ Managing-problems skills

3. Relationships

_____ Ability to own your thoughts, feelings and actions in relationships
_____ Talking about yourself verbally
_____ Having good vocal skills
_____ Using body language well
_____ Starting relationships
_____ Developing relationships
_____ Defining and asserting yourself
_____ Good listening
_____ Helpful responding
_____ Managing anger
_____ Managing conflict
_____ Skills for specific roles: for example, parenting, community participation, work, leisure (please stipulate role and skills)

4. Study

_____ Making educational choices wisely
_____ Goal setting and planning
_____ Managing time effectively
_____ Ability to meet deadlines
_____ Effective reading
_____ Writing skills
_____ Coping with achievement/examination anxiety

_____ Coping with maths/statistics anxiety
_____ Ability to be creative
_____ Ability to think critically
_____ Participating in groups
_____ Speaking in public

5. *Working/handling unemployment*
_____ Accurately identifying your interests
_____ Realistically appraising your abilities and skills
_____ Awareness of opportunities
_____ Information gathering skills
_____ Decision-making skills
_____ Written self-presentation skills
_____ Interview skills
_____ Skills for realistically appraising negative feedback
_____ Preparing for and handling transition skills
_____ Ability to develop/make the most of your work setting
_____ Business/money related skills
_____ Skills for specific roles: for example, managing, supervising
                (please stipulate role and skills) _____

6. *Leisure*
_____ Ability to value leisure time highly
_____ Awareness of personally rewarding interests and
                activities
_____ Awareness of opportunities to engage in rewarding activi-
                ties
_____ Information gathering skills
_____ Decision-making skills
_____ Ability to participate actively in rewarding activities
_____ Ability for passive relaxation
_____ Having adequate and enjoyable holidays

7. *Health*
_____ Assuming responsibility for your health
_____ Eating nutritionally and in moderation
_____ Adequate control of alcohol consumption
_____ Avoidance of smoking
_____ Avoidance of addictive drugs
_____ Keeping physically fit
_____ Managing stress well
_____ Observing a good balance between work, relationship,
                family and recreational activities

Conclude the exercise by writing out a summary statement, as specifically
as possible, of the areas in which you consider you could:
1.   develop your own life skills; and
2.   train others in life skills.

B   *In pairs*
   Either independently complete the questionnaire, then discuss your
   answers with your partner. Also, identify life skills in which you might train
   others;
   or go through the questionnaire discussing your answers together. Also,
   identify life skills in which each of you might train others.
C   *In a training group*
   The trainer introduces the topic of life skills and encourages members to
   assess and explore their current level of skills. The trainer gets group
   members to write out their self-assessments as singles or pairs (possibly as
   homework), prior to conducting a plenary sharing and discussion session.
   Part of this discussion is focused on identifying skills in which group
   members might train others.

Attitude, Knowledge and Skills

It can be helpful to think of specific life skills as comprising three
dimensions: attitude, knowledge and skill.

- *Attitude.*   An appropriate attitude to any life skill is that you assume
  personal responsibility for acquiring, maintaining, using and developing it. You may lose some or all of a life skill if you fail to work at using
  and developing it. A personally responsible attitude is the motiv-
  ational or 'wanting to do it' dimension of a life skill.
- *Knowledge.*   Any life skill involves knowledge concerning what are
  the correct choices to make. People who have been exposed to good
  models may possess the requisite knowledge implicitly rather than
  explicitly. Though they may not be able to articulate them, they know
  the correct choices to make, for example in being a good listener.
  People with deficits in skills areas are likely to require the relevant
  knowledge clearly articulated or 'spelled out'. This then can guide
  their actions. This is the 'knowing how to do it' dimension of a life
  skill.
- *Skill.*   The skill dimension entails the application of attitude and
  knowledge to practice. In appropriate circumstances, you translate
  your 'wanting to do it' and 'knowing how to do it' into 'actually doing
  it'.

STAGES IN LIFE SKILLS TRAINING GROUPS

It is possible to think of life skills training groups as having the same four stages as counselling groups: preparatory, initial, working and ending. Many of the facilitator skills for group counselling are similar to, if not the same as, the trainer skills for life skills training. In this chapter, I focus on skills that are more specifically relevant for life skills trainers.

Stage One: Preparatory Stage Skills

Later in the chapter, I cover designing a life skills programme. This is an important skill for the preparatory stage. Here I mention some other preparatory considerations that differ for life skills training and group counselling. However, all the preparatory considerations for counselling groups are also pertinent for life skills training groups.

● *Number of trainers.* You may conduct life skills training groups on your own or with others. Co-training may mean that a larger group is viable. There can be whole group presentations followed by sub-groups for skills acquisition and development. Sometimes these subgroups could be led by trainer aides. Additionally, there is opportunity for a team teaching approach that best utilizes some of the different strengths of individual trainers. Needless to say, all the trainers involved would share in the preparation of a life skills training group.

● *Clientele.* The clientele for life skills training groups differs from that for counselling groups in two main ways. First, by definition they are homogeneous groups composed of people who are together to acquire specific skills or clusters of skills. Second, people frequently select themselves for membership, unlike that of counselling groups, by responding to advertising. Additionally, sometimes people may be assigned to attend life skills training groups as part of either their jobs (for example managers) or their custodial condition (for example, juvenile delinquents).[9]

● *Group size.* Life skills training is best conducted in relatively small groups, say six to eight.[10] This allows the trainer to focus on the skills of individual members. Where there are two trainers or one or more trainer aides, the overall size of the group can be considerably larger. Nevertheless, for 'how-to-do-it' skills to be acquired, the overall group will still require breaking down into smaller groups each with their own trainer.

● *Duration of group and frequency and length of sessions.* Life skills training often takes place in fixed length groups lasting six to ten sessions. The length of individual sessions varies greatly. For instance in a school setting, it may be one or two forty-minute sessions per week. With adults, weekly sessions of from ninety minutes to three hours each are more likely. Sometimes five or six sessions are offered as a weekend workshop. A disadvantage of such workshops is that participants are not able to do between-sessions homework in which they practise and integrate their new skills into their daily lives.

● *Location, physical setting and facilities.*   Life skills training groups may be held in outreach settings, for instance, classrooms.[11] There may be little choice over physical setting and facilities. Where possible, try to get a room which is large enough to allow the group to subdivide into pairs, threes and so on without interfering with each other. Alternatively, have a room in which the whole group meets, and smaller rooms for subgroups. Space needs to allow for flexibility. Trainers should endeavour to have access to suitable training material, such as manuals, and audiovisual aids, such as a training whiteboard and facilities for audio- or, preferably, video-recording and playback.

Stage Two: Initial Stage Skills

All of the skills of facilitating the initial stage of a counselling group are relevant to the initial session of a life skills training group. These include: structuring, encouraging participation, encouraging responsibility, empathic responding, and further facilitation skills such as questioning, confronting, disclosing and summarizing.

However, you are a *trainer* rather than a *facilitator*. Consequently, you may also choose to use structured group skills like: breaking the ice exercises, collecting baseline data and encouraging self-assessment, presenting your programme and setting homework. I deal with giving presentations and setting homework in the section on working stage skills. Here I discuss both breaking the ice exercises and also collecting baseline data and encouraging self-assessment.

Life skills trainers often use 'getting acquainted' exercises to start their programme and sometimes to start each session. Their purpose is to loosen people up, break down barriers, and energize them for active participation in the group. The following are some options for starting a group. You may use more than one method.

● Seated in a circle, trainees introduce themselves. Either then or in a second go around they share their expectations and fears concerning the training programme.

● Trainees pair off, get to know their partners, and introduce their partners to the whole group.

● Every couple of minutes the group reforms into different pairs as trainees walk around and meet as though at a cocktail party. Each time trainees shake hands on meeting. They can either be given a choice as to what they reveal or be directed to reveal something about themselves in a relatively safe 'getting acquainted' area.

● Each trainee is given a card and asked to print what they like to be called in the top left-hand corner. In the top right-hand corner, they list three pieces of information about themselves (for example, age, marital status, birthplace). In the bottom left-hand corner they list three adjectives that describe them as a person (for example, likeable, sporty, disorganized). In the bottom right-hand corner they list three of their main recreational activities (for example, dancing, tennis, gardening). The trainer also fills out a card. Participants are asked to pin their cards to the front of their clothes. They then go round holding conversations in pairs about their cards as if getting acquainted at a party.

Exercise 10.2   Breaking the ice

This exercise may be done in a number of ways.

A   *On your own*
Write out your answers to the following questions.
1.   What are the main considerations to take into account when getting people acquainted in the initial session of a life skills training group?
2.   What are some of the most effective ways to encourage breaking the ice in the group's initial session?

B   *In pairs*
Either do the above exercise independently, then discuss;
or do the above exercise together from the start.

C   *In a training group*
The trainer introduces the topic of breaking the ice in a life skills training group. The group discusses considerations and ways of going about this. Then the trainer gets the group to participate in simulations of a number of different approaches so that they can experience the impact of each. Either each simulation is followed by a discussion or there is a plenary sharing and discussion session at the end of all the simulations.

Collecting baseline data and encouraging self-assessment

There are a number of reasons why, in initial life skills training sessions, assessment can play an important part. First, it involves collecting data that form the basis for later comparisons to see whether the targeted goals, both for individuals and the group, are being attained. Second, it encourages trainees to assess and monitor their behaviours in the skills area. This helps them develop an attitude of personal responsibility for acquiring and using the skills. Third, assessment tends to break the skills down into some of their component parts so trainees acquire knowledge about what is involved in the skills. Fourth, initial assessment may provide you, as a trainer, with insights into the skills resources and deficits of both the group as a whole and of the individuals in it. This feedback assists in designing and reformulating the training programme. Fifth, assessment can be handled in initial sessions in such a way as to encourage group participation.

There are a number of ways in which you may collect baseline data and encourage self-assessment. Needless to say, these should both closely reflect the goals of your programme and also be valid ways of measuring them. For instance, a life skills programme aimed at reducing smoking requires different measures from a programme for reducing shyness and increasing friendship behaviours. Assessment measures include the following:

- *Questionnaires.* These may be existing self-report questionnaires or ones that you have tailored to measure the targeted goals.
- *Critical incidents.* You might ask trainees to describe a given number of critical incidents illustrating their present resources and deficits in a skills area.
- *Self-observation.* As mentioned in Chapter 8, self-observation usually involves collecting quantitative data on observable behaviour by means such as charts, tally sheets, wrist counters and pocket counters. However, client self-observation may also involve charting feelings and thoughts as well as observable behaviours.
- *Ratings by others.* Ratings by others may be useful not just for measuring behaviour within a life skills training group but also for measuring behaviour outside the group. For instance, in a making friends training group in a school setting, ratings might be provided by peers, teachers and even parents and family members.
- *Trainer ratings.* As a trainer, you may devise rating scales to be filled in by yourself regarding members' behaviour in the group's target area. You may either observe behaviour or actively collect data

by means of questions, confrontations and role plays.

● *Using role plays.* Valuable observations and self-observations may be gained from role plays. For instance, in a managing conflict training group, couples might be video-recorded as they demonstrate their usual ways of trying to resolve a conflict in their relationship. The playback might be assessed by the trainer, by the couple and by the other group members. Use of role plays is likely to be time-consuming since it focuses on only one or two trainees at a time. Nevertheless, as mentioned earlier, role plays have the value of highlighting vocal and body as well as verbal messages. In relationship skills, *how* you communicate is frequently much more important than *what* you communicate.[12,13]

Some of the initial assessment work can be carried out as homework. For instance, trainees could be asked to complete a questionnaire and chart their behaviour either before they come to the initial session or between the first and second sessions.

A final point is that in life skills training there may be value in obtaining feedback at the end of each session. This might focus on how trainees react to the session just ending. Also, trainees can assess their progress in the targeted skill and their involvement in the group. Feedback may be gathered either verbally or, more systematically, by handing out and collecting feedback cards.

Exercise 10.3 Collecting baseline data and encouraging self-assessment

This exercise may be done in a number of ways.

A   *On your own*
Think of conducting a life skills training programme focused on a skill of your choice. Write out how you might collect baseline data and encourage self-assessment in the initial session or sessions.

B   *In pairs*
Either do the above exercise independently, then discuss;
or do the above exercise together from the start.

C   *In a training group*
The trainer runs a demonstration initial session of a life skills training group in which he or she collects baseline data and encourages self-assessment. The trainees then perform either of the exercises in Parts A and B, prior to coming together for a plenary sharing and discussion session.

Introducing the notion of skills

As a life skills trainer, you cannot assume a shared starting point: namely, that people think in terms of skills when approaching various areas of their personal lives. For instance, three-quarters of a group of sixteen-to-seventeen-year-old Australian boys attending a private school answered 'no' to the question: 'Have you ever before been encouraged to look at the way you relate to others as involving a set or repertoire of skills?' [14] This was a predominantly middle-class group. In a lower-class group, the proportion answering 'no' is likely to be even higher. Consequently, especially with trainees who are not volunteers, you may need to co-orient the group to the approach taken in your training programme. This may be in the face of resistance.

One way of co-orienting your group is to help them clarify and articulate their personal goals for the programme. Once this is done, they can be encouraged to look at the skills required for attaining these goals. In my life skills training groups, I make it clear that I regard skills as sequences of choices, and also that people can have both deficits and resources in any skills area. The overall goal of the programme is to increase trainees' resources relative to their deficits in the skills area or areas in question. A related goal is to help them acquire the requisite knowledge and inner speech to guide their behaviour after the programme ends. The idea that life skills are self-help skills, rather than trainer-offered skills, is emphasized from the start and throughout the groups.

Stage Three: Working Stage Skills

Though you also use group *facilitator* skills, here I focus on some of the *trainer* skills you require in the working stage. I prefer the term 'training' to 'teaching' since it has more of a connotation of imparting applied skills. Nevertheless, there is considerable overlap between training and teaching skills.

Presentation skills

At many stages of a life skills training programme, you will be required to make presentations. For instance, in the initial session you probably would outline the proposed programme. In subsequent sessions, you are likely to give a presentation in regard to each skill or subskill you introduce. Below are some considerations in making presentations.[15]

- *Have manageable goals.* Beginning life skills trainers often try to cover too much ground in their presentations. As a consequence, the presentations become too diffuse.
- *Communicate your goals clearly.* Be specific as to what you expect trainees to achieve by the end of a session.
- *Break the task down and clearly identify each step.* Clear identification of steps is important. You are not only trying to teach trainees the skill now, but to help them acquire the language and inner speech to guide their behaviour once the programme has ended.
- *Be prepared to intersperse presentation with rehearsal and practice.* For instance, if your goal is to teach reflection of content you might: (1) state your goal, including clearly defining what you mean by reflection of content; (2) give a presentation on the *receiver* skills of reflection of content; (3) rehearse and practise trainees in the *receiver* skills; (4) give a presentation on the *sender* skills of reflection of content; and (5) rehearse and practise trainees in these *sender* skills.
- *Have a high 'doing to talking' ratio.* It is easy to talk too much as a life skills trainer. Though good presentations are important, much of your skill as a trainer lies in providing practical learning experiences that allow for coaching, feedback and self-observation.
- *Use public speaking skills.* These skills are verbal, vocal and bodily. Verbal skills include: well-structured presentation, clarity, use of simple language and humour. Vocal skills include: communicating enthusiasm in your voice, good pacing, audibility and appropriate variations in intonation. Body skills include: maintaining good eye contact and avoiding distracting arm gestures.
- *Use modelling.* Always see if you can build modelling into your presentations. Modelling, or 'a picture is worth a thousand words', is critically important in skills training. For further information you are referred back to the discussion in modelling in Chapter 8.
- *Use audiovisual aids.* Audiovisual aids such as videocassettes and films are helpful when demonstrating a skill. However, even when imparting knowledge and information, endeavour to use visual as well as verbal presentation. I regard a training whiteboard and felt tip pen as essential. Other possible training materials are: blackboard and chalk; flip charts; overhead projectors; large sheets of paper and Blu-tack; and preprinted charts.
- *Use written aids.* If trainees do not each possess a skills manual, provide clearly structured handouts that summarize the main points

in your presentations. Use worksheets and questionnaires as necessary. Where appropriate, provide references for relevant reading.

● *Use checking skills.*   Check that your audience understands your presentation. This may be done by either allowing for questions or asking questions. Additionally, you discover whether you have been received loud and clear by observing trainees practising the skill in question.

● *Build in homework.*   Give your presentation in such a way that trainees expect to do between-session homework on the skill. The homework assignment can be clearly and specifically stated at the end of any handout you provide.

Exercise 10.4   Presenting a life skill

This exercise may be done in pairs or a training group.

A   *In pairs*
Choose a specific life skill. Prepare and make a fifteen- to twenty-minute presentation to your partner concerning one or more dimensions of that skill. Aim to impart both knowledge and 'how to do it' information. Observe the following guidelines:
1.   have manageable goals;
2.   communicate your goals clearly;
3.   break the task down and clearly identify each step;
4.   be mindful of opportunities to intersperse presentation with rehearsal and practice (though in this exercise keep your main focus on presentation);
5.   use verbal, vocal and body public speaking skills;
6.   use modelling;
7.   use audiovisual aids;
8.   prepare a handout;
9.   use checking skills; and
10.   build in homework.

Afterwards, discuss your presentation with your partner. Then your partner has the opportunity to make a fifteen- to twenty-minute presentation to you concerning one or more dimensions of either the same or another life skill. Both presentations could be independently prepared at the same time. It may help to video- or audio-record and play back each presentation.

B   *In a training group*
The trainer demonstrates the exercise. Each group member then prepares

a fifteen- to twenty-minute presentation, with the topics being negotiated with the trainer. The trainer then has various options, including letting trainees make presentations in these ways: to the whole group who act as trainees; to the whole group in a fishbowl format, with the inner circle being trainees and the outer circle observing and providing feedback; to sub-groups (for example, fours); or in pairs. Where possible, presentations should be video-recorded to allow trainees to observe their performance later. As appropriate, the trainer holds a plenary sharing and discussion session. Trainees are encouraged to identify their presentation skills resources and deficits and to work on both, especially their deficits.

Using the group creatively

Life skills training is often best done in groups of six to eight. However, in their book on training in microcounselling skills, Ivey and Authier write: 'Groups of four tend to be most effective and provide ample opportunity for role-playing.'[16] The difficulty in focusing on individual members' skills is only one of the problems caused by large group size. Another problem is that of holding the attention of the group. This can be especially a problem with children and adolescents. Here you may not only have a *training* function, but also a *class control* or *discipline* function. For instance, any extended live modelling of a skill may be sabotaged by distracting chatter. Also, if you work with one subgroup, you may have little control over what goes on in the other subgroups.

One way of mitigating or getting round the problems of large group size is to use more people as trainers: for instance, two trainers, trainer aides or a team of trainers. However, this is not always possible. Another way is to use good pre-prepared audiovisual presentations. You then use your energy for managing the group. A third way is to be creative in your use of the group. This is recommended even with a small group.

Table 10.1 lists different ways, apart from giving formal presentations, that you can work with a group. First, you can vary the size of the working groups. Second, you can vary the seating arrangements. Indeed, as in some of the earlier breaking the ice exercises, trainees may be standing rather than sitting. Third, you can vary the tasks in which the group engages. This is not to mention the many possible permutations in varying numbers, seating and task.

Table 10.1   *Variations in use of the group in life skills training*

Variations	
Numerical variations	*Task variations*
The focus can be on:	Task variations include:
whole group	use of exercises and games
small groups	use of worksheets
quartets or triads	behaviour rehearsal
pairs	dramas
singles	discussion groups
	trainees as panel members
Seating variations	seminars led by trainees
The seating pattern can be:	trainees as skills trainers: for example,
circular	in pairs
horseshoe	task groups reporting back to whole
fishbowl (inner and outer rings)	group
rows (generally not recommended)	focusing on critical incidents/case
two chairs for demonstration in front	studies
chairs for panel in front	watching/listening to audiovisual
	material
	setting and reviewing homework

Using and designing exercises and games

Life skills training programmes tend to contain many structured learning experiences. Depending on the extent to which they involve play, they may be called either exercises or games. For instance, in relationship skills training it is possible to turn a structured exercise about sending 'I' messages into a game by having the sender toss a ball to the receiver along with the 'I' message. Try speeding this up and it may become even more of a game! Especially when working with children there is much to be said for using or creating relevant games. Inclusion of humour and fun assists learning for any age group.

There are two main sources of exercises and games; either using other people's or making your own up. Using the relationship skills area as an example, existing sources of exercises include those in: Hopson and Hough's *Exercises in Personal and Career Development*,[17] Egan's *You and Me*,[18] Johnson's *Reaching Out*,[19] my own *Human Relationship Skills*,[20] and the Pfeiffer and Jones' series *Structured Experiences for Human Relations Training*.[21] Also, you might get a catalogue from a company like Lifeskills Associates which specializes in structured training packages.[22]

Why stop at using other people's material which may not be tailor-made for your purposes? I encourage you not only to use existing material, but also to tap your creativity and design some exercises for any training group that you run. Some guidelines in designing exercises include the following:

- Clear, specific and relevant goals.
- Simple presentation including, wherever possible, modelling.
- Simple, clear instructions that participants can use as inner speech to guide their activities.
- Creative use of the group.
- Learning by doing.
- Where possible, opportunity for coaching, rehearsal and practice.
- Attention paid to homework and to transfer of skills to outside settings.
- If possible, piloting of the exercise to see whether it works and to refine it if necessary.

Exercise 10.5   Designing an exercise or game

This exercise can be done on your own, in pairs or in a training group.

A   *On your own*
Pick a learning that you wish to impart in a life skills area of your choice. If possible, familiarize yourself with existing exercises and games in that area. Then, following the guidelines mentioned in the text, design and write an exercise or game that helps a group of eight trainees achieve your learning objective.

B   *In pairs*
Either do the above exercise independently, then discuss;
or, working together from the start, jointly design a life skills training exercise or game.

C   *In a training group*
The trainer introduces the topic of being creative in designing exercises and games to help attain life skills training objectives. The trainer breaks the group down into small groups, each of which has an area in which to design an exercise or game. The groups are given thirty minutes to work together to come up with something.

   Afterwards, there is a plenary session in which representatives from each group present their group's exercise and receive feedback. If there is time, the whole group might do each exercise as it is presented. The trainer and group try to identify and articulate the principles of well-designed exercises and games.

Setting and reviewing homework

There are two main reasons why life skills trainers set homework. First, it can speed up the learning process. Second, it can help with the transfer of skills to outside life. In your initial presentation of the training programme, you can let participants know both that they are expected to complete homework assignments and why this is the case.

Homework assignments are more likely to be completed if the following conditions apply:

● *Clarity.* The task requirements are clear. Earlier it was suggested that you might finish your session handout with the homework assignment to be completed by the next session.
● *Relevance.* The task is not only relevant but also *perceived* by trainees to be relevant to attaining their personal goals.
● *Consolidation of earlier training.* The homework builds on and consolidates learning within the previous session or sessions.
● *Appropriate difficulty level.* The tasks are relevant to trainees' level of readiness. Trainees have a good idea how to do what is expected of them. Where appropriate, graded task assignment is used.
● *Realistic amount.* You can work out with your trainees what is a realistic amount of between-session homework.
● *Reviews of progress.* You can review how trainers have fared in their homework at the start of the next session. This has numerous functions: acting as a reward for doing homework, offering trainer and group support, targeting difficulties and helping you plan subsequent sessions.
● *Constructive group norms.* Where possible, encourage the development of constructive group norms in regard to homework: for instance, the expectancy that it gets done, the open discussion of successes and failures, and trainees being encouraged for their efforts rather than ridiculed for their mistakes.

There are numerous reasons why people fail to do homework. For instance, in a school setting, a life skills training class may be ungraded whereas 'academic' subjects are graded. Sometimes trainees may be in life skills training classes compulsorily rather than voluntarily. Homework may entail taking risks in trying out new behaviours outside the group. As a life skills trainer, you have both to acknowledge and also deal with any such difficulties and resistances as best you can.

Stage Four: Ending Stage Skills

A major issue in life skills training is that of how to ensure that it has lasting effect. Marzillier reviewed social skills training outcome studies, mainly those for college student and psychiatric populations, and concluded: 'To date there is a lack of evidence with any client populations which can be said to support the conclusion that SST produces lasting and significant improvement in competency in everyday interactions.'[23] His comments merit attention for trainers of other life skills as well.

Most life skills training programmes are of limited duration, say six to ten sessions. Dealing with end-of-group emotional issues is generally not as important as in group counselling. The most important task is that of consolidating self-help skills. The ending stage should therefore be built into the programme from the start. In various ways you encourage trainees not to regard the programme as an end in itself. Rather, it is a means of acquiring skills primarily for use once the programme is over.

Ways of consolidating self-help skills *during* a programme include the following:

- Imparting an attitude of personal responsibility. Trainees need to become clear that ultimately the buck stops with them, not their trainers, for *choosing* to acquire, use and develop their skills.
- Ensuring that trainees have the requisite understanding and inner speech to guide their later behaviour. Good life skills trainers do not just do things *to* trainees. Rather, they work *with* trainees to develop the trainees' self-help skills. Part of this collaboration is ensuring that they know what are the operations involved in a skill so that they can implement these operations on their own.
- Setting and reviewing appropriate homework.

Ways of consolidating self-help skills *at the end of* a programme include helping trainees do the following activities:

- Make an accurate assessment of their resources and deficits in the skills area.
- Develop action plans for maintaining, using and developing their skills. Part of such an action plan may be to develop strategies for coping with barriers to maintaining and using skills. Additionally, trainees should have clear ways, including feedback from significant others (e.g. friends, relatives), of monitoring their use of skills.
- Review their understanding of the skills. Trainer and trainee together may review the learnings from the programme.
- Have access to a skills manual or handouts. Trainees may be enco

aged to review written material after the group has ended.
- Attend one or more follow-up sessions. Where possible, follow-up sessions are highly recommended. Such sessions might be either three or six months after the end of a programme. They act as motivators and ways of identifying problems, and make it easier for further action plans to be formulated.

Another agenda at the end of a life skills training group is that for obtaining feedback. This feedback may be about the degree to which outcomes have been obtained. This is impossible to do adequately if baseline data were not initially collected. Feedback should also focus on processes as well as outcomes: for instance, which interventions in the training programme did trainees find helpful and why? Saying goodbye and ensuring that adequate attention is paid to the needs of any still vulnerable trainees are other agendas in the ending stage.

Exercise 10.6   Assisting transfer of skills to outside life

This exercise may be done in a number of ways.

A   *On your own*
Think of a life skill in which you might train others. Write out answers to the following questions.
1. What do you consider to be the main barriers to trainees transferring the skills acquired in your programme to use in their outside lives?
2. List as many strategies as you can think of to assist trainees in transferring any skills learned in your programme to use in their outside lives.
3. Rank in order of importance the main transfer of skills strategies in your list.

B   *In pairs*
Either do the above exercise independently, then discuss;
or do the above exercise together from the start.

C   *In a training group*
The trainer introduces the topic of the importance of trainees transferring the use of newly acquired skills into their outside lives. The trainer divides the group into task groups. Each task group is allowed twenty to thirty minutes to answer the questions in Part A above. This is followed by a plenary session in which representatives from the task groups report back to the whole group, followed by further discussion as appropriate.

DESIGNING A LIFE SKILLS TRAINING PROGRAMME

A major skill of the preparatory stage is that of designing a life skills training programme. Much of the design of individual sessions may be best left until after the previous session. Nevertheless, you require an overall vision or plan. Let's take as an example designing eight sessions, each of one and a half hours, for a weekly group on the topic of 'how to make friends'. There is one trainer. The group is run in a school setting and comprises eight volunteers who have agreed to attend the sessions out of class. Their age range is fifteen to sixteen and there are four girls and four boys, none of whom have had much contact with each other.

The overall goal of the group is to help members become more effective in making friends, especially of the opposite gender. The focus is on starting rather than developing friendships. The trainer operationalizes the concept of making friends into a series of subskills.

The *thinking skills* to be focused on are:

● assuming responsibility for your relationships;
● having realistic inner rules, especially in regard to rejection;
● ability to use coping inner speech to manage anxiety and stay task-relevant.

The *action skills* to be focused on mainly relate to one-to-one interaction and are as follows:

● making contact;
● holding, maintaining and ending a brief conversation;
● telephone skills.

The trainer decides to collect baseline data and to initiate self-assessment before the first session. This comprises three elements. Trainees are asked to fill out a 'making friends' questionnaire in their own time and independently. This assesses their existing thinking and action skills and their pattern of friendships. Additionally, the trainer arranges to video each trainee holding a ten-minute conversation with a peer trained to behave in a fairly standard way. Trainees are rated on four scales: listening, talking about self, loudness of voice and amount of eye contact. There is no control group since the collection of data is more for feedback to the trainer than as part of a rigorous research project. The third element consists of collecting teacher ratings of each trainee friendship behaviour.

In the initial session, the trainer outlines the proposed program though not in as much detail as in Table 10.2. The group's wishes ma tàken into account in the sequencing of material. The trainer allows sufficient flexibility to adjust the programme in the light of feedback and the pace of learning of the group. Trainees are expected to do between-session homework. The trainer is very conscious that much of the learning in the programme will come from what trainees teach each other. A handout is provided for each session. It includes: the goals for the session; a session outline; a summary of relevant knowledge; any exercises for the session; and the homework assignment to be completed by the next session. Trainees are provided with a workbook in which to keep course materials.

In the Table 10.2 programme, trainees were asked to complete the 'making friends' questionnaire again after the seventh session so that their answers generated material for the final session. Teacher ratings of trainees' friendship behaviour were collected again on a post-test basis at the time of the final session. Additionally, within a couple of days of the final session, each trainee was videoed again holding a ten-minute conversation with a peer confederate. The trainer then had four different assessments of the effects of the programme: pre- and post-tests of the 'making friends' questionnaire, teacher ratings, and ratings of the videoed conversations; and responses to the end-of-programme feedback questionnaire.

Exercise 10.7   Designing a life skills training programme

This exercise is perhaps best done on your own so that it forces you to think through some of the numerous issues in designing a life skills training programme. However, it can also be done either with a partner or as a small group exercise.

Design a life skills training programme for a skill of your choice. Assume that you have eight one-and-a-half-hour sessions available; there are eight trainees; you are the only trainer; the group meets once a week; and the programme is conducted in an agency or setting of relevance to you. Formulate and write out the following items:

1.   the overall goal of your programme;
  .   an operationalization of the overall goal into subskills; and
     a session-by-session outline of your programme, along the lines of Table 10.2, using the following headings: *Session, Objectives* and *Training methods.*

Table 10.2   *An outline for a life skills training programme on how to make friends*

Session	Objectives	Training methods
1.	Creation of a safe learning climate and enhancement of motivation	Breaking the ice exercises Boys and girls task groups discuss responses to 'making friends' questionnaire, and report back to whole group
	Greater understanding of targeted skills	Trainer presents programme outline Discussion and feedback *Homework*: Keep diary of friendship behaviour
2.	Increase awareness of influence of thinking on making friends	Review of homework Exercise on gender roles Group discussion Exercise on internal rules and rejection Discussion and feedback *Homework*: Keep diary on feelings when relating to peers Complete 'coping with rejection' worksheet
3.	Increase awareness of personal responsibility and of skills of making initial contact	Review of homework Game on making 'I' statements Lecturette on being a chooser in life Mixed task groups on how to meet and make initial contact with others, followed by reporting back to whole group Opportunity for feedback *Homework*: Practise making 'I' statements in daily life Observe and keep diary on ways in which people make initial contact
4.	Increase both making and receiving initial contact skills	Review of homework Lecturette on making and receiving initial contact, emphasizing body and vocal as well as verbal communication Behaviour rehearsal, coaching and video feedback Discussion and feedback *Homework*: Practise making initial contact skills on the basis of graded task assignment Where possible, use rewarding receiving initial contact skills Keep diary of progress
5.	Improve holding, maintaining and ending a conversation skills	Review of homework Lecturette on conversational skills, illustrate with demonstration video Exercise on talking about yourself Exercise on being a rewarding listener Discussion and feedback

Table 10.2   (*contd.*)

		Homework: Observe skills of good conversationalists Practise conversation skills (in mixed pairs) Use conversation skills in daily life Keep diary of progress
6.	Improve holding, maintaining and ending a conversation skills	Review of homework Lecturette on assertively ending conversations Brief conversations: behaviour rehearsal, coaching and video feedback Discussion and feedback *Homework*: Use of conversation skills in daily life, possibly using graded tasks Keep diary of progress
7.	Increase coping inner speech and telephone conversation skills	Review of homework Lecturette on coping inner speech, including audio-recorded modelling of skills in relation to asking someone for a date on the phone Behaviour rehearsal and coaching of thinking and action skills concerning asking/being asked for a date Discussion and feedback *Homework*: Practise inner speech and skills for dating phone calls (mixed pairs who phone each other up) Retake 'making friends' questionnaire Keep diary of progress
8.	Consolidate self-help skills Obtain feedback about programme	Review of homework, including retake of 'making friends' questionnaire Trainees feedback to trainer the central teachings of the programme Exercise on planning to maintain, use and develop making friends skills Discussion Completion of brief feedback questionnaire regarding the programme Arrangement of follow-up session Saying goodbye.

11 Maintaining and Developing your Skills

Question: What is the similarity between computers and Australians?
Answer: You have to punch information into both of them.

The point I try to make with this highly unwarranted joke (told by a New Zealander, you might have guessed) is that all of us have to discipline ourselves to become better helpers. If, for the benefit of our clients, this involves punching information into ourselves, so be it. In this chapter I make suggestions about how to assume responsibility for maintaining and further developing your helping potential.

PRACTICAL, PERSONAL AND ACADEMIC DIMENSIONS

Training in helping consists of three interrelated dimensions: practical, personal and academic. Consequently, you may wish to explore ways of increasing your helping effectiveness by paying some attention to one or more of these dimensions. The *practical dimension* consists of a dire focus on helping skills: for example, both skills training in laborate settings prior to client contact, and supervised work with clients placements. However, helping relationships are not conducted ju technicians but by people. Therefore actual or prospective helpe experience difficulties in listening and communicating outside ar to have similar difficulties in their relationships with clients. Tho skills training may help with such difficulties, the time and atte can be devoted to them in such practical training may be insu number of programmes for training helpers include a separate *personal dimension* in which trainees can focus directly on their own problems of living and relationships skills. All helpers implicitly or explicitly operate from theoretical assumptions. Furthermore, some view what they do as an applied science in which it is very important to pay attention to research findings concerning the process and outcomes of helping. Thus the *academic dimension* of being an effective helper includes knowledge of relevant theory and research. I now make some suggestions regarding the practical and personal dimensions. I omit the academic dimension since the main focus of this book is on practice.

The Practical Dimension

You may maintain and further develop your helping skills by means of self-help, training courses and workshops, supervised practical experience, and helping skills reading.

Self-help

'Self-help' is a term that I use to encompass all activities that develop your skills without the aid of a trainer. Self-help ways of maintaining and developing your helping skills come under the broad categories of *observing models* and *practising*.

Ways of maintaining and developing your helping skills by *observing models* include the following:

- *Listening to cassettes and tapes.*   Cassettes and tapes of interviews conducted by leading counsellors and helpers are available in Britain, North America and Australasia. One possibility is to listen to the whole session and focus on the helper, the client and the process. Another possibility is to rate the helper's level of either empathy or performance on some other skill by rating segments of interviews, say three or four minutes. Also, for breadth and for comparative purposes, it is best to listen to interviews of helpers working from different theoretical frameworks and on different problems.
  Looking at video recordings and films.   All the possibilities mentioned for audiocassettes are relevant for videocassettes, with the added possibility of observing and rating body messages. Films are available. However, sometimes they are difficult to screen. Furthermore, they *are* less flexible than video recordings for stopping

and playing back. In Britain, films and videos may be hired from the British Association for Counselling.[1]

- *Reading transcripts.* Transcripts of interviews by leading helpers are available, sometimes accompanying a cassette. Transcripts may be read in their entirety. Alternatively, you may wish to look either at smaller segments or for illustrations of particular skills.
- *Being a client.* Try to obtain the experience of being the client of a very skilled helper for at least a few sessions, more if possible. You may learn a lot about creating a working relationship, pacing, timing and about some specific interventions.

Ways of maintaining and developing your helping skills by *practising* include the following:

- *Composing an internal dialogue.* Write out an internal dialogue in which you act as your own helper.
- *Responding to transcripts.* Get a transcript of a session by someone like Rogers and go down the page covering up Rogers' responses, formulating your own, then checking Rogers' responses.
- *Responding to cassettes.* Get an interview cassette of an experienced helper and, immediately after a client statement, switch off the cassette and formulate your own response. Then listen to the helper's response and compare it with your own. Focus on vocal as well as on verbal communication.
- *Co-counselling.* Practise your helping skills with a colleague on a co-counselling basis using audio and video feedback where appropriate.
- *Working with real clients.* Monitor your use of helping skills with real clients by cassette-recording your sessions and later playing them back and reviewing them.
- *Comparison with experienced helpers.* Have available a cassette-recording of one of your sessions and one of the interview of a experienced helper. Listen alternatively to brief segments from ea of the cassettes and review any significant differences.
- *Become part of a learning helping skills peer self-help group.* may be able to form or become part of a learning helping skil self-help group in which you work with, comment on and each other as you develop your skills.

Training courses and workshops

There are no hard and fast distinctions between train'

workshops. If anything, however, training courses are spread out over a longer period, say two months or more, whereas workshops are relatively intense experiences lasting a day, a weekend, a week or possibly two weeks. Training courses may be full-time, half-time, day-release or a few hours a week. Workshops tend to, but do not necessarily, require full-time attendance. An illustration of the lack of a clear distinction between the two is that sometimes workshops are called short courses.

It may be possible to obtain details of training courses and workshops from national professional associations in counselling, in psychology and in other relevant areas. For instance, in Britain, the British Association for Counselling (BAC) publishes a list of courses entitled *Training in Counselling: a Dictionary*.[2] Furthermore, details of short courses, workshops and conferences are provided in BAC's quarterly *Newsletter* as well as in the British Psychological Society's monthly *Bulletin*. In Australia, details of short courses, conferences and workshops are sometimes promulgated in the *Bulletin of the Australian Psychological Society*, but are more likely to be found in the newsletters of the Society's branches. Table 11.1 lists the names and addresses of national counselling and psychology professional associations in Australia, Britain, Canada, New Zealand and the USA. Each of these may provide information on where to look for relevant training experiences.

Conferences are also run by international counselling associations. Prominent among these are the *International Round Table for the Advancement of Counselling* (IRTAC)[3] and the *Association of Psychological and Educational Counsellor of Asia* (APECA).[4]

If you are interested in developing your skills in a particular approach to helping, it may pay you to make enquiries about whether there is an agency to train people in the approach. For instance, training in facilitating person-centred groups and in transactional analysis has reached the stage where it is conducted on an international basis with local trainers. Additionally, if you are interested in developing your skills in a particular ─a of helping, for example marital or careers, again it is advisable to ─ke specific inquiries.

─sed practical experience

─ practical experience is an excellent way for you to develop
─g skills. Some people may have ready access to suitable
─eas for others access to clients may be a major stumbling
─uate supervision. Helper training courses of reasonable

Table 11.1   *Names and addresses of national professional associations for counselling and for psychology in Australia, Britain, Canada, New Zealand and the USA*

Area	Names and addresses
Australia	
Counselling	The Australian Guidance and Counselling Association, PO Box 3, Geebung, Queensland 4034
Psychology	The Australian Psychological Society, National Science Centre, 191 Royal Parade, Parkville, Victoria 3502
Britain	
Counselling	British Association for Counselling, 37A Sheep Street, Rugby CV21 3BX
Psychology	The British Psychological Society, St Andrews House, 48 Princess Road East, Leicester LE1 7DR
Canada	
Counselling	Canadian Guidance and Counselling Association/Société Canadienne d'Orientation et de Consultation, PO Box 13059, Kanata, Ontario K2K 1X3
Psychology	Canadian Psychological Association/Société Canadienne de Psychologie, 588 King Edward Avenue, Ottawa, Ontario K1N 7N8
New Zealand	
Counselling	New Zealand Counselling and Guidance Association, 16 Claude Road, Epsom, Auckland
Psychology	New Zealand Psychological Society, PO Box 4092, Wellington
USA	
Counselling	American Association for Counseling and Development, 5999 Stevenson Avenue, Alexandria, Virginia 22304
Psychology	American Psychological Association, 1200 Seventeenth Street, N.W., Washington D.C. 20036

duration are remiss if they do not attempt to ensure that their trainees, when ready, have enough access to clients. Also, trainees require good support and supervision especially when first assuming responsibility for clients. In settings where the focus is on less formal helping (for example nurses in hospitals), the more experienced can help the less experienced to develop their skills. However, for many reasons, even experienced helpers may find it beneficial to have some supervision. These reasons include: guarding against falling into bad habits; updating their knowledge and skills; obtaining assistance with difficult clients; and, if necessary, receiving personal and/or professional support.

Much of the value of supervised practical experience depends on the quality of supervision. Robert Carkhuff has both suggested and provided evidence to support his position that the level of skills of t trainer is perhaps the most critical element determining the effectiveness of practical skills training.[5] Of all methods of supervising trainees' practical work, I consider listening to and commenting on cassette-recordings of their interviews to be by far the most effective. Clients' permission for cassette-recording can usually be obtained so long as they are assured that the material will be treated as confidential and scrubbed clean in the reasonably near future. Without this cassette evidence, the supervisor is unable to focus on how the trainee responds to the client. Consequently, the very important area of responding choices is largely lost to supervision. Other possible elements in supervision include focusing on: trainees' ability to operationalize problems; their intervention skills; their thoughts and feelings towards their clients and about their interviewing; and their understanding and effectiveness within the institutional or agency context in which they work.

Options differ about whether supervision is best done with just one person at a time, in twos, in threes or with even larger numbers. Reasons for keeping supervision on an individual basis include the time-consuming nature of listening to cassette-recordings, and the possibility that trainees explore themselves as helpers more deeply on a one-to-one basis. Reasons for supervising groups of two, three or more include making it possible for trainees both to comment on other people's work and to learn from each other. Also, there are the obvious reasons of economy and practicability if there is a shortage of supervisors.

For practising helpers there is much to be said for peer supervision in which you facilitate, confront and learn off each other. *Co-counselling* is one model of peer supervision. For instance, you may each occupy one hour, reversing supervisor/supervisee roles at the end of the first hour. Furthermore, you can negotiate the role you wish your supervisor to play – facilitator, trainer, personal support, etc. – so that you 'control' your supervision. *Peer supervision groups* are another model of peer supervision. The group can decide how best to use the talents and resources of members. Again, individual members who present material can be given the opportunity of stating what kind of assistance they want from the group.

skills reading

... de the theoretical literature that contributes to underpinning ... re are two main sources of helping skills reading: skills *books* ... research and continuing education *journals*.

... es section of this *book* cites numerous other helping skills *books.* Additionally, you may wish to do more focused reading both on the skills of a particular approach and also on the application of skills to specific problems and populations.

Journals provide an excellent means of keeping abreast of counselling and helping skills developments. Journals specifically focused on *counselling* include: the *British Journal of Guidance and Counselling*, published by the Careers Research and Advisory Centre; *Marriage Guidance*, published by the British National Marriage Guidance Council; BAC's journal *Counselling*; the American Association of Counseling and Development's *Journal of Counseling and Development* and *Counselor Education and Supervision;* the Canadian Guidance and Counselling Association's *Canadian Counsellor*; the *New Zealand Counselling and Guidance Association Journal*; and the International Round Table for the Advancement of Counselling and the International Association for Educational Vocational Guidance's *International Journal for the Advancement of Counselling.*

Psychological society journals include: *The Australian Counselling Psychologist*, the journal of the Australian Psychological Society's Board of Counselling Psychologists; the *Review*, the journal of the British Psychological Society's Counselling Psychology Section; and the American Psychological Association Division of Counselling Psychology's *The Counseling Psychologist*, geared to the continuing education of practitioners, and *Journal of Counseling Psychology*, which publishes research papers. *Cognitive Therapy and Research* and *Behavior Therapy* are two other American applied research journals that I find useful. Also, in 1988, *Counselling Psychology Quarterly* commenced publication by Carfax Press in Britain.

There are numerous other journals which have papers relevant to practical counselling and helping skills, without having them as a primary focus. Some of these are psychological journals, some are journals of other groups: for example personnel managers, social workers, nurses and teachers.

The Personal Dimension

Another way in which you can maintain and develop yourselves as counsellors and helpers is to pay attention to your personal effectiveness. An assumption here is that all people, not just clients, have to work at being effective in their lives. The old adage 'Physician heal theyself' also applies to helpers. Four approaches to maintaining and developing yourself as a person are self-help, individual counselling, group counselling and life skills training.

Self-help

Effective living is a continuous process of psychological self-help. Much of the knowledge and skills you acquire in learning about counselling and helping can be applied to helping yourself. For example, you can consciously try to become better at listening to your own feelings. Furthermore, your skills of focusing on clients' faulty habits of thinking can easily be transferred to exploring your own difficulties and disciplining yourself to think more realistically. Also, if you experience problems in acting effectively, you should have some insight into ways of changing your behaviour. Sometimes the notion of self-help is extended to include knowing how to utilize resources in the environment, be they friends, relatives or even other counsellors, on an ad hoc basis. Further suggestions for self-help include engaging in regular co-counselling with a suitable person and becoming a member of a self-help group.

Helpers who do not take responsibility for looking after themselves and managing the stresses in their work and personal lives tend to be excellent candidates for *burnout*, if not *breakdown*.[6,7,8] Most helpers face sufficient pressures in their jobs without further burdening themselves with the self-induced varieties. There are many skills deficits that contribute to helper burnout. These include the following:

- Inability to set limits on others and say no to unreasonable requests.
- Inability to set limits on yourself and, as far as possible, establish a manageable workload.
- Perfectionist tendencies in regard to your work.
- Undue needs for external approval.
- Assuming too much responsibility in the helping relationship.
- Inability to build or create variety in the helping role.
- Poor skills at relating to colleagues and administrators.
- Poor administrative skills.
- Poor skills at building a support network.
- Poor skills at maintaining and developing practical helping skills.
- Poor skills at realizing that there is a life outside helping which, if insufficiently attended to, can drain away the energy and resilience necessary for being a skilled helper.

Individual counselling

Some helping approaches, such as psychoanalysis, make the experience of being a client a mandatory part of training. This is partly to improve the personal effectiveness of trainees and partly to help them understand the application of the approach for 'professional' purposes. In developing yourself as a helper you may wish to receive counselling from a competent professional. You are then faced with choosing such a person. In a number of countries, terms like 'psychotherapist' and 'counselling psychologist' are used in addition to the term 'counsellor'. Counselling psychologists are people with recognized psychological qualifications who perform counselling. The terms 'counselling' and 'psychotherapy' are often used interchangeably. Attempts to differentiate the two terms are never wholly successful and, if anything, they denote differing emphases rather than separate skills. For example, psychotherapists, probably more than counsellors, work with moderately to severely disturbed clients in medical settings. Indeed, many psychotherapists are psychiatrists, who are doctors with psychological as well as medical training.

Whether you seek counselling from a counsellor, psychotherapist, psychiatrist or from some other helping professional, my message is '*caveat emptor*', or 'buyer beware'. Think through your goals in seeking counselling. Be prepared to ask and shop around for a counsellor who meets your criteria. If you then get into counselling with someone who does not match up to your criteria, do not be afraid to look elsewhere. Unfortunately, there are huge differences in competence amongst professional counsellors. Your selection process *must* take this into account.

Group counselling

As with individual counselling, participation as a client in group counselling may help both your personal effectiveness and your helping skills. There are usually opportunities for those living in large cities to become members of counselling groups. However, people living in small towns and rural areas are likely to find such opportunities much more limited. In Chapter 9, I discussed some of the advantages and disadvantages of group counselling. Also, I mentioned some criteria for assessing counselling groups. Both those sections are as relevant when considering group counselling for yourself as they are when making decisions in regard to your clients.

Life skills training

There may be opportunities in your area for working on specific life skills.

Again, you have the dual agenda of being a trainee not only in the skill itself but also in how to train others in it. In the remainder of the twentieth century, life skills training is likely to be a burgeoning area in the provision of counselling and helping services. Though programmes may be unavailable in your locality now, hopefully the situation will soon alter.

Exercise 11.1 Maintaining and developing your helping skills

This exercise may be done in a number of ways.

A *On your own*
Design a plan for maintaining and developing your helping skills. Write down as specifically as possible:
1. your goals;
2. the methods you intend to use to achieve your goals: for example, details of self-help, training courses and workshops, supervised practical experience, practical skills reading and personal development;
3. a realistic time schedule for achieving each sub goal; and
4. how you intend to monitor and evaluate your progress.

B *In pairs*
Either do the exercise in Part A above independently, then discuss it; or do it jointly. Another option is for you to act as counsellor and first facilitate your partner's exploration regarding developing his or her helping skills, and then help him or her to design and write down a plan to achieve his or her goals. Afterwards, reverse roles.

C *In a training group*
The trainer illustrates with examples of how people in the area of helping for which the group is being trained go about developing their skills. The trainer may self-disclose about his or her own professional skills development. The trainer may conduct a demonstration interview and facilitate a group member exploring how to develop his or her skills and then formulating of a plan to do so. Another option is for the trainer to ask the group to do the exercise in Part A or Part B. Afterwards, there is a plenary sharing and discussion session about the development of helping skills during the training course and/or after it is finished.

THE CHALLENGE TO COUNSELLORS AND HELPERS

As counsellors and helpers, your assuming responsibility for maintaining and developing your skills may seem so obvious that it scarcely merits mention. However, a note of realism, if not pessimism, is in order.[9] The obstacles are considerable and some have already been mentioned. Others include the following:

- The pressures and compromises in earning a living that impinge on your helping work: for instance, the obvious and sometimes subtle pressures on either school counsellors or private practitioners.
- The pressure of a heavy case load and the risks of burnout and breakdown.
- The dangers of institutionalization, for those working in institutions, and of isolation, for those working on their own.
- The blinkers provided you by your trainers through their own possibly narrow allegiances.
- The tendency to associate in networks of like-minded helpers, possibly sustaining allegiances to narrow positions.
- The effects of professional and voluntary agency hierarchies, with preferment sometimes being more a matter of allegiance to a particular hierarchy than recognition of ability.
- The fact that developing your helping skills often has financial costs: for example, fees, purchase of books, income foregone.
- The heavy expenditure of time and effort required to keep abreast of the relevant helping literature.
- The likelihood that some of your clients will reward your skills deficits and not just your resources.
- Any personal deficiencies that you bring to your job: for instance, a tendency to filter out negative feedback.

The challenge to counsellor and helpers is the same as the challenge to clients. It is that of *affirming* your existence, despite the various pressures that might diminish you. I sincerely hope that you have found reading and working with this book a rewarding experience. I wish you every success in living up to the challenge to make the choices that define you as effective counsellors and helpers.

A Glossary of Helping Terms

Acceptance   Unconditional approval of or by another. Absence of rejection.

Acute   Sharp, critical, intense. Often contrasted with chronic.

Advanced empathic responding   Responses to clients' statements that expand or advance their awareness yet still remain primarily within their frame of reference. See also *Empathic responding*.

Advising   Telling others how they might think, feel or act rather than letting them come to their own conclusions.

Affection   Experiencing and being able to show fond and tender feelings toward another.

Aggression   Hostile or attacking behaviour which is an overreaction to a perceived provocation, and involves putting down another.

Anger management   Being able to cope with feelings of anger in ways that are constructive rather than destructive.

Anticipating risk and gain   Assessing the positive and negative consequences of future behaviour and events.

Antidepressant drugs   Drugs which are used primarily to elevate mood and to relieve depression.

Anxiety   Feelings of fear or apprehension which may be either general or associated with specific people and situations.

Anxiety management   Being able to acknowledge feelings of anxiety and then, if necessary, adopt appropriate strategies for coping with them.

Assertion   Stating positive and oppositional thoughts and feelings, accompanied by appropriate actions if necessary, in ways that are neither aggressive nor inhibited.

Assessment   Collecting and analysing data about clients in order to make treatment choices. Monitoring progress and evaluating outcomes. Frequently a collaborative exercise with clients.

Attributing responsibility   Ascribing or making causal inferences about the responsibility for one's own or other people's feelings, thoughts and actions and for external events.

Avoidance   Thinking and acting in ways that avoid dealing directly with the realities of life: for example, by withdrawal.

Awareness   Consciousness of and sensitivity to oneself, others and the environment.

Behaviour rehearsal   Rehearsing clients in appropriate behaviour by means of role-playing, coaching and feedback. Clients may also rehearse appropriate thoughts and images.

Body messages   Sending messages with your body about thoughts and feelings in ways that either do not accompany words or frame the use of words: for example, facial expression. See also *Verbal messages* and *Vocal messages*.

Burnout   Depletion of motivation, energy, resilience and, ultimately, of effectiveness on the part of helpers.

Catharsis   Release and discharge of emotional tension by talking about and expressing it.

Chronic   Lingering, lasting. Sometimes also with the connotation of not being so severe as when the term *acute* is used.

Concreteness   Responding to clients' utterances in a clear and specific manner. Clear and specific communication by clients.

Confidentiality   Keeping trust with others by not divulging personal information about them unless granted permission.

Confrontation   Challenging another person's view of themselves, of you, or of a situation. Focusing on discrepancies in people's thoughts, feelings and actions.

Congruence   Genuineness or lack of facade. Having and being seen to have your thoughts, feelings, words and actions match each other.

Continuation messages   Brief responses designed to give another person the message 'I am with you. Please continue.'

Contracting   Making agreements with others which may be either implicit, or verbal, or written and countersigned.

Coping   Dealing with situations by managing them adequately without necessarily mastering them completely.

Coping inner speech   Self-talk that helps clients to manage situations both by keeping focused on the task at hand and also by calming their anxieties.

Counselling and helping   Counselling and helping (usually called 'helping' in this book) is a process whose aim is to help clients, who are mainly seen outside medical settings, to help themselves by making better choices and by becoming better choosers. The counsellor or helper's repertoire of skills includes those of forming an understanding relationship as well as interventions focused on helping clients change specific aspects of their feeling, thinking and acting.

Co-counselling   Taking turns with another person in counselling each other.

Couples counselling   Counselling two partners in a relationship either jointly or with a mixture of counselling them both separately and jointly.

Crises   Situations of excessive stress in which people feel that their coping resources are severely stretched or inadequate to meet the adjustive demands being made upon them.

Crisis management   Coping with and helping clients cope with crises. Working to help clients handle anxieties and develop self-help skills and strategies.

Defensive thinking   The processes by which people deny and distort information that varies from their picture of themselves when this information threatens their feelings of adequacy and worth.

Delusions   Strongly held false ideas: for example, delusions of being persecuted.

Demonstration   Either intentionally or unintentionally showing someone how to think or behave by doing it yourself. See also *Modelling*.

Denial   A defensive process by which people protect themselves from threatening aspects either of themselves or of external reality by refusing to recognize them.

Dependency   Relying on support from another or others rather than on self-support.

Depression   Feelings of sadness and of loss. Symptoms may include apathy, withdrawal, disturbed sleep, lack of appetite and lowered sexual interest.

Didactic/interpretive confronting   Challenging clients' existing perceptions to help them understand how these may sustain their problems. See also *Facilitative confronting*.

Directiveness   Behaving in ways that give direction to others whether or not they wish it.

Distortion   A defensive process involving 'working on' aspects of reality in order to make them less threatening and more consistent with existing self-pictures. Positive as well as negative feedback may be distorted.

Eclecticism Basing one's helping practice on interventions drawn from more than one theoretical position.

Empathic responding Accurately understanding, from their frames of reference, what your clients tell you and then sensitively communicating back your understanding in a language attuned to their needs. More colloquially, being a good listener and then responding with understanding. See also *Advanced empathic responding.*

Encounter groups An intensive method of group counselling with an emphasis on focusing on feelings and group interaction.

Endogenous depression Depression predominantly originating within the physiology of the organism; e.g. manic-depression.

Extinction The weakening or disappearance of a response when it is no longer rewarded or reinforced.

Facilitative confronting Challenging clients' existing frames of reference in a relatively non-threatening manner. See also *Didactic/interpretive confronting.*

Family counselling Counselling involving working with members of a family, either together or in varying combinations, and focusing on improving communication between them.

Feedback Receiving messages from others about yourself and sending messages to others about themselves. See *Denial* and *Distortion.*

Feelings Emotions, affective states of varying degrees of positiveness and negativeness.

Feelings words Words used to label, describe, and express feelings.

Focused exploration Helper and client together explore a specific area or areas of a client's feeling, thinking and/or acting.

Gay A colloquial word for homosexual. People of varying degrees of bisexuality are much more common than exclusively homosexual people.

Genuineness Absence of facade and insincerity. See *Congruence.*

Goals The implicit or explicit objectives of helpers, clients, and specific helping interventions.

Graded task assignment Identifying and setting progressively more difficult tasks.

Group counselling The relationships, activities and skills involved in counselling two or more people at the same time.

Guilt Feelings of distress, involving self-devaluation and anxiety, resulting from having transgressed a code of behaviour to which you subscribe.

Habit A tendency based on learning to respond in a consistent way to person or situation.

Hallucination Illusions regarding external objects which are actually present. Most commonly these are auditory: for example, hearing voices.

Helper   Person who uses counselling and helping skills in a paid, voluntary or informal capacity. See *Counselling and helping*.

Helpful responding   Responding in ways that help others listen to themselves, feel understood, and clarify problem areas.

Hierarchies   Lists of progressively more anxiety-evoking scenes (for example, in systematic desensitization), and lists of progressively more difficult tasks.

Homework   Tasks assigned inside to be completed outside and usually between helping sessions.

Hypnotic drugs   Drugs that induce sleep.

'I' statements   Owning and directly stating what you think and feel, starting with the words 'I think . . .' or 'I feel . . .', etc. See also *'You' statements*.

Illusion   False perception or belief.

Imaginal goal rehearsal   Using imaging as a coping skill for both containing anxiety and also imagining and rehearsing successful execution of tasks. See also *Behaviour rehearsal*.

Immediacy   Helper and, possibly, client comments that focus on the 'here and now' of the helping relationship, perhaps by focusing on what has previously been left unsaid. Sometimes expressed as 'you–me' talk. See also *Open mutual feedback*.

Information   Material relevant to clients' concerns and decisions which they may seek out for themselves or which may be provided by their helpers: for example, careers information.

Inhibition   Restraining, weakening, inadequately acknowledging and shrinking from an impulse, desire or action.

Inner empathy   The capacity to listen accurately to your own feelings and thoughts.

Inner rules   Self-standards, beliefs. Possessing an inner rule book about appropriate behaviour for yourself and others.

Inner speech   Self-talk, or thinking aloud to yourself, often taking the form of an internal dialogue. See also *Coping inner speech*.

Intellectualizing   Using thoughts to avoid dealing with feelings.

Internal frame of reference   The subjective world of a person rather than an external viewpoint. Understanding how another person thinks and feels as if you were them.

Interpretation   Explanations from another's frame of reference of a person's feelings, thoughts, words, dreams and actions.

Interventions   Specific methods by which helpers intervene and work with clients.

Intimacy   Sharing and being attuned to each other's thoughts and feelings, including those likely to be too threatening to reveal in other contexts. May include physical intimacy.

Introjection   Taking something from another person or other people and treating it as part of oneself. See also *Projection*.

In vivo   Taking place in real-life or laboratory settings and not in imagination.

Life skills   The skills required for effective living: for example, relationship skills.

Listening   Not just hearing but understanding another.

Listening, sources of interference   Everything that gets in the way of messages being received accurately. Sources of interference may be in the helper, the client or in the environment.

Managing anger   See *Anger management*.

Managing anxiety   See *Anxiety management*.

Managing crises   See *Crisis management*.

Managing stress   See *Stress management*.

Manipulation of feedback   A defensive process whereby individuals place open or subtle pressure on others to provide feedback that is consistent with their conceptions of themselves.

Marital counselling   Counselling marital partners or people thinking of marrying, and possibly providing a conciliation service for divorced people in the interests of their children.

Medication   Medically prescribed drugs used either independently or in conjunction with helping.

Misattributing responsibility   Inaccurately ascribing or making causal inferences about the responsibility for one's own or other people's feelings, thoughts and actions and for external events.

Modelling   Demonstrating before another feelings, thoughts and actions. Much modelling is unintentional.

Monitoring   Observing and keeping a check on your own or others' feelings, thoughts and behaviour. Keeping a record of behaviour.

Nervous breakdown   A reaction to excessive stress involving marked physiological and psychological debilitation as well as a drastic lessening of ability to cope with life.

Nonverbal communication   See *Body messages* and *Vocal messages*.

Open mutual feedback   Honest two-way feedback about either an overall relationship or any interaction in it, with special reference to the immediate present. See also *Immediacy*.

Openers   Remarks which indicate both attention and interest and also permission and psychological space to talk.

Operational definition   Defining a problem in terms of the skills deficits that contribute to sustaining it.

Ownership   Acknowledging to yourself and/or to others your feelings, thoughts and actions as your own. See also *'I' statements*.

Peer self-help groups   Groups of people with similar characteristics or with similar problems who meet regularly for mutual help.

Permissions to talk   See *Openers*.

Personal and social education   Educating pupils, students and others in life skills.

Personal responsibility   The process of making the choices that maximize your happiness and fulfilment.

Plan   A step-by-step outline, verbal or written, of the specific actions necessary to obtain your goals.

Possessiveness   Wishing to control others (for example, clients) for your own ends rather than to help them develop as unique individuals.

Problem management helping   Short-term collaboration with clients to help them develop the skills required to cope better with specific problems.

Problem management training   Training clients in the self-help skills of managing their problems.

Projection   Taking something from oneself and treating it as part of another person or other people. See also *Introjection*.

Psychiatry   The branch of medicine dealing with understanding, treating and preventing mental disorders.

Psychodrama   A helping approach involving the use of dramatic enactments of scenes.

Psychological education   Primarily, educating people in psychological or life skills. Otherwise, humanistic education and paraprofessional training.

Psychology   The science and study of human behaviour.

Psychophysiological disorders   Disorders caused and maintained primarily by psychological and emotional rather than by physical or organic factors. Previously called psychosomatic disorders.

Psychosis   Severe mental disorder involving loss of contact with reality and usually characterized by delusions and/or hallucinations.

Psychotherapy   Often used as another term for counselling. May have connotations of moderately to severely disturbed clients seen in medical settings, but not necessarily so. More accurate is 'psychotherapies', since there are many theoretical and practical approaches to psychotherapy.

Questions   Questions may be used to help clients elaborate, specify, give personal reactions, and explore and evaluate different perceptions.

Reactive depression Depression which is a disproportionate and continuing reaction to a precipitating event, such as a bereavement or setback. Reactive depressions are often contrasted with endogenous depressions, though depressions may contain both elements.

Realistic standards Standards for behaviour and self-evaluation which are functional in helping individuals to cope with their lives and meet their needs.

Records Helpers may keep records focusing on initial assessment, progress during helping, and termination details. Records may also take the form of statistical summaries.

Reflection Mirroring the verbal and/or emotional content of the client's communications through empathic responding.

Regard Non-possessive liking or prizing of another (for example, the client). Unconditional acceptance of the other as a person.

Regulating thinking Working on thinking both to make it more effective and also to lessen or eliminate negative feelings.

Reinforcement See *Reward*.

Rejection Either not accepting or not being accepted by another person in whole or in part.

Relationship Being connected in some way with another. Often used to describe a close connection between helper and client.

Relationship skills The skills of relating to others effectively. See also *Skills*.

Relaxation A restful state, or one of numerous approaches to gaining that state: for example, tensing and relaxing various muscle groupings, imagining restful scenes, etc.

Reluctant clients Clients who have been referred or assigned to helping against their will.

Repression A defensive process by means of which anxiety-evoking material and memories are kept out of awareness or consciousness.

Resistances All processes in clients that oppose their progress towards self-awareness and psychological wellbeing.

Responding choices Helper choices about how best to respond to single client statements or to a series of them.

Responsibility avoidances All the ways in which people avoid assuming personal responsibility for their lives.

Reward Something that increases the probability of a behaviour being repeated.

Role choices Helper choices about how best to allocate their time and energy between various options.

Role-playing Enacting behaviours in simulated settings or in imagination. See also *Behaviour rehearsal*.

Schizophrenia   A psychosis characterized by the disintegration of personality, emotional withdrawal and disorders of perception, thought and behaviour.

Self-acceptance   Accepting yourself as a person while remaining aware of your strengths and limitations.

Self-awareness   Being aware of your significant thoughts, feelings and actions and of the impact that you make on others.

Self-concept   The way in which people see themselves and to which they attach terms like 'I' or 'me'.

Self-definition   Making the choices that define you both to yourself and to others.

Self-disclosure   Revealing personal information and expressing thoughts and feelings.

Self-esteem   Sense of adequacy. Positive and negative evaluation of yourself as a person. Sense of your own worth.

Self-evaluation   The process of placing positive and negative values on your personal characteristics.

Self-help   Acquiring, maintaining, using and developing the skills of helping oneself.

Self-instruction   The process of talking to yourself with coping statements that reduce anxiety and facilitate the performance of tasks. See also *Inner speech*.

Self-protective thinking   See *Defensive thinking*.

Self-reward   Use of reward by clients to influence their actions through either modifying their environments so as to control their behaviour or by administering a reward to themselves after behaving in a desired way.

Self-standards   The standards or inner rules by which you lead your life and which form the basis of your positive and negative evaluations of yourself. See also *Inner rules*.

Shaping of behaviour   The fashioning of new patterns of behaviour by rewarding successively close approximations until the desired behaviour is attained. See also *Behaviour rehearsal* and *Graded task assignment*.

Shyness   Anxiety in social situations.

Skills   Areas in which you can make and implement an effictive sequence of choices to achieve a desired objective.

kills deficit   A predisposition to make poor choices in a skills area.

ills resource   A predisposition to make good choices in a skills area.

ial skills   Skills for communicating in personal and work relationships and in social groupings.

ficity   Responding to others' (for example clients') utterances in a clear and specific manner. Avoidance of vague generalities. Clear and specific communication by others (for example, clients).

Stress   Perceived demands on energy and coping abilities.

Stress management   Coping with stress constructively by understanding it and then developing and implementing appropriate strategies to deal with it.

Stressor   An individual item that causes stress.

Structuring   The behaviours by which helpers let clients know their respective roles at various stages of the helping process.

Summarizing   Making statements which clarify what you and/or another has been saying over a period of time. Summaries may include feedback from you.

Support   Giving strength and encouragement to another.

Support networks   Networks of people available to support each other, especially when in difficulty.

Systematic desensitization   An intervention aimed at reducing anxiety by presenting items from a hierarchy of progressively more anxiety-evoking scenes to clients when they are relaxed.

Thinking errors   Faulty habits of thinking that contribute to negative feelings and poor performance.

Threat   Perception of real or imagined danger.

Timing   The 'when' of helper responses and of making and implementing treatment choices.

Toxic   Poisonous. Most commonly used regarding the unwanted side-effects of drugs, but sometimes used to describe people!

Tranquillizing drugs   Drugs for the reduction of anxiety and tension.

Transference   The process by which people transfer feelings and thoughts from previous to present relationships.

Transition   Changes which people undergo during the course of their lives: for example, the birth of a first child or retirement.

Treatment choices   Choices of what interventions to adopt with whom, how and when.

Trust   Faith and confidence in the honesty and reliability of another.

Trustworthy   Being honest and reliable.

Tunnel vision   A narrowing of perception under threat so that the individual focuses only on certain factors in a situation and excludes others which may be important.

Unconscious   Beneath the level of conscious awareness.

Unrealistic standards   Standards or inner rules for behaviour a self-evaluation which are dysfunctional in helping people cope with and meet their needs.

Uptight   A colloquial word describing someone who exudes tension and anxiety.

Values   Deeply held internal rules or beliefs.

Verbal messages   What people actually say with words as contrasted with what they say by their vocal messages and body messages.

Vicarious reward   An observed event which, when following a response by another, strengthens the possibility of that response recurring in the other. This may in turn influence the observer.

Vocal messages   Sending messages, often about feelings, by means of the voice in ways that frame words. However, sometimes vocal messages (for instance, a sigh) can be independent of words. See also *Body messages* and *Verbal messages*.

Vulnerability   Being psychologically at risk, especially when faced with negative occurrences and feedback. A tendency to contribute to, if not cause, your own difficulties.

Withdrawal   Retreating or pulling back with one's feelings, thoughts and/or actions.

Working through   Facing up to a problem or decision and working on it until a satisfactory resolution or adjustment is reached.

'You' statements   Statements starting with the word 'you' by which people label or blame others. See also *'I' statements*.

References

CHAPTER 1 COUNSELLING, HELPING AND SELF-HELP

1. Murgatroyd, S. (1985) *Counselling and Helping*. London: Methuen.
2. Kanfer, F.H. and Goldstein, A.P. (1986) Introduction. In Kanfer, F.H. and Goldstein, A.P. (eds) *Helping People Change* (3rd edn). Oxford: Pergamon Press, 1–18.
3. Rogers, C.R. (1961) *On Becoming a Person*. Boston: Houghton Mifflin.
4. Egan, G. (1986) *The Skilled Helper* (3rd edn). Monterey, Calif.: Brooks/Cole.
5. Perloff, R. (1987) Self-interest and personal responsibility redux. *American Psychologist*, 42 (1), 3–11.
6. Nelson-Jones, R. (1984) *Personal Responsibility Counselling and Therapy: An Integrative Approach*. Sydney and London: Harper and Row.
7. Frankl, V.E. (1969) *The Doctor and the Soul*. Harmondsworth: Penguin Books.
8. Strong, S.R. (1968) Counseling: an interpersonal influence process. *Journal of Counseling Psychology*, 15, 215–24.
9. Bowlby, J. (1979) *The Making and Breaking of Affectional Bonds*. London: Tavistock.
10. Ellis, A. (1980) An overview of the clinical theory of rational-emotive therapy. In Grieger, R. and Boyd, J. (eds) *Rational-emotive Therapy: A Skills Based Approach*. New York: Van Nostrand Reinhold, 1–31.
11. Nelson-Jones, R. (1982) The counsellor as decision-maker: role, treatment and responding decisions. *British Journal of Guidance and Counselling*, 10 (2), 113–24.
12. Maslow, A.H. (1971) *The Farther Reaches of Human Nature*. Harmondsworth: Penguin Books, 47.
13. Nelson-Jones, R. (1986) *Human Relationship Skills: Training and Self-help*. London: Cassell, and Sydney: Holt, Rinehart and Winston.
14. Zaro, J.S., Barach, R., Nedelman, D.J. and Dreiblatt, I.S. (1977) *A Guide for Beginning Psychotherapists*. Cambridge: Cambridge University Press.

15. Rogers, C.R. (1957) The necessary and sufficient conditions of therapeutic personality change. *Journal of Consulting Psychology*, 21, 95–104.

CHAPTER 2   BECOMING A GOOD LISTENER

1. Holmes, O.W. (1872) *The Poet at Breakfast.* Quotation reprinted in *The Oxford Dictionary of Quotations* (3rd edn) (1979). Oxford: Oxford University Press.
2. Gordon, T. (1970) *Parent Effectiveness Training.* New York: Wyden.
3. Rogers, C.R. (1975) Empathic: an unappreciated way of being. *The Counseling Psychologist*, 5(2), 2–10. Reprinted in Rogers, C.R. (1980) *A Way of Being.* Boston: Houghton Mifflin, 137–63.
4. Barrett-Lennard, G.T. (1981) The empathy cycle: refinement of a nuclear concept. *Journal of Counseling Psychology*, 28, 91–100.
5. Elliott, R. (1985) Helpful and nonhelpful events in brief counseling interviews: an empirical taxonomy. *Journal of Counseling Psychology*, 32, 307–22.
6. Strong, S.R. (1968) Counseling; an interpersonal influence process. *Journal of Counseling Psychology*, 15, 215–24.
7. Strong, S.R. (1978) Social psychological approach to psychotherapy research. In Garfield, S.L. and Bergin, A.E. (eds) *Handbook of Psychotherapy and Behavior Change: An Empirical Analysis.* New York: Wiley.
8. Sue, S. and Zane, N. (1987) The role of culture and cultural techniques in psychotherapy. *American Psychologist*, 42, 37–45.
9. Rogers, C.R. (1959) A theory of therapy, personality and interpersonal relationships, as developed in the client-centered framework. In Koch, S. (ed.) *Psychology: a Study of Science.* (Vol. III). New York: McGraw-Hill, 184–256.
10. Rogers, C.R. (1961) *On Becoming a Person.* Boston: Houghton Mifflin.
11. Porter, E.H. (1950) *An Introduction to Therapeutic Counseling.* Boston: Houghton Mifflin.
12. Heppner, R.E., Rogers, M.E. and Lee, L.A. (1984) Carl Rogers: reflections on his life. *Journal of Counseling and Development*, 63, 14–20. (Carl Rogers died in 1987.)
13. Bugental, J.F.T. (1978) *Psychotherapy and Process: The Fundamentals of an Existential-humanistic Approach.* Reading, Mass.: Addison-Wesley.
14. Gray, K. (1979) Aspects of counsellor vulnerability. *British Journal of Guidance and Counselling*, 7, 188–98.
15. Egan, G. (1986) *The Skilled Helper* (3rd edn). Monterey, Calif: Brooks/Cole.
16. Carkhuff, R.R. (1983) *The Art of Helping* (5th edn). Amherst, Mass.: Human Resource Development Press.
17. Burley-Allen, M. (1982) *Listening: The Forgotten Skill.* New York: John Wiley.

CHAPTER 3   COMMUNICATING AND FACILITATING UNDERSTANDING

Gendlin, E.T. (1981) *Focusing* (2nd edn). New York: Bantam Books.

2. Haase, R.F. and Tepper, D.T. (1972) Nonverbal components of empathic communication. *Journal of Counseling Psychology*, 19, 417–24.
3. Shapiro, J.G., Foster, C.P. and Powell, T. (1968) Facial and bodily cues of genuiness, empathy and warmth. *Journal of Clinical Psychology*, 24, 233–6.
4. Barrett-Lennard, G.T. (1981) The empathy cycle: refinement of a nuclear concept. *Journal of Counseling Psychology*, 28, 91–100.
5. Rogers, C.R. (1951) *Client-centered Therapy*. Boston: Houghton Mifflin.
6. Rogers, C.R. (1975) Empathic: an unappreciated way of being. *The Counseling Psychologist*, 5(2), 2–10. Reprinted in Rogers, C.R. (1980) *A Way of Being*. Boston: Houghton Mifflin, 137–63.
7. Gendlin (1981).
8. Lee, D.Y. and Uhlemann, M.R. (1984) Comparison of verbal responses of Rogers, Shostrum and Lazarus. *Journal of Counseling Psychology*, 31, 91–4.
9. Truax, C.B. and Carkhuff, R.R. (1967) *Toward Effective Counseling and Psychotherapy: Training and Practice*. Chicago: Aldine.
10. Carkhuff, R.R. (1969) *Helping and Human Relations*. Volume 1, *Selection and Training*. New York: Holt, Rinehart and Winston.
11. Egan, G. (1986) *The Skilled Helper* (3rd edn). Monterey, Calif.: Brooks/ Cole.
12. Truax, C.B. and Mitchell, K.M. (1971) Research on certain therapist interpersonal skills in relation to process and outcome. In Bergin, A.E. and Garfield, S.L. (eds) *Handbook of Psychotherapy and Behavior Change: An Empirical Analysis*. New York: Wiley, 299–344.
13. Barkham, M. and Shapiro, D.A. (1986) Counselor verbal response modes and experienced empathy. *Journal of Counseling Psychology*, 33, 3–10.
14. Barrett-Lennard, G.T. (1962) Dimensions of therapist response as causal factors in therapeutic change. *Psychological Monographs*, 76 (43, Whole No. 562).
15. Nelson-Jones, R. (1986) The language of counselling, life skills training and self-help: an exploratory study. Unpublished manuscript.
16. Elliott, R., Filipovich, H., Harrigan, L., Gaynor, J., Reimschuessel, C. and Zapadka, J.K. (1982) Measuring response empathy: the development of a multicomponent rating scale. *Journal of Counseling Psychology*, 30, 379–87.
17. Maurer, R.E. and Tindall, J.H. (1983) Effect of postural congruence on client's perception of counselor empathy. *Journal of Counseling Psychology*, 30, 158–63.
18. Ivey, A.E. and Authier, J. (1978) *Microcounseling: Innovations in Interviewing, Counseling, Psychotherapy and Psychoeducation* (2nd edn). Springfield, Ill.: Charles C. Thomas.

CHAPTER 4   FURTHER FACILITATION SKILLS

1. Gordon, T. (1970) *Parent Effectiveness Training*. New York: Wyden.
2. Levitsky, A. and Perls, F.S. (1970) The rules and games of gestalt the In Fagan, J. and Shepherd, I.K. (eds) *Gestalt Therapy Now*. Palo Calif.: Science and Behavior Books, 140–49.
3. Brammer, L.M. (1985) *The Helping Relationship: Process and Sk edn). Englewood Cliffs, NJ: Prentice Hall.

4. Frankl, V. (1975) *The Unconscious God*. New York: Simon and Schuster.
5. Sklare, G., Portes, P. and Splete, H. (1985) Developing questioning effectiveness in counseling. *Counselor Education and Supervision*, September, 12–20.
6. Carkhuff, R.R. and Berenson, B.G. (1967) *Beyond Counseling and Therapy*. New York: Holt, Rinehart and Winston.
7. Berenson, B.G., Mitchell, K.M. and Laney, R.C. (1968) Level of therapist functioning, types of confrontation and type of patient. *Journal of Clinical Psychology*, 24, 111–13.
8. Berenson, B.G., Mitchell, K.M. and Moravec, J.A. (1968) Level of therapist functioning, patient depth of self-exploration, and type of confrontation. *Journal of Counseling Psychology*, 15, 136–9.
9. Perls, F.S. (1973) *The Gestalt Approach and Eyewitness to Therapy*. New York: Bantam Books.
10. McKee, J.E., Moore, H.B. and Presbury, J.H. (1982) A model for teaching counselor trainees how to make challenging responses. *Counselor Education and Supervision*, December, 149–53.
11. Carkhuff, R.R. (1969) *Helping and Human Relations*. Volume 1, *Selection and Training*. New York: Holt, Rinehart and Winston.
12. Loughary, J.W. and Ripley, T.M. (1979) *Helping Others Help Themselves: A Guide to Counseling Skills*. New York: McGraw-Hill.
13. Kennedy, E. (1977) *On Becoming a Counsellor*. Dublin: Gill and Macmillan.
14. McCarthy, P.R. (1982) Differential effects of counselor self-referent responses and counselor status. *Journal of Counseling Psychology*, 29, 125–31.
15. Carkhuff (1969).
16. Walker, A.M., Rablen, R.A. and Rogers, C.R. (1960) Development of a scale to measure process changes in psychotherapy. *Journal of Clinical Psychology*, 16, 79–85.
17. Truax, C.B. and Carkhuff, R.R. (1967) *Toward Effective Counseling and Psychotherapy: Training and Practice*. Chicago: Aldine, 206.

CHAPTER 5   A MODEL FOR MANAGING PROBLEMS

1. Egan, G. (1986) *The Skilled Helper* (3rd edn). Monterey, Calif.: Brooks/Cole.
2. Ivey, A.E. (1983) *International Counseling and Interviewing*. Monterey, Calif.: Brooks/Cole.
3. Ivey, A.E. and Mathews, W.J. (1984) A meta-model for structuring the clinical interview. *Journal of Counseling and Development*, 63, 237–43.
4. Carkhuff, R.R. (1983) *The Art of Helping* (5th edn). Amherst, Mass.: Human Resource Development Press.
'. D'Zurilla, T.J. and Goldfried, M.R. (1971) Problem solving and behavior modification. *Journal of Abnormal Psychology*, 78, 107–26.
    Lazarus, A.A. (1981) *The Practice of Multimodal Therapy*. New York: McGraw-Hill.
    Wolpe, J.E. (1982) *The Practice of Behavior Therapy* (3rd edn). Oxford: Pergamon Press.

8. Beck, A.T., Rush, A.J., Shaw, B.F. and Emery, G. (1979) *Cognitive Therapy of Depression*. New York: John Wiley.
9. Nelson-Jones, R. (1984) *Personal Responsibility Counselling and Therapy: An Integrative Approach*. Sydney and London: Harper and Row.
10. Nelson-Jones, R. (1982) *The Theory and Practice of Counselling Psychology*. Sydney and London: Holt, Rinehart and Winston.
11. Corsini, R.J. (ed.) (1984) *Current Psychotherapies* (3rd edn), Itasca, Ill.: Peacock.
12. Patterson, C.H. (1985) *Theories of Counseling and Psychotherapy* (4th edn). New York: Harper and Row.
13. Corey, G. (1985) *Theory and Practice of Counseling and Psychotherapy* (3rd edn). Monterey, Calif.: Brooks/Cole.
14. Hansen, J.C., Stevic, R.R. and Warner, R.W. (1982) *Counseling: Theory and Process* (3rd edn). Boston: Allyn and Bacon.
15. American Psychiatric Association (1980) *Diagnostic and Statistical Manual of Mental Distorders* (3rd edn). Washington D.C.: American Psychiatric Association.
16. Webb, L.J., DiClemente, C.C., Johnstone, E.E., Sanders, J.L. and Perley, R.A. (1981) *DSM-III Training Guide*. New York: Brunner/Mazel.
17. Trethowen, W.H. and Sims, A.C.P. (1983) *Psychiatry* (5th edn). London: Baillière Tindall.
18. Willis, J. (1984) *Lecture Notes on Psychiatry* (6th edn). Oxford: Blackwell.
19. Coleman, J.C. and Butcher, J.N. (1984) *Abnormal Psychology and Modern Life* (7th Edn). Glenview, Ill.: Scott, Foresman.
20. Davison, G.C. and Neale, J.M. (1986) *Abnormal Psychology* (4th edn). New York: John Wiley and Sons.
21. Beck et al. (1979).
22. Barkham, M. and Shapiro, D.A. (1986) Counselor verbal response modes and experienced empathy. *Journal of Counseling Psychology*, 33, 3–10.
23. Egan (1986).
24. Ellis, A. (1962) *Reason and Emotion in Psychotherapy*. New York: Lyle Stuart.
25. Egan (1986).
26. Carkhuff (1983).
27. Marx, J.A. and Gelso, C.J. (1987) Termination of individual counseling in a university counseling center. *Journal of Counseling Psychology*, 34, 3–9.
28. Ward, D.E. (1984) Termination of individual counseling: concepts and strategies. *Journal of Counseling and Development*, 63, 21–5.

CHAPTER 6 FOCUSING ON FEELING

1. Rogers, C.R. (1975) Empathic: an unappreciated way of being. *Counseling Psychologist*, 5(2), 2–10. Reprinted in Rogers, C.R. (19... *Way of Being*. Boston: Houghton Mifflin, 137–63.
2. Perls, F.S. (1973) *The Gestalt Approach and Eyewitness to Thera...* York: Bantam Books.
3. *Ibid.*
4. Masters, W.H. and Johnson, V.E. (1970) *Human Sexual I...* London: J.A. Churchill.

5. Kaplan, H.S. (1974) *The New Sex Therapy: Active Treatment of Sexual Dysfunctions.* Harmondsworth: Penguin.
6. Nelson-Jones, R. (1986) Towards a people centred language for counselling psychology. *The Australian Counselling Psychologist,* 2(1), 18–23.
7. Gendlin, E.G. (1981) *Focusing* (2nd edn). New York: Bantam Books.
8. Bassoff, E.S. (1984) Healthy aspects of passivity and Gendlin's focusing. *The Personnel and Guidance Journal.* January, 268–70.
9. Jacobson, E. (1929) *Progressive Relaxation.* Chicago: University of Chicago Press.
10. Wolpe, J.E. (1982) *The Practice of Behavior Therapy* (3rd edn). Oxford: Pergamon.
11. Bernstein, D.A. and Borkovec, T.D. (1973) *Progressive Relaxation Training: A Manual for the Helping Professions.* Champaign, Ill.: Research Press.
12. Goldfried, M.R. and Davison, G.C. (1976) *Clinical Behavior Therapy.* New York: Holt, Rinehart and Winston.
13. Tasto, D.L. and Hinkle, J.E. (1973) Muscle relaxation treatment for tension headaches. *Behaviour Research and Therapy,* 11, 347–9.
14. Hoelscher, T.J., Lichstein, K.L., Fischer, S. and Hegarty, T.B. (1987) Relaxation treatment of hypertension: do home relaxation tapes enhance treatment outcome? *Behavior Therapy,* 18, 33–7.
15. Wolpe, J. (1958) *Psychotherapy by Reciprocal Inhibition.* Stanford: Stanford University Press.
16. Wolpe (1982).
17. Wolpe (1982).
18. Goldfried and Davison (1976).
19. Goldfried, M.R. (1971) Systematic desensitization as training in self-control. *Journal of Consulting and Clinical Psychology,* 37, 228–34.
20. Meichenbaum, D.H. (1977) *Cognitive-behavior Modification.* New York: Plenum.
21. Selye, H. (1974) *Stress Without Distress.* Sevenoaks: Hodder and Stoughton.
22. Fujimura, L.E., Weis, D.M. and Cochran, J.R. (1985) Suicide: dynamics and implications for counseling. *Journal of Counseling and Development,* 63, 612–15.
23. Murgatroyd, S. and Wolfe, R. (1982) *Coping with Crisis: Understanding and Helping People in Need.* London: Harper and Row.
24. Pearson, J.E. (1986) The definition and measurement of social support. *Journal of Counseling and Development,* 64, 390–5.

CHAPTER 7   FOCUSING ON THINKING

Lazarus, A. (1984) *In the Mind's Eye.* New York: Guilford Press.
Meichenbaum, D.(1986) Cognitive-behavior modification. In Kanfer, F.H. and Goldstein, A.P. (eds) *Helping People Change* (3rd edn). Oxford: Pergamon Press, 346–80.
s, A. (1962) *Reason and Emotion in Psychotherapy.* New York: Lyle t.
well, R.T., Galassi, J.P., Galassi, M.D. and Watson, T.E. (1985) Are ve assessment methods equal? A comparison of think aloud and

thought listing. *Cognitive Therapy and Research*, 9, 399–413.

5. Dobson, K.S. and Shaw, B.F. (1986) Cognitive assessment with major depressive disorders. *Cognitive Therapy and Research,* 10, 13–29.
6. Beck, A.T., Rush, A.J., Shaw, B.F. and Emery, G. (1979) *Cognitive Therapy of Depression*. New York: John Wiley.
7. Jacobson, N.S., McDonald, D.W., Follette, W.C. and Berley, R.A. (1985) Attributional processes in distressed and nondistressed married couples. *Cognitive Therapy and Research*, 9, 35–50.
8. Beck et al. (1979).
9. Seligman, M.E.P., Abramson, L.Y., Semmel, A. and von Baeyer, C. (1979) Depressive attributional style. *Journal of Abnormal Psychology*, 88, 242–7.
10. Meichenbaum, D. (1977) *Cognitive-behavior Modification*. New York: Plenum.
11. Meichenbaum, D. (1983) *Coping with Stress*. London: Century Publishing.
12. Meichenbaum (1986).
13. Ellis (1962).
14. Ellis, A. (1980) An overview of the clinical theory of rational-emotive therapy. In Grieger, R. and Boyd, J. (eds) *Rational-emotive Therapy: A Skills Based Approach*. New York: Van Nostrand Reinhold, 1–31.
15. Ibid.
16. Beck, A.T. (1976) *Cognitive Therapy and the Emotional Disorders*. New York: International Universities Press.
17. Beck et al. (1979).
18. Beck, A.T., Emery, G. and Greenberg, R.L. (1985) *Anxiety Disorders and Phobias: A Cognitive Perspective*. New York: Basic Books.
19. Ibid.
20. D'Zurilla, T.J. and Goldfried, M.R. (1971) Problem solving and behavior modification. *Journal of Abnormal Psychology*, 78, 107–26.
21. Ibid.
22. Hagga, D.A. and Davison, G.C. (1986) Cognitive change methods. In Kanfer and Golstein (1986), 236–82.

CHAPTER 8 FOCUSING ON ACTION

1. Egan, G. (1986) *The Skilled Helper* (3rd edn) Monterey, Calif.: Brooks/Cole.
2. Perry, M.A. and Furukawa, M.J. (1986) Modeling methods. In Kanfer, F.H. and Goldstein, A.P. (eds). *Helping People Change* (3rd edn). Oxford: Pergamon Press, 66–110.
3. Bandura, A. (1969) *Principles of Behavior Modification*. New York: Holt, Rinehart and Winston.
4. Loughary, J.W. and Ripley, T.M. (1979) *Helping Others Help Themselves. A Guide to Counseling Skills*. New York: McGraw-Hill.
5. Perry and Furukawa (1986).
6. Skinner, B.F. (1953) *Science and Human Behavior*. New York: Macmillan.
7. Skinner, B.F. (1969) *Contingencies of Reinforcement*. New York: Appleton-Century-Crofts.
8. Lewinsohn, P.M., Munoz, R.F., Youngren, M.A. and Zeiss, A.

Control Your Depression (rev. edn). New York: Prentice Hall Press. This book contains a copy of the Pleasant Events Schedule.

9. MacPhillamy, D.J. and Léwinsohn, P.M. (1982) The Pleasant Events Schedule: studies on reliability, validity and scale intercorrelation. *Journal of Consulting and Clinical Psychology*, 50, 363–80. This article contains form III-S of the Schedule as an appendix.

10. Daley, M.F. (1969) The 'reinforcement menu': finding effective reinforcers. In Krumboltz, J.D. and Thorensen, C.E. (eds) *Behavioral Counseling: Cases and Techniques*. New York: Holt, Reinhart and Winston, 42–5.

11. Truax, C.B. (1986) Reinforcement and non-reinforcement in Rogerian psychotherapy. *Journal of Abnormal Psychology*, 71, 1–9.

12. Beck, A.T., Rush, A.J., Shaw, B.F. and Emery, G. (1979) *Cognitive Therapy of Depression*. New York: John Wiley.

13. Kanfer, F.H. and Gaelick, L. (1986) Self-management methods. In Kanfer and Goldstein (1986), 283–345.

14. Thoresen, C.E. and Mahoney, M.J. (1974) *Behavioral Self-Control*. New York: Holt, Rinehart and Winston.

15. Kanfer and Gaelick (1986).

16. Thoresen and Mahoney (1974).

17. Cautela, J.R. (1967) Covert sensitization. *Psychological Reports*, 20, 459–68.

18. O'Farrell, T.J. and Keuthen N.J. (1983) Readability of behavior therapy self-help manuals. *Behavior Therapy*, 14, 449–54.

19. McFall, R.M. and Dodge, K.A. (1982) Self-management and interpersonal skills learning. In Karoly, P. and Kanfer, F.H. (eds) *Self Management and Behavior Change*. Oxford: Pergamon Press, 353–92.

20. Goldfried, M.R. and Davison, G.C. (1976) *Clinical Behavior Therapy*. New York: Holt, Rinehart and Winston.

21. Nelson-Jones, R. (1986) Towards a people centred language for counselling psychology. *The Australian Counselling Psychologist*, 2(1), 18–23.

22. Howe, M.A. (1986) *Imaging*. Melbourne: Spiral.

23. Lazarus, A. (1984) *In the Mind's Eye*. New York: Guildford Press.

24. Beck et al. (1979).

CHAPTER 9   FACILITATING GROUPS

1. Mahler, C.A. (1969) *Group Counseling in the Schools*. Boston: Houghton Mifflin.

2. Yalom, I.D. (1986) *The Theory and Practice of Group Psychotherapy* (3rd edn). New York: Harper and Row.

3. Mahler (1969).

4. Corey, G. and Corey, M.S. (1982) *Groups: Process and Practice* (2nd edn). Monterey, Calif.: Brooks/Cole.

Rogers, C.R. (1970) *Encounter Groups*. London: Penguin Press.

Landreth, G.L.(1984) *Encountering Carl Rogers: his views on facilitating groups. Personnel and Guidance Journal*, 62, 323–6.

arkhuff, R.R. (1969) *Helping and Human Relations*. Volume 1, *Selection d Training*. New York: Holt, Rinehart and Winston.

, A.E. and Authier, J. (1978) *Microcounseling: Innovations in Inter-ng, Counseling, Psychotherapy and Psychoeducation* (2nd edn). field, Ill.: Charles C. Thomas.

9. Higgins, W., Ivey, A. and Uhlemann, M. (1970) Media therapy: a programmed approach to teaching behavioural skills. *Journal of Counseling Psychology*, 17, 20–6.

10. Egan, G. (1977) *You and Me: The Skills of Communicating and Relating to Others.* Monterey, Calif.: Brooks/Cole.

11. Egan, G. (1986) *The Skilled Helper* (3rd edn). Monterey, Calif.: Brooks/Cole.

12. Nelson-Jones, R. (1986) Relationship skills training in schools: some fieldwork observations. *British Journal of Guidance and Counselling*, 14(3), 292–305.

13. Nelson-Jones, R. (1986) *Human Relationship Skills: Training and Self-help.* London: Cassell, and Sydney: Holt, Rinehart and Winston.

14. Bates, B. and Goodman, A. (1986) The effectiveness of encounter groups: implications of research for counselling practice. *British Journal of Guidance and Counselling*, 14, 240–51.

15. Pearson, J.E. (1986) The definition and measurement of social support. *Journal of Counseling and Development*, 64, 390–5.

16. Ashinger, P. (1985) Using social networks in counseling. *Journal of Counseling and Development*, 63, 519–21.

17. Murgatroyd, S. (1985) *Counselling and Helping.* London: Methuen, 150–9.

CHAPTER 10   LIFE SKILLS TRAINING

1. Daws, P.P. (1973) Mental health and education: counselling as prophylaxis. *British Journal of Guidance and Counselling*, 1, 2–10.

2. Working Party on Marriage Guidance (1979) *Marriage Matters.* London: HMSO.

3. *The Age* (Melbourne), 21 December 1985.

4. Duck, S. (1986) *Human Relationships: An Introduction to Social Psychology.* London: Sage Publications.

5. Havighurst, R. (1979) *Developmental Tasks and Education* (3rd edn). New York: David McKay.

6. Blocher, D. (1974) *Developmental Counseling* (2nd edn). New York: Wiley.

7. Egan, G. and Cowan, M.A. (1979) *People in Systems: A Model for Development.* Monterey, Calif.: Brooks/Cole.

8. Nelson-Jones, R. (1984) *Personal Responsibility Counselling and Therapy: An Integrative Approach.* Sydney and London: Harper and Row.

9. Hollin, C.R. and Trower, P. (eds) (1986) *Handbook of Social Skill Training.* Volume 1. Oxford: Pergamon Press.

10. Argyle, M. (1984) Some new developments in social skills training. *Bull of the British Psychological Society*, 37, 405–10.

11. Cartledge, G. and Milburn, J.F. (eds) (1986) *Teaching Social Sk Children.* Oxford: Pergamon Press.

12. Argyle, M., Salter, V., Nicholson, H., Williams, M. and Burgess, P The communication of inferior and superior attitudes by verbal verbal signals. *British Journal of Social and Clinical Psychology,*

13. Haase, R.F. and Tepper, D.T. (1972) Nonverbal components communication. *Journal of Counseling Psychology*, 19, 417–

14. Nelson-Jones, R. (1986) Relationship skills training in s

fieldwork observations. *British Journal of Guidance and Counselling*, 14(3), 292–305.

15. Hopson, B. and Scally, M. (1981) *Lifeskills Teaching*. London: McGraw-Hill.

16. Ivey, A.E. and Authier, J. (1978) *Microcounseling: Innovations in Interviewing, Counseling, Psychotherapy and Psychoeducation* (2nd edn). Springfield, Ill.: Charles C. Thomas.

17. Hopson, B. and Hough, P. (1973) *Exercises in Personal and Career Development*. Cambridge: CRAC.

18. Egan, G. (1977) *You and Me: The Skills of Communicating and Relating to Others*. Monterey, Calif.: Brooks/Cole.

19. Johnson, D.W. (1986) *Reaching Out* (3rd edn). Englewood Cliffs, NJ: Prentice Hall.

20. Nelson-Jones, R. (1986) *Human Relationship Skills: Training and Self-help*. London: Cassell; Sydney: Holt, Rinehart and Winston.

21. Pfeiffer, J. and Jones, J. (1969–85) *Structured Experiences for Human Relations Training*. Volumes 1–10. Iowa City: University Associates Press.

22. Lifeskills Associates, Ashling, Back Church Lane, Leeds LS16 8DN, England.

23. Marzillier, J.S. (1978) Outcome studies of skills training: a review. In Trower, P., Bryant, B. and Argyle, M. (eds) *Social Skills and Mental Health*. London: Methuen.

CHAPTER 11   MAINTAINING AND DEVELOPING YOUR SKILLS

1. Audio Visual Aids Unit (1986) *Film and Video Hire Catalogue* (4th edn). Rugby: British Association for Counselling.

2. Ackroyd, A. (ed.) *Training in Counselling: A Directory*. Rugby: British Association for Counselling. Updated regularly.

3. The Secretary of the International Round Table for Counselling (IRTAC) is Dr Derek Hope, Brunel University, Uxbridge UB8 3PH, England.

4. The Secretary of the Association of Psychological and Educational Counsellors of Asia (APECA) is Rev Jovita de Sousa, c/o St Joseph's Church, 143 Victoria Street, Singapore 0718.

5. Carkhuff, R.R. (1969) Critical variables in effective counselor training. *Journal of Counseling Psychology*, 16, 238–45.

6. Savicki, V. and Cooley, E.J. (1982) Implications of burnout research and theory for counselor educators. *The Personnel and Guidance Journal*, 60, 415–19.

7. Maher, E.L. (1983) Burnout and commitment: a theoretical alternative. *The Personnel and Guidance Journal*, 61, 390–52.
   Savicki, V. and Cooley, E. (1987) The relationship of work environment and client contact to burnout in mental health professionals. *Journal of Counseling and Development*, 65, 249–52.
   Nelson-Jones, R. (1984) *Personal Responsibility Counselling and Therapy: Integrative Approach*. Sydney and London: Harper and Row.

Name Index

Subject Index